Ghosts in the Consulting Room

Ghosts in the Consulting Room: Echoes of trauma in psychoanalysis delves into the overwhelming, often unmetabolizable feelings related to mourning. The book uses clinical examples of people living in a state of liminality or ongoing melancholia. The authors reflect on the challenges of learning to move forward and embrace life over time, while acknowledging, witnessing, and working through the emotional scars of the past.

Bringing together a collection of clinical and theoretical papers, *Ghosts in the Consulting Room* features accounts of the unpredictable effects of trauma that emerge within clinical work, often unexpectedly, in ways that surprise both patient and therapist. In the book, distinguished psychoanalysts examine how to work with a variety of 'ghosts', as they manifest in transference and countertransference, in work with children and adults, in institutional settings, and even in the very founders and foundations of the field of psychoanalysis itself. They explore the dilemma of how to process loss when it is unspeakable and unknowable, often manifesting in silence or gaps in knowledge, and living in strange relations to time and space.

This book will be of interest to psychotherapists and psychoanalysts, as well as to social workers, family therapists, psychologists, and psychiatrists. It will appeal to those specializing in bereavement and trauma and, on a broader level, to sociologists and historians interested in understanding means of coping with loss and grief on both an individual and larger-scale basis.

Adrienne Harris is on the faculty and is a supervisor at the NYU Postdoctoral Program in Psychotherapy and Psychoanalysis. She published *Gender as Soft Assembly* in 2005. She writes about gender and development, about analytic subjectivity, about ghosts, and about the analysts developing and writing around the period of the First World War.

Margery Kalb is a psychologist and psychoanalyst in private practice in New York City. She is on the faculty at the NYU Postdoctoral Program in Psychotherapy and Psychoanalysis. She also teaches and supervises clinical work for the doctoral psychology program at Pace University. Dr. Kalb is the author of several papers on ghosts.

Susan Klebanoff is a clinical psychologist and psychoanalyst in private practice in New York City. She is on the faculty of the Stephen Mitchell Center and is an adjunct clinical supervisor at the Ferkauf School of Yeshiva University. Klebanoff has previously co-authored a book on depression for middle school aged children and a chapter in a book on uncertainty in psychoanalysis.

RELATIONAL PERSPECTIVES BOOK SERIES

LEWIS ARON & ADRIENNE HARRIS
Series Co-Editors

STEVEN KUCHUCK & EYAL ROZMARIN
Associate Editors

The Relational Perspectives Book Series (RPBS) publishes books that grow out of or contribute to the relational tradition in contemporary psychoanalysis. The term *relational psychoanalysis* was first used by Greenberg and Mitchell[1] to bridge the traditions of interpersonal relations, as developed within interpersonal psychoanalysis and object relations, as developed within contemporary British theory. But, under the seminal work of the late Stephen Mitchell, the term *relational psychoanalysis* grew and began to accrue to itself many other influences and developments. Various tributaries—interpersonal psychoanalysis, object relations theory, self psychology, empirical infancy research, and elements of contemporary Freudian and Kleinian thought—flow into this tradition, which understands relational configurations between self and others, both real and fantasied, as the primary subject of psychoanalytic investigation.

We refer to the relational tradition, rather than to a relational school, to highlight that we are identifying a trend, a tendency within contemporary psychoanalysis, not a more formally organized or coherent school or system of beliefs. Our use of the term *relational* signifies a dimension of theory and practice that has become salient across the wide spectrum of contemporary psychoanalysis. Now under the editorial supervision of Lewis Aron and Adrienne Harris with the assistance of Associate Editors Steven Kuchuck and Eyal Rozmarin, the Relational Perspectives Book Series originated in 1990 under the editorial eye of the late Stephen A.

1 Greenberg, J. & Mitchell, S. (1983). *Object relations in psychoanalytic theory.* Cambridge, MA: Harvard University Press.

Mitchell. Mitchell was the most prolific and influential of the originators of the relational tradition. He was committed to dialogue among psychoanalysts and he abhorred the authoritarianism that dictated adherence to a rigid set of beliefs or technical restrictions. He championed open discussion, comparative and integrative approaches, and he promoted new voices across the generations.

Included in the Relational Perspectives Book Series are authors and works that come from within the relational tradition, extend and develop the tradition, as well as works that critique relational approaches or compare and contrast it with alternative points of view. The series includes our most distinguished senior psychoanalysts, along with younger contributors who bring fresh vision.

A full list of titles in this series is available at https://www.routledge.com/series/LEARPBS. Recently published titles:

Vol. 68
Somatic Experience in Psychoanalysis and Psychotherapy: In the Expressive Language of the Living
William F. Cornell

Vol. 69
Relational Treatment of Trauma: Stories of loss and hope
Toni Heineman

Vol. 70
Freud's Legacy in the Global Era
Carlo Strenger

Vol. 71
The Enigma of Desire: Sex, Longing, and Belonging in Psychoanalysis
Galit Atlas

Vol. 72
Conservative and Radical Perspectives on Psychoanalytic Knowledge: The Fascinated and the Disenchanted
Aner Govrin

Vol. 73
Immigration in Psychoanalysis: Locating Ourselves
Julia Beltsiou

Vol. 74
The Dissociative Mind in Psychoanalysis: Understanding and Working With Trauma
Elizabeth Howell & Sheldon Itzkowitz

Vol.75
Ghosts in the Consulting Room: Echoes of Trauma in Psychoanalysis
Adrienne Harris, Susan Klebanoff and Margery Kalb

Vol.76
Demons in the Consulting Room: Echoes of Genocide, Slavery and Extreme Trauma in Psychoanalytic Practice
Adrienne Harris, Susan Klebanoff and Margery Kalb

Ghosts in the Consulting Room

Echoes of trauma in psychoanalysis

Edited by Adrienne Harris, Margery Kalb, and Susan Klebanoff

LONDON AND NEW YORK

First published 2016
by Routledge
2 Park Square, Milton Park, Abingdon, Oxon OX14 4RN

and by Routledge
711 Third Avenue, New York, NY 10017

Routledge is an imprint of the Taylor & Francis Group, an informa business

British Library Cataloguing in Publication Data
A catalogue record for this book is available from the British Library

Library of Congress Cataloging in Publication Data
Names: Harris, Adrienne, editor. | Kalb, Margery, editor. | Klebanoff, Susan, editor.
Title: Ghosts in the consulting room : echoes of trauma in psychoanlysis / Adrienne Harris, Margery Kalb, Susan Klebanoff (editors).
Description: Abingdon, Oxon ; New York, NY : Routledge, 2016.
Identifiers: LCCN 2015039175| ISBN 9780415728652 (hbk) | ISBN 9780415728676 (pbk)
Subjects: LCSH: Psychic trauma. | Psychoanalysis.
Classification: LCC BF175.5.P75 G46 2016 | DDC 155.9/3—dc23
LC record available at http://lccn.loc.gov/2015039175

ISBN: 978-0-415-72865-2 (hbk)
ISBN: 978-0-415-72867-6 (pbk)
ISBN: 978-1-315-64180-5 (ebk)

Typeset in Times New Roman
By Swales & Willis Ltd, Exeter, Devon, UK

Printed and bound in Great Britain by
TJ International Ltd, Padstow, Cornwall

Contents

Author biographies ix

Introduction 1
ADRIENNE HARRIS, MARGERY KALB, AND SUSAN KLEBANOFF

Clinical **17**

1 "I always wished I could stop time": an adolescent girl, unresolved mourning, and the haunted third 19
SUSAN KLEBANOFF

2 Ghostly intrusions: unformulated trauma and its transformation in the therapeutic dyad 36
HEATHER FERGUSON

3 Travel fever: transgenerational trauma and witnessing in analyst and analysand 52
MICHAEL J. FELDMAN

4 Shadows, ghosts, and Chimaeras: on some early modes of handling psycho-genetic heritage 76
JOSHUA DURBAN

5 Vaginal ghosts: memorializing the disappeared 97
SUE GRAND

Community & culture **113**

6 Ghosts in psychoanalysis 115
ADRIENNE HARRIS, MICHAEL S. ROTH, JACK DRESCHER, DANIEL G. BUTLER, DOUGLAS KIRSNER, AND DON TROISE

7 Empty arms and secret shames: reverberations of relational trauma in the NICU 139
SUSAN KRAEMER AND ZINA STEINBERG

8 Mourning in the hollows of architecture and psychoanalysis 156
MARIA MCVARISH AND JULIE LEAVITT

9 First kiss, last word: stairway to heaven 181
ADRIENNE HARRIS

Afterword 199
SAM GERSON

Index 204

Author biographies

Daniel G. Butler, MA, is a psychoanalytic psychotherapist at Access Institute for Psychological Services in San Francisco. Forthcoming publications include a paper on psychoanalytic training in a neoliberal age and a book chapter on the figure of the child in Ferenczi's metapsychology. Mr. Butler's interests span psychoanalysis, continental philosophy, queer studies, and medical and psychological anthropology.

Jack Drescher, MD, is a psychiatrist and psychoanalyst in private practice in New York City as well as Training and Supervising Analyst at the William Alanson White Institute, Clinical Professor of Psychiatry & Behavioral Sciences at New York Medical College, and Adjunct Professor at New York University's Postdoctoral Program in Psychotherapy and Psychoanalysis. He was a member of the DSM-5 Workgroup on Sexual and Gender Identity Disorders and presently serves on the World Health Organization Working Group on Classification of Sexual Disorders and Sexual Health and the Honorary Scientific Committee of the Psychodynamic Diagnostic Manual (PDM-2). Dr. Drescher is author of *Psychoanalytic Therapy and the Gay Man* (Routledge) and Emeritus Editor of *Journal of Gay and Lesbian Mental Health.*

Joshua Durban is a training and supervising child and adult psychoanalyst at the Israeli Psychoanalytic Society and Institute, Jerusalem. He is a member of the faculty at the Sackler School of Medicine, Tel-Aviv University, The Psychotherapy Program, Early Mental States unit, and a co-founder of Post-Graduate Kleinian Studies there. He is scientific editor of the Hebrew edition of the collected works of Melanie Klein. He works in private practice with children, adolescents, and adults, specializing in the psychoanalysis of ASD and psychotic children and adults. He is founder and co-chair of the Israeli Psychoanalytic

Inter-Disciplinary Forum for the study of ASD: a joint venture of the Israeli psychoanalytic Society and the NHS.

Michael J. Feldman is a psychoanalyst and board-certified adult and child psychiatrist with a private practice in New York City. He participates widely regarding gender and sexuality and trauma and resilience at regional, national, and international psychoanalytic meetings. He is a member of the American Psychoanalytic Association and co-authored its Position Statement opposing attempts to change gender and sexual identity. He is on the teaching faculty at the Columbia University Center for Psychoanalytic Training and Research and Assistant Professor of Clinical Psychiatry at Columbia University. An earlier version of this manuscript was published in *Psychoanalytic Dialogues* (2016).

Heather Ferguson, LCSW, is a psychoanalyst and group therapist in private practice in New York City. She is on the faculty at the Institute for Expressive Analysis and on the faculty and a coordinating committee member of the Institute for the Psychoanalytic Study of Subjectivity, New York City. With Sarah Mendelsohn, LCSW, she co-authored, "Full of Yourself: How Eating Disorders Encode a Relational History," in the *International Journal of Psychoanalytic Self Psychology* in 2011 and with Dr. Klebanoff, "The Enigma of Ana: Lost and Found in Cyberspace?," in the *Journal of Infant, Child, and Adolescent Psychotherapy* in 2014. She teaches and writes about a range of topics related to eating disorder treatment, trauma, and grief.

Sam Gerson, PhD, is a founder, past president, and a training and supervising analyst at the Psychoanalysis Institute of Northern California.

Sue Grand is a member of the faculty and a supervisor at the NYU Postdoctoral Program in Psychotherapy and Psychoanalysis; a member of the faculty for the NYU Pd program in Couples and Family therapy, the Mitchell Center for Relational Psychoanalysis, and the National Institute for the Psychotherapies. She is a visiting scholar at the Psychoanalytic Society of Northern Calif and a fellow at The Institute for The Psychology of the Other. She is an associate editor for *Psychoanalytic Dialogues and Psychoanalysis, Culture and Society*. She is the author of *The Reproduction of Evil: A Clinical and Cultural Perspective* and *The Hero in the Mirror: From Fear to Fortitude*. Dr. Grand is in private practice in New York City and in Teaneck NJ.

Adrienne Harris, PhD, is a member of the faculty and a supervisor at New York University Postdoctoral Program in Psychotherapy and Psychoanalysis. She is on the faculty at the Psychoanalytic Institute of Northern California. In 2009, she, Lewis Aron, and Jeremy Safron established the Sandor Ferenczi Center at the New School University. She has published *Rocking the Ship of State: Women and Peace Politics* (1985); *Gender as Soft Assembly* (2005). She edited, with Muriel Dimen, *Storms in her Head*, with Lewis Aron, *The Legacy of Sandor Ferenczi*, with Steven Botticelli, *First Do No Harm: Psychoanalysis, Warmaking and Resistance*, and in 2015 with Steven Kuchuck, *The Legacy of Sandor Ferenczi: From Ghost to Ancestor*.

Margery Kalb is a psychologist and psychoanalyst in private practice in New York City. She is faculty at the NYU Postdoctoral Program in Psychotherapy and Psychoanalysis. She also teaches and supervises clinical work for the doctoral psychology program at Pace University. Dr. Kalb is the author of several papers, on ghosts, loss, and clinical process.

Douglas Kirsner, PhD, is Emeritus Professor at Deakin University where he previously held a personal chair in Philosophy and Psychoanalytic Studies. He was elected an Honorary Member of the American Psychoanalytic Association in 2015. His publications include *Unfree Associations: Inside Psychoanalytic Institutes* (Rowman and Littlefield, 2009), *The Schizoid World of Jean-Paul Sartre and RD Laing* (Other Press, 2003), numerous journal articles, book chapters, and edited collections. He is associate editor of the *International Journal of Applied Psychoanalytic Studies* and *Organisational and Social Dynamics*, and editorial advisor for *Psychoanalysis and History*.

Susan Klebanoff is a clinical psychologist in private practice in New York City. She is on the faculty of the Stephen Mitchell Center and an adjunct clinical supervisor at the Ferkauf School of Yeshiva University. She is the co-author, with Ellen Luborsky, of *Ups and Downs: How to Beat the Blues and Teen Depression* (Price Stern Sloan, 1999). She is also the co-author, with Heather Ferguson, of "The Enigma of Ana: Lost *or* Found In CyberSpace?" in the *Journal of Infant, Child and Adolescent Psychotherapy* (Volume 13, Issue 3, 2014). She is the author of a chapter titled "Six Degrees of Separation…When Real Worlds Collide in Treatment," in *Knowing, Not Knowing, and Sort of Knowing:*

Psychoanalysis and the Experience of Uncertainty (Karnac, 2010). She has presented at numerous psychoanalytic conferences on topics such as eating disorders, family relations, immigration, and intergenerational transmission of trauma.

Susan Kraemer, a clinical psychologist and psychoanalyst, serves as consultant and supervisor in the neonatal intensive care unit at Morgan Stanley Children's Hospital. She has consulted to the hospital's Pediatric Advanced Care Team and is a member of the faculty at the Parent-Infant Psychotherapy Training Program, Columbia University. She writes and teaches about the psychic impact of working in a pediatric intensive care setting and the cascading impact of infertility, premature birth, and perinatal loss on maternal identity and family relationships.

Julie Leavitt, MD is a member and faculty at the Psychoanalytic Institute of Northern California, is in private practice and is medical director at Access Institute for Psychological Services in San Francisco. She teaches on inter-disciplinary collaboration, ethics and the psychoanalytic-sociocultural interface. She has written about spatial/material memory, gender, and community effects of ethical violations, and is currently writing on "geographic transference" and U.S. cultural melancholy via a review of *The Warmth of Other Suns: The Epic Story of America's Great Migration* by Isabel Wilkerson.

Maria McVarish is an architect, artist, and visual researcher practicing in San Francisco. She has lectured in architecture at UC Berkeley's College of Environmental Design and, since 1996, teaches interdisciplinary studies, critical theory, and design at California College of the Arts. She is currently a doctoral student in modern thought and literature at Stanford University, where her research centers on the role of spatial representation in economic development and on the effects of long-held ideas about space and place within communities. Her essays, drawings and sculpture have been published in *Memory Connection Journal, Diacritics, Zyzzava, How(ever), Architecture California: the Journal of the American Institute of Architects*, and *The Art of Description: Writings on the Cantor Collections*. Her architectural work has been featured in *California Home and Design, Southface Journal*, and CNN's television series *Earth-Wise*.

Michael S. Roth is president of Wesleyan University and the author, most recently, of *Beyond the University: Why Liberal Education Matters*

(Yale University Press, 2014) and *Memory, Trauma, and History: Essays on Living With the Past* (Columbia University Press, 2011).

Zina Steinberg, EdD, is Assistant Clinical Professor of Medical Psychology (in Pediatrics and Psychiatry), Columbia University College of Physicians and Surgeons. Thirteen years ago she created an ongoing project providing consultation to families and staff in the neonatal intensive care unit at Morgan-Stanley Children's Hospital, New York-Presbyterian. She works with the National Perinatal Association and with a nationwide consortium of psychologists to increase and intensify services for families of critically ill newborns. She is on the faculty of the Stephen Mitchell Center for Relational Studies and the Parent-Infant Psychotherapy Training Program, Columbia University Center for Psychoanalytic Training and Research. She is in private practice in New York seeing individuals, couples, and families.

Don Troise, LCSW, is a faculty member, and training and supervising analyst at the Institute for Contemporary Psychotherapy; he is also in private practice in New York City. He has published in *Contemporary Psychoanalysis* and *Psychoanalytic Dialogues*. His paper, The Traumatic Field: Psychoanalysis as Trauma Translated, will soon be published in a collection entitled *Unknowable, Unspeakable and Unsprung*.

Introduction

Adrienne Harris, Margery Kalb, and Susan Klebanoff

This book and its companion, edited collections of essays on "ghostliness" and demonic prescences in psychoanalytic and cultural life, emerged from the collective work of a group of analysts. Both collaboratively and individually, we were struck by the way uncanny and spectral presence, or absent presence, entered minds, bodies, and consulting rooms. The attention to ghosts did not stop just in the clinical dyad. We found ghosts haunting our theories, our practices, and our training institutes. We found them in many interstices of cultural and social life, too. There is no dearth of spectral presences. In addition to familial, intrapsychic, and relational ghosts, ghosts emerge from war and catastrophes that cannot easily be assimilated in the surrounding cultures and communities or in the minds and bodies of individuals.

Ghosts emerge in and as unwitnessed silences, and surely, from actual deaths. The body may be the absorber and also the communicator of ghosts. We draw on the term "ghosts" to capture the sense of objects that are neither internal nor external solely, that may disturb the atmosphere, the soma, the mind, temporality, and the surrounding fields.

We came to this topic unexpectedly. Or should we say, uncannily. We,[1] are seven psychoanalysts, different in backgrounds and in formation, who came together to discuss clinical work. The group formed out of the supervisory experience of one member and was made up of people new to each other, if not new to Adrienne Harris who formed the group.

We began a group process by reading Sam Gerson's "When the Third is Dead," (2009) his prize-winning essay on witnessing and its vicissitudes. The paper focuses on the oddness whereby historic injuries accrue around, between, and within persons as "present absences." Gerson was concerned with what happens culturally and personally when there is no registration of a catastrophe that has happened, is happening, seems always already to be happening. He was interested in bearing witness and he was also interested in what happened when such witnessing failed, when registration becomes beyond the capacity of an individual or the collective. He has written afterwords to both books, a mark for us of expanding influence on how we understand witnessing loss and its absence or failure or destruction.

Gerson deploys an evocative term for this lack of registration, "present absences." This concept appears, too, in the work of Bollas (1994), Caruth (1996), and Ogden (1992). The phrase has been a guiding force in our group work. "Present absences" refer to just that—absences that can be emotionally, viscerally, or even unconsciously felt in the patient, in the analyst, and in their interaction. These present absences grow from overwhelming but under-processed feelings about loss (frequently, though not necessarily, an actual death), and often emerge in gaps in factual information, narrative or affect—things mysteriously missing. We can think of this un-knowledge as a perpetual struggle between mourning and melancholia (Freud, 1917). Something is under wraps, a secret too dangerous to be disturbed—and thus oftentimes discovered in the enacted sphere of the transference/countertransference matrix.

Reading Gerson was a way to begin a group process. This was thought of just in a rather instrumental way. We picked a common task, thinking that such common work binds people, but we must hold and ponder the question of uncanny prescience in making such a transformative choice.

The Gerson paper stimulated many interesting associations and clinical concerns in the group and as the cases began to pile up, so too did bodies, losses—conscious and unconscious—deep uncertainties, intergenerational transmissions of trauma and, we all came to agree, ghosts. And, in a way that certainly marked the group and shaped our collective and internal growth, there have been, over six years, four staggeringly difficult deaths experienced by members in the group, and the demands of serious illnesses carried privately and also borne by everyone. We have also had two weddings, joyous occasions carrying their own ghosts as well.

We offer these personal details because we suspect that they are not really very atypical. Part of the work on analytic subjectivity has been to comprehend the complexity of the interrelationship of the use of the analytic instrument and the demands of daily life (Deutsch, 2014; Harris and Sinsheimer, 2008). A commitment to a field, to a bi-personal unconscious and conscious transmission across the analytic dyad requires that we widen our view as to what enters and affects the analytic process. In the processing of the personal and the clinical, the theoretical and the historical, we were also able to, and really needed to, include our own histories and countertransferences in our group process and in our individual clinical work.

Our hope is that in the clinical work we did on ghostly presences in treatments, and the writing it is stimulating, we can find ways to talk and think about the manner we and patients are haunted, and how these hauntings might be imagined and transformed. How do such possessions highjack lives and often treatments? Where are there demons? Are there good ghosts? Even as the presence of ghosts has historically signified the presence of unmetabolizable loss, are there limits to mourning? Is mourning, to some extent, an idealization and specters, whether grim or wishful, inevitable legacies of loss.

As the group's project has evolved to include an expanded group of authors, we ask and have been asked. Why ghosts? Why demons? Why not internal objects, why not dissociation or disavowal? Why do we need this new/old perhaps melodramatic language? In evolving answers to these questions, are we struggling towards a new conception that lives liminally in different sectors of clinical life, cultural thought, and practices?

Theorists have thought of these phenomena differently: intergenerational transmission of trauma (Davoine, 2007; Davoine and Gaudilliere, 2004), telescoping of generations (Faimberg, 2004), witnessing and Thirdness (Benjamin, 2004; Gerson, 2009), encrypted identifications (Abraham and Torok, 1994), or radioactive identifications (Gampel, 1992; Puget,1989, 2002). Freud (1919), Loewald (1960), and more contemporaneously Reis (2011) and Grand (2010) have written about the impactful presence of ghosts, vampires, and other kinds of haunting objects that enter the analytic field.

Working on ghosts and demons required an expansion of vocabulary and imagination. There are ghosts that protect, that hold us hostage; ghosts that we protect and cannot separate from (Baranger, and Baranger, 2009). But there is a murderous side to this; demons and vampires, dybbuks, and monstrous and grotesque forms that often represent the impossibility of containing and metabolizing loss and trauma. The body and the mind can be the site of attack and invasion. Eros and Thanatos can intermingle and disturb individuals and cultures.

In this book, we hope to explore the actual and psychic legacy of loss, of violence, phobic hatreds, and migrations that bear so heavily on the lives, minds, and bodies of contemporary patients. In tracking the present-absence and absent-presence of ghosts and various forms of hauntings within psychoanalytic treatments, we are tracking the power of hidden and often shame-laden histories to enter and shape the clinical work.

You could think of the ghost world as the place to manage excess, to find a skin of strangeness and uncertainty in which to imbed things hard to bear or hard to fathom. This is another melancholy solution but rich and engaging also. In some of the chapters, particularly the clinical ones, we have found ourselves in deep engagement with the differences and meanings of melancholy and mourning, ultimately wanting to expand the space and scope and duration of melancholy, while not avoiding or reifying its pathological aspects.

Harris (2013) wrote about Bion's well-known ideas about death in life in the context of his advice to analysts to work without memory or desire.

> This is Bion's famous instruction to the analyst: work in the present moment, without reference to history and desire. (Bion, 1967, p. 612)

As a sentence, an invocation, a call, this sentence is charming, evocative, interesting, putting us in touch with the foundational Freudian injunction of "evenly hovering attention." Yet, we might remember Racker's reworking of this injunction as a call to meditative states, states of altered consciousness. And we also can evoke now Ferro's idea of the task of analysis as one of inducing dreaming. It is a goal of analytic work to arrive at primary process. All these ideas seem to be exceedingly useful injunctions to analysts, pushing us to be attuned to bodies, minds, affects and to try (never fully successfully) to entertain experiences "outside the sentence" (Barthes, 1975).

But let us introduce another Bion quote to add to the complexity of Bion's relationship to temporality. To wit:

> I died on August 7th, 1917, on the Amiens-Roye Road. (Bion 1982, p. 265.)

He meant it.

So, Bion, in every waking minute, including the careful unfolding minutes of analytic sessions, is both changing, remembering, and still walking on that road, where his friend is still, in every present minute, being killed and he (Bion) not moving, or saving, or helping. And so forever, walking and dying on that road, both men. And, if so, we might say that the living man (Bion) is actually then conducting analyses from what Francoise Davoine (2007) refers to as "the bridge world," a space between the living and the dead" (Harris, 2013).

Bion was haunted, surely, but his haunting underwrote his vocation. Looked at from this biographical perspective, then, working with no history and no future, is actually at base the work of a traumatized, ghost-riddled analyst, a person working with time suspended, usefully and tragically. This might be so for all of us, even if our traumas are significantly less acute than Bion's. Loewald (1989) too, talks about this and so we might include him in this account of the impact of trauma on theory building, wondering what was carried personally for him, from the death of his father and the bereavement of his mother, in the injunction to turn a ghost into an ancestor.

Here is another Bion notion. Patients and analysts are working always at the edge of the abyss, the terror at the moments of transition. (Goldberg, 2008). James Grotstein, Bion's analysand, thinks that Bion remained stymied, stuck, hopelessly lost in the wake of the death of that beloved friend in 1917. Grotstein ends his discussion of Bion's memoir with this comment:

> Someone once said that Bion was "miles behind his face." I take this to mean that he was withdrawn, lonely, and unreached. (Grotstein, 1998, p. 613)

If you are a psychoanalyst caught up in this way of seeing the task or problem of analysis, history is necessary but history is also an albatross. Sometimes the ghostliness seems embodied in spectral presences, in figures actually dead or missing. Fascinating psychic processes underlie the deeply committed attempts patients make to keep the dead alive, close down space, or alternatively keep it open and ready for habitation. Killing and saving seem often too close to each other.

Rey (1988) has an intriguing way of thinking about this: the task of the analysand is to have the analyst cure the damaged objects he/she brings to the work. And, as Harris (2009) has argued, in clinical impasses, we often see how the analyst similarly arrives in the work to cure old injuries, bury the undead, undertake the final repair of history.

The task of repair of internal objects, laced into our countertransferences, is the source and wellspring of powerful sublimations and transformations into work ethics and skill. But there remains in anyone conducting this work, the residue of uneasy spirits and unfixed figures. Part of the shared task of analytic work is the transformation of melancholy into mourning, an always partially incomplete task. Many chapters in this book attest to the unending exhausting task of mourning. Margaret Little's (1985) pronouncement seems apt, "Mourning is for life."

It was in considering our clinical work and the complexity of encryption that we found it necessary to consider the profound role of the body and embodiment. In the current theoretical work on reconsidering levels of representation and registration of experience (Botella and Botella, 2005; Levine, Reed, and Scarfone, 2013; Stern, 2015) we are reaching for an account of what the body carries and communicates that builds on different models of mind and body, more integrated ideas of mental and bodily life and the complex structures in which experience is carried. As variable phenomena as body image, somatic illnesses, affect storms, gait, posture, the set of the face and gaze, the experience of weather, of space and time, are all saturated in meaning. Indeed, each and every one of our clinical chapters encompasses some form of unstable somatic dimension. We have found it useful to see these phenomena as ghostly, spectral, and ambiguous.

Although we began in the consulting room we found we could not entirely stay there. In many traditional cultures, ghosts and the spirit world can live both easily and strangely within daily life. Looking back now, it is fascinating to realize that the popular culture following the First World War seemed full of ghosts and vampires, creatures popping out of movies and television and popular novels. Was this popular depiction an attempt to contain or perhaps express the cultural level of melancholy and mourning? Did these effects and influence come from the past (slavery, wars, historical trauma, gulags) or, as some might say, from the future already present (climate change, terrorism, economic pain)?

In thinking of the long shadow of war (in both familial and cultural intergenerational transmission of trauma), we encountered some other interesting material on ghosts. Ghosts, sightings, séances, attempting to reach and speak to the dead, appear very powerfully in Western Culture in the wake of loss on a mass scale. The Civil War, in the United States, particularly the South (see Gilpin, 2009), and World War I in Europe, brought of an astonishing outbreak on spiritism. Visions of the dead and sightings of religious figures haunted battlefields and post war settings. Freud and Fernczi were engaged in discussions about the occult and "thought transference," over quite a long period. Their discussions were a mix of fascination, skepticism, and anxiety (see Freud-Ferenczi correspondence, Vol 1 Brabant, Falzeder and Giampieri-Deutsch 1993; Meszaros, 2014).

We are in the complex domain of unconscious communication. But words like uncanny and haunted are required, the words and language of object relations and internal objects seem too orderly for the experiences the authors in these books are describing.

Despite these cautionary notes, there is the triumph when narrative enters treatment, when fragments and chaos are ordered through naming and genealogy. This has been Davoine and Gaudilliere's (2004) perspective, seeing the long hand of history. It takes a half-century, they felt, to process a war. Unprocessed historical trauma was a prime engine of psychotic functioning. So there is, in the permanent tasks of mourning, both triumph and despair and this must be parsed and held by analyst for the patient and for him/herself.

Consistent with Davoine's thinking, some fifty-plus years after World War II, we are absolutely deluged with memoirs and novels, movies and plays, dances and operas, which are attempting to work through the emotional/psychological aftermath of the Holocaust. Some of these artistic projects have been initiated by second- and third-generation survivors in an effort to bear witness to their parents' and grandparents' previously unmetabolized wartime experiences. Some stories take the form of realistic historically accurate retelling; others are more intuitive and sensory near, like the French film *Le Secret*. In this movie, a boy is born after the war to survivor parents who had lost a son but agreed never to speak about the experience to anyone. Nevertheless, their post-war child is haunted by the spectral presence of his dead brother. Only when his parents finally reveal their loss can their child let go of his brother's ghost, which he had been unconsciously holding for his parents. We wonder if this outpouring of trauma-based artistic endeavours has both a containing and a retraumatizing effect in its conscious effort to put into narrative what is often beyond explaining with words.

We think here of Maya Lin's Vietnam war memorial in Washington DC, with its miles of engraved names of all who were killed. Or the 9/11 memorial in NYC which similarly offers up the engraved names of each of the 2,977 victims on the stone rim surrounding the dramatic multilayered descending memory pools. Perhaps our need for these memorials intensifies as our media-fueled barrage of trauma—absent much space for genuine containment or witnessing—intensifies. In all likelihood, the presence of these memorials does help to counteract absence (Slochower, 2011). But while such public memorials, and the rituals that surround them, are useful, they cannot substitute, says Gaines (1997), for the necessary language and affect accessed through private, internal, personal mourning.

Our attention was drawn both to the wider and larger cultures but also to something closer to home. Ghosts in psychoanalysis, in our profession, our institutes and our theories signify unburied, unmourned losses. In 2014 we read a news story, front page in the *New York Times*, about the discovery of 55,000 psychiatric patients in unmarked graves in New York. "In New York, more than 55,000 deceased psychiatric patients lie in unmarked graves. Near the former Willard Asylum, a small committee has spent the past three years fighting to memorialize the dead" (Bracken, 2014).

What kind of professional PTSD in our field allowed this to happen, so silently, over a period of so many years? We found ourselves, too, struggling and too often failing to be able to hold on to the specters and fearful shadows that haunt very many psychoanalytic institutes in regard to boundary violations and other moral matters.

The more open we were to looking for ghosts, the more we found them, lurking inside both our patients and ourselves, inside our personal and historical pasts, our internal and external spaces and the architecture of our lives. Ghosts and their ilk (vampires, demons, etc.) are widespread in contemporary popular culture. The television series *Lost*, for example, involves a constant oscillation between fantasy and reality, with none of the containing real-world limits of time and space. People die and reappear and ghosts wander about with an alternating comforting and alarming presence, as they simultaneously revisit their pasts, which are filled with dark secrets and unresolved trauma. Numerous other television series also explore similar experiences of people traumatically gone missing, and the psychological impact on those left behind.

We wonder why contemporary culture seems, right now, particularly strongly pulled toward the world of ghosts, of haunting? Could it be that we are living in a time of greater general uncertainty and chaos in the world—socially, economically, around the globe? Could it be the accumulated mass traumas and losses of modern day warfare, in concert with the fact that these events are no longer reported in a contained way on the 6 o'clock news and in the morning newspaper, but instead broadcast incessantly in excruciating, lurid detail on 24-hour news channels and across countless portholes on the internet all day and night long? It is harder—for better and worse—to shut out what is going on in the world. But it is also harder to metabolize the abundant and raw exposure.

The internet may play a role in another context. "Ghosting" is a common term in online parlance. It refers to someone (usually within a dating context) who simply disappears on another person, after extensive online talking or several dates or even months of dating. The use of "ghosting" to describe this common occurrence indicates a familiarity with the language and experience of ghosts, and an increasing familiarity with ghosts, and in fact both more awareness of and literally more ghosts in people's lives. It emphasizes the there/not there of present absences and absent presences of relationships both fostered and maintained on line, even post break up. This use of the term is also about loss that cannot be processed—because people simply disappear without explanation, because they remain both here—visible online, but not here. These are also absences that haunt.

This book was written with a companion book in mind: *Demons in the Consulting Room: Echoes of Genocide, Slavery and Extreme Trauma in Psychoanalytic Practice*. The two books are distinctly different yet also overlapping. They are enigmatic in their differences, much like the feel of ghosts themselves. We like to think of the two books as mutable: sometimes very distinct, sometimes dopplegangers. A doppleganger is defined loosely as a ghostly apparition, or alter ego, of a living person. The word originates from the German, literally meaning double-goer or double walker. Further definitions include a ghostly double of a living person that haunts its living counterpart, or the wraith (e.g., astral body or shadow). We want to emphasize the doubleness or existence of the shadow of the other. Much like figure/ground matrices, which can be fluid and shifting, it is often difficult—and intended to be difficult—to tell ghosts and demons apart. What on the surface may seem to be dichotomous categories are actually overlapping in complex, most certainly non-dichotomous ways. Trauma occurs on a continuum. Yet we hope the subtle conceptual distinctions help to illuminate the manner in which one is haunted by ghosts, and demons, distinct and overlapping.

Another of the many potential ways to think of the differences between ghostly present absences and demonic absent presences is to think of the major clinical tasks at hand. In this book and its companion, we are talking about the need to process overwhelming pain and resolve mourning, oftentimes trauma and mourning that have been put off from one generation to another. In this book we are trying to address the difficulties and challenges and sometimes limits of mourning. In the companion book, *Demons in the Consulting Room*, we are writing about the near-impossibilities of mourning, the stuckness in intractable melancholia (Freud, 1914). Seen through the lens of language, many authors in this book tend to emphasize verbalization of sorrow and grief, while authors in *Demons in the Consulting Room* tend to use language having to do with the realm of vampires, dybbuks, demons, and other states of deep and often distorted melancholy, "undeadness" or non-being, elements or substances, organic or inorganic that are not-fully-dead, but rather anti-mourning hauntings.

The power of the melancholic state seemed markedly evident to us, personally, clinically, and culturally. Most explicitly, we had to notice the tremendous aid that witnessing provides and the alternative difficulties of silence and solitude. This has continued to be part of Gerson's project, tracking the great dangers to witnessing's absence. A great many of our clinical accounts hold absence and silence at the heart of the clinical trauma. Absence and silence are the forms in which ghosts and demons, the wistful, the desperate, and the grotesque may proliferate. Narrative and witnessing are possibly the antidote to haunting. There are places and situations and persons and families where knowledge of trauma is refused, where the questions of what happened are turned back unanswered. Perhaps it is there the spirits howl loudest?

Another way to conceptualize differences between the two books is to use the terms developed by Durban (this book). In working with patients who are haunted by specters, however lurid or enigmatic, he suggests there are three types of patient experiences: those who are haunted by external shadows, those who are haunted by an internal presence of the shadow, and those who *are* the shadow. This book can be seen as describing those people and situations in which there is external or internal haunting, or both. Inevitably, these distinctions hold and they wobble and partially dissolve. It is surely fitting that enigma and uncertainty haunt these writings.

The consulting room

Ghosts haunt analyst and analysand, participating in impasses and uncanny experiences in the countertransference and in the transference, while more traditional spiritual practices involving hauntings seek to expel ghosts and demons. It is intriguing and important to us to stress that psychoanalysis and psychotherapies—drawing on trauma work—rather seek to have ghosts readmitted and repatriated.

In her chapter, Grand makes clear, that when a history of violence makes an appearance in our consulting room, we must hold, mourn, and contain the destructive aspects of the "borrowed wounds" and "terrors of generations past." In his chapter, Durban gives us two case illustrations to elucidate the clinical differences between his concepts of "living *with* the shadow of one's heritage" (being internally haunted, persecuted – similar to our idea of present absences) and *being* the shadow (a more chaotic, pathological self—similar to absent presences). An autistic boy is infused and almost consumed with shapes and indeterminate forms, full of affect and mystery. A middle-aged man, the son of a camp survivor who carried both injury and criminality (both traumatic), carries this parent with some conscious awareness but huge violence and cruelty turned against himself and others.

Across different theoretical traditions, each of these writers is trying to be mindful of the residue of trauma held unconsciously, often over several generations.

The chapters by Klebanoff and Ferguson each consider cases where actual history—the deaths of their patients' mothers—figure prominently in revivifying but also stalling and stultifying loss and mourning in both patient and therapist. In Klebanoff's work with her patient, she became struck by the strange disruptions in temporality, the freezes and odd lingering and time-stops that her patient practiced mostly unconsciously. For Ferguson's patient, time was also halted, and the idealized and lost beloved ghost remained untouchable, out of reach but endlessly longed for. In both these cases, micro and macro aspects of temporality were radically disrupted.

The task of repair of internal objects, is often laced into our countertransferences, where it can be the source and wellspring of powerful sublimations and transformations into work ethics and skill. But there remains in anyone conducting this work the residue of uneasy spirits and unfixed figures. Part of the shared task of analytic work is the transformation of melancholy into mourning, an always partially incomplete task. Ghosts remain in various forms and to reprise the insight of Abraham and Torok (1994) in their idea of encrypted identifications, sometimes the secrets passed remain unknown to bearer or receiver. This will be true for patient and to some degree in analyst as well. Feldman explores the case of a patient in a dissociated manic-like state, fleeing from the known/unknown gaps of his family's traumatic exile story, which he eventually learns in treatment to acknowledge, narrativize and express creatively in his work. The work developed within a parallel process in which the analyst found he had to attend to his own history, secret and half known. It is an assumption of contemporary work that stresses the intersubjective and the intrapsychic that this kind of countertransference work creates the ground for the clinical work.

What perhaps most profoundly links all of the chapters in our clinical sections in this book is the way that unprocessed gaps, breaches, breaks, opacity, disruptions, cracks, present absences/absent presences—actual, fantasied, inherited—lodged in our hearts, bodies, and minds, result in unmetabolized ghosts that haunt our lives and our treatment relationships. It is our human challenge and analytic endeavour to strive to witness, contain, hold, grow from, and try to mourn these ghosts.

The culture and the community

This project, beginning in a tight clinical focus, inevitably morphed into a consideration of ghosts in the culture and in the community. We had to notice, as many are suggesting (Caruth, 1996; Dimen 2011; Gerson, 2009; Grand and Salberg, 2015; Rozmarin, 2011, among others) that the haunting residues of cultural and social surround leak into the familial and individual experiences.

Ghosts haunt collectivities. Certainly, in our profession, with its, too frequent beheading of opponents and repression of conflict and dissidence, spectral "absent presences" abound. In the chapter on the ghosts of psychoanalysis, which is multiply authored, we try to think about some of these gaps. Roth speaks to the haunting presence Freud continues to have on all of us in our profession, as well as on the culture at large. Troise speaks in his essay to the unprocessed personal traumas that haunted Freud and Jung and speculates about how their personal hauntings may have in turn been influential in creating the very theories on which psychoanalytic work is based. Harris gets behind the ghostly and caricatured revival of Spielrein in the 1990s, as the tortured soul, to focus on the smart, scholarly teacher, clinician, researcher, and theorist. Butler writes about Trigant Burrow, the first American-born psychoanalyst, largely unknown in contemporary circles, but whose specter can be glimpsed sans credit in the ideas of many post-Freudian thinkers. And Kirsner discusses the ghost of Marilyn Monroe and how her suicide has haunted the field ever since. Drescher writes about psychoanalysis' traumatic history of prejudice and exclusion in regard to dealing with homosexuality in our patients as well as our own professional community.

McVarish and Leavitt explore this intermingling of personal and historical ghosts in their chapter about the mysterious Winchester House. The house was built by the heiress to the Winchester Rifle fortune, who was herself haunted by many tragic losses. Those losses were recreated and embedded over time in the nooks and crannies and secret passageways of the house's architecture, evoking as well the many ghosts that have resulted from the use of those firearms.

Kraemer and Steinberg write, in this book, about their clinical work in another haunted community: a neonatal intensive care unit. They inhabit a space that uncomfortably intertwines vulnerabilities at birth—including the experience-near potential for devastating loss—with reverberations of past traumas in the lives of the affected parents, as well as in the lives of the authors. Here is where Gerson's work is so helpful, his attunement to the potency of contained witnessing, witnessing that allows reflection and linkage, witnessing that is not retraumatizing, witnessing that can facilitate the transformation of present absences and absent presences.

Social and psychic ghosts have, naturally, also taken up fertile residence in the arts. Harris threads a moving personal story of loss with a reading of a wartime film about ghosts, *Stairway to Heaven* (1946). This chapter reads ghostliness as an aspect of melancholy, noting how powerfully the pull to omnipotence trumps the acceptance of limit and some form of acceptance of reality. Freud's great project (1917) in Mourning and Melancholia turns out to be hard to follow, as he himself knew and sometimes could say (Freud, 1929).

We circle back to conclude this section of our Introduction with a reprise, a conclusion that resonates deeply with all of our writers. Absence and silence are the forms in which ghosts and demons, the wistful, the desperate, and the grotesque may proliferate. Narrative and witnessing are possibly the antidote to haunting. There are places and situations and persons and families where knowledge of trauma is refused, where the questions of what happened are turned back unanswered. Perhaps it is there that the spirits howl loudest?

Note

1 Galit Atlas, Michael Feldman, Heather Ferguson, Arthur Fox, Adrienne Harris, Margery Kalb, and Susan Klebanoff.

Bibliography

Abraham, N. & Torok, M. (1994). *The Shell and the Kernel*. Chicago, IL: University of Chicago Press.

Baranger, M. & Baranger, W. (2009). *The Work of Confluence: Listening and Interpreting in the Psychoanalytic Field*. London: Karnac Books.

Barthes, R. (1975). *The Pleasure of the Text*. New York: Hill and Wang.

Benjamin, J. (2004). Beyond Doer and Done to: An Intersubjective View of Thirdness. *Psychoanal. Quart*. 73: 5–46

Bion W.R. (1982). *The Long Weekend: 1897–1919 (Part of a Life)*. (Edited by F. Bion). Abingdon: The Fleetwood Press.

Bollas, C. (1994). Aspects of the Erotic Transference. *Psychoanal. Inq*., 14: 572–590.

Botella, S. & Botella, C. (2005). *The Work of Psychic Figurability: Mental States without Representation*. London: Routledge

Brabant, E., Falzeder, E., & Giampieri-Deutsch, P. (1993). *The Correspondence of Sigmund Freud and Sandor Ferenczi, Vol. 1. 1908–1914*. Cambridge, MA: Harvard University Press.

Bracken, K. (2014). An Asylum's Final Secrets. *New York Times*. Nov 28, 2014.

Caruth, C. (1996). *Unclaimed Experience: Trauma, Narrative, and History*. Baltimore, MD: Johns Hopkins Press.

Casement, P.J. (1982). Samuel Beckett's Relationship to His Mother-Tongue. *International Rev. of Psychoanal*, 9: 35–44.

Davoine, F. (2007). The Characters of Madness in the Talking Cure. *Psychoanal. Dial*., 17: 627–638.

Davoine, F. & Gaudilliere, J.M. (2004). *History Beyond Trauma*. London: Other Press.

Deutsch, R. (2014). *Traumatic Ruptures: Abandonment, Betrayal and the Analytic Relationship*. London: Taylor and Francis.

Dimen, M. (2011). (Ed.) *With Culture in Mind: Psychoanalytic Stories*. New York: Routledge.

Durban, J. (2011). Shadows, Ghosts, and Chimaeras: On Some Early Modes of Handling Psycho-genetic Heritage. *Int. J. Psycho-Anal*., 92: 903–924.

Faimberg, H. (2004). *Telescoping of Generations*. London: Karnac Books.

Fraiberg, S. (with Adelson, E., & Shapiro, V.) (1975/1987). Ghosts in the Nursery: A Psychoanalytic Approach to the Problems of Impaired Infant-Mother Relations. In: Louis Fraiberg (Ed.), *Selected Writings of Selma Fraiberg* (1987), Columbus, OH: Ohio State Press, 100–136.

Freud, S. (1909). Analysis of a Phobia in a Five-Year-Old Boy. *Standard Edition*, Vol.10. 1–150. London: Hogarth Press.

Freud, S. (1915). Mourning and Melancholia. *Standard Edition*, Vol. 14. London: Hogarth Press.

Freud, S. (1919). The Uncanny. *Standard Edition*, Vol, 17, pp. 217–256. London: Hogarth Press.

Freud, S. (1929). Letter from Sigmund Freud to Ludwig Binswanger, April 11, 1929. *Letters of Sigmund Freud 1873–1939*. London: The Hogarth Press. 386.

Gaines, R. (1997). Detachment and Continuity. *Contemporary Psychoanalysis*, 33: 549–571.

Gampel, Y. (1992). Psychoanalysis, Ethics and Actualities. *Psychoanal. Inq*. 12: 526–550.

Gerson, S. (2009). When the Third Is Dead: Memory, Mourning and Witnessing in the Aftermath of the Holocaust. *Int. J. Psycho-Anal*. 90: 1341–1357.

Gilpin, D.F. (2009). *The Republic of Suffering: Death and the American Civil War*. New York: Vintage.

Goldberg, P. (2008). Catastrophic Change, Communal Dreaming and the Counter-catastrophic Personality. Paper Read at 4th EBOR Conference, Seattle, WA, Nov 1, 2008.

Grand, S. (2010). *The Hero in the Mirror: From Fear to Fortitude*. New York: Routledge.

Grotstein, J. (1998). Review of W. R. Bion, War Memoirs, 1917–1918. *Journal of Analytical Psychology*. 43: 610–613.

Harris, A. (2005). Conflict in Relational Treatment. *Psychoanal. Quart*. 74: 267–293.

Harris, A. (2009). You Must Remember This. *Psychoanal. Dial*. 19: 2–21.

Harris, A. (2013). Time: Stopped, Started, Frozen, Thawed. *The Candidate*. 3: 59–61.

Harris, A. and Sinsheimer, K. (2008). The Analyst's Vulnerability: Finetuning and Preserving Analytic Bodies. In: F. Anderson (Ed.) *Bodies in Treatment*. New York. Routledge.

Laub, D. (2005). Traumatic Shutdown of Narrative and Symbolization: A Death Instinct Derivative? *Contemp. Psychoanal*., 41: 307–326.

Levine, H., Reed, G. & Scarfone, D. (2013). *Unrepresented States and the Construction of Meaning: Clinical and Theoretical Contributions*. London: Karnac.

Little, M. (1985). Working with Winnicott Where Psychotic Anxieties Prevail. *Free Association*. 5: 1–19.

Loewald, H. (1960). On the Therapeutic Action of Psychoanalysis. In: *Papers on Psychoanalysis* Hagerstown, MD: University Publishing Group 221–256.

Loewald, H. (1989). *Papers on Psychoanalysis*. New Haven, CT: Yale University Press.

Meszaros, J. (2014). *Ferenczi and Beyond: Exile of the Budapest School: Solidarity in the Psychcoanalytic Movement in the Nazi Years*. London: Karnac.

Ogden, T. (1992). The Dialectically Constituted/Decentered Subject of Psychoanalysis. *Int. J. Psycho-Anal*., 73: 517–526.

Puget, J. (1989). Social Violence and Psychoanalysis in the Argentinian Context. *Brit. J. Psychother*., 5: 363–369.

Puget, J. (2002). The State of Threat and Psychoanalysis: From the Uncanny That Structures to the Uncanny That Alienates. *Free Associations*, 9: 611–648.

Reis, B. (2011). Zombie States: Reconsidering the Relationship between Life and Death Instincts. *Psychoanalytic Quarterly*, 80: 269–286.

Rey, J.H. (1988). That which Patients Bring to Analysis. *Int. J. Psycho-Anal*., 69: 457–470.

Rozmarin, E. (2011). To Be Is to Betray: On the Place of Collective History and Freedom in Psychoanalysis. *Psychoanal. Dial*., 21: 320–345.

Slochower, J. (2011). Out of the Analytic Shadow: On the Dynamics of Commemorative Ritual. *Psychoanal. Dial*., 21: 676–690.

Stern, D. (2015). *Relational Freedom: Emergent Properties in the Relational Field*. London: Routledge.

Goldberg, J. (2008) [illegible] Communal [illegible] and [illegible] Goodbye Catastrophic Personality. Paper Read at 4th [illegible] Conference [illegible] (2008).
[illegible] (20[illegible]) The [illegible] to [illegible]. [illegible] Routledge.
[illegible], L. (1998) [illegible] W. R. [illegible] Memoir. [illegible] Psychology [illegible]
Harris, A. (2007) Conflict in [illegible] Treatment. Psychoanalytic Quarterly, 76: 207-233.
Harris, A. (20[illegible]) [illegible]
Harris, A. (2013) [illegible] Stanford [illegible] Journal [illegible]
Harris, A. and Sklar, J. (2008) The [illegible] Compassion [illegible]
[illegible] Books [illegible] Review [illegible]
[illegible] Journal of [illegible] 41: 307-[illegible].
Leving, H. B., Reed, G. S. and Scarfone, D. (2013) [illegible] the Unconscious [illegible]
[illegible]
Little, M. (19[illegible]) [illegible] Psychoanalysis [illegible]
[illegible]
[illegible] (19[illegible]) [illegible] Psychoanalysis [illegible]
[illegible]
[illegible] (19[illegible]) [illegible] New [illegible]
[illegible] (2014) [illegible]
[illegible]
[illegible] (19[illegible]) [illegible] of Psychoanalysis [illegible]
[illegible]
[illegible] (19[illegible]) [illegible]
[illegible]
[illegible] (19[illegible]) [illegible] Supervision [illegible]
[illegible]
[illegible] (20[illegible]) [illegible] between [illegible] and [illegible]
[illegible] Psychoanalytic Quarterly, [illegible]: 209-[illegible].
[illegible] (19[illegible]) [illegible] 427-[illegible].
[illegible] (19[illegible]) [illegible]
[illegible] 21: 320-[illegible].
[illegible] (19[illegible]) [illegible] Psychoanalysis [illegible]
[illegible]
[illegible] (20[illegible]) [illegible]
[illegible]

Clinical

Chapter 1

"I always wished I could stop time"

An adolescent girl, unresolved mourning, and the haunted third

Susan Klebanoff

> *"I wander now among names of the dead: my mother's name, stone pillow for my head."* (Trethewey, 2006, p.8)[1]

Days before I presented this case for the first time, I had the following dream. *"I am buried in a plain wooden coffin. My eyes are open and I am staring straight up at the lid of the box. I can't move and I can't breathe. I know this is me, but I have platinum blonde hair in big ringlets and big blue eyes and wear a girl's cotton jumper with a Peter Pan collar. I am aware that I am in my patient Sophie's body. I am at the same time both inside the coffin and outside, feeling myself being Sophie and observing Sophie being herself. In the dream, I am thinking, 'So this is what it feels like to be buried alive.'"*

Six years earlier, Sophie entered my office in a free fall of panic and despair. Thin with pale, almost translucent, skin she made a ghostly appearance, and told her story, between sobs, sounding more like a lost child than a 26-year-old accomplished musician. "I don't know where to go," she said, "and I don't know what to do."

Sophie was reeling from the effects of several recent losses. She had been fired from her job in a small professional orchestra and had been dumped by her boyfriend of several years. She was behind on her rent and her roommate had asked her to leave. She had already gotten a job as a receptionist to tide her over financially, but she was so humiliated by her loss in stature that she was unable to maintain eye contact with the customers. During breaks, she would hide out in the stockroom, hitting her head against the wall until she was bloody and bruised. Then she would cover her injuries with makeup and return to her desk. Sophie was scared she was going insane. "And if I do," she said, "no one will be there to take care of me."

In assessing the need for imminent hospitalization, I contacted the referring therapist, who had seen Sophie as a child. "Sophie's parents," she said, "they're the salt of the earth. They did everything right. But Sophie, there's always been something wrong with Sophie. Maybe it's chemical." Next, with Sophie's permission, I contacted her dad, who was about to leave the country for a two-week vacation. He reluctantly agreed to come in for a session. "I have four other children," he announced in the first five minutes of our meeting, "and I don't believe in coddling. I spent years taking care of my brother with all his mental health problems," he continued, "and that's not happening here." I explained my serious concerns for Sophie's emotional state, but this tough, middle-aged, retired marine just didn't understand what made things so difficult. "If Sophie has failed," he said, "then she can come home with me. That's the best I have to offer. Otherwise, she needs to make sure she gets a job with benefits. Her mother got sick and died young. She needs to remember that."

By the time he left, Sophie's story was beginning to take shape.

Sophie's recent string of losses had piled up, until together they triggered a delayed post-traumatic stress reaction, awakening long frozen feelings about her mother's death over a decade earlier, when Sophie was just fourteen. Sophie's father had been determined that the family move forward as if nothing had changed. He allowed Sophie and her siblings only one day off from school for the funeral. What he was unable to provide was any true guidance as to how to mourn. Consequently, Sophie froze up, in a way that preserved her dead mother in a static psychic space where time stood still. In addition, after her mother's death, she became haunted by the collective and, more importantly, unspeakable grief that belonged to the entire family, until finally, the ice broke, and with it, her capacity, as a precocious child, to carry it alone. In time, it became clear that holding her family's grief had set Sophie voluntarily on a toxic errand that was slowly pulling her toward extinction. I came to understand that my job, as her therapist, was "to extract the ambush toward extinction and to undergo the unpleasant drudgery of constantly managing the mandate to die . . . in order to find new and more flexible forms of adaptation" (Apprey, 1999. p.131). For Sophie, the pull toward "extinction" was seductive on many levels. It offered the possibility of reuniting with her dead mother, as well as the possibility of sparing herself the painful feelings of loss she so desperately wanted to ward off.

My position as Sophie's therapist would also mean dealing with spectral hauntings of my own. Like any analyst, I too bring my own ghosts into the room. My father, a Russian Jew born and raised in China, lost his own father as a very young child, and an older sister a few years later, both to sudden and deadly diseases. In 1937, he boarded a boat in Shanghai to escape the Japanese invasion and immigrated to America. Communication with his family in China was cut off for years. When it was restored, he learned that his mother had died during the period of government-mandated silence. With all these losses, my father focused on "making it" in his new adopted country, never speaking of his past, except in a joking manner, and never taking the time to grieve. I remember approaching him when I was around ten years old, about a family tree project I had to complete for Hebrew school. I asked him to name his siblings in birth order and his reaction was to stare off into space for a few minutes before finally saying quietly, "Impossible, ask your mother." As a child, I found his reaction strange and chalked it up to yet another example of my foreign-born dad's oddity. As an adult and a psychoanalyst, I understand his reaction as defensive and dissociative; there was simply too much loss to process. Over time, I came to learn that, like Sophie, those losses had haunted him throughout his life in an unconscious and unspeakable way, and eventually, came to haunt me too.

As the sensitive child in the family, I came to realize that growing up I functioned unconsciously as a container for my father's unformulated trauma (Faimberg, 2005) and, as a result, identified easily with Sophie's position in *her* family. Both daughters of authoritarian figures who suffered from their own unspoken PTSD—my father's, from innumerable early losses, and Sophie's father's, from wartime experiences and a childhood with his own marine father and a cold, punitive mother. Over time, it became clear that the two of us were similarly tied up in and weighed down by our respective ancestral ghosts, both holding "deposits" from our fathers. Traveling to China five years ago gave me an opportunity to move forward, to get to know my father, who passed away long ago, from a more nuanced and more adult perspective. I saw pieces of him in the sounds and colors and even the dance movements of the culture, and discovered that many of the strange tales he told, which my family had assumed were comic caricatures, were actually borne of his true experience. But most importantly, I got to turn the family errand *I* was unconsciously carrying into a positive one. During a Jewish tour of Shanghai with an Israeli journalist, who spent the last eight years searching for and collecting gravestones from the Jewish cemeteries desecrated during the Cultural Revolution, I got to watch a video of one such excavation from a muddy river outside the city. As the headstone was pulled out of the ground, the camera zoomed in on the name, carved in Hebrew and in Russian. Uncannily, it read Zippa Klebanoff. The gravestone turned out to be that of my paternal grandmother, a woman I never knew, but whom I am named after. I was quite literally putting ancestors to rest, and left with a sense of calm and closure that on a conscious level I didn't even know I was missing. As Davoine and Gaudilliere (2004) explain, it is necessary for the therapist to mourn his own ghosts before helping his patients mourn theirs. My personal journey to China made me even more committed to actively helping Sophie find a new adaptation because I understood firsthand the peace that results from finally burying the emotionally undead.

At first, treatment with Sophie was chaotic. She arrived late for appointments or missed them entirely. Mostly I came to think of her difficulty settling in as a reenactment of Sophie's most significant experience in life. But this time, Sophie would be the one disappearing, like her mother, and I would be the one left alone, holding both the "presence of her absence" (Green, 1972; Gerson, 2009) and my own anxiety, worrying if she were okay and if she would return. It was a necessary game of hide and seek, and I needed to prove I could stay alive and keep looking for her, unlike her emotionally withdrawn father, or her dying mother (Winnicott, 1958, 1974). Eventually, we addressed this reenactment in the room and the significance of Sophie's need to switch roles. This time, I got to be the frightened child, who had to deal with the uncertainty of impending loss, and she got to be the abandoning mother. Sophie took in this interpretation with wide eyes and a profound sense of relief for my offer to contain the emotions that were too much for her child self to process. It was as if I had offered her deceased mother a seat at the table. I told her we could speak of both her mother's life and her death and promised I would be there to help hold her overwhelming affects for as long as she needed.

This invitation had a calming effect on Sophie and the treatment and allowed us symbolically to hold her mother's ghost together in a shared experience, with no expectation that Sophie let go on anyone's schedule but her own. At times, these early sessions had the feeling of a séance. There could have been a sign on the door: ghosts welcome here. Because, for Sophie, this haunting was the opposite of unwanted; her ghost world was familiar, a source of identity and continuity, a place of comfort, like the mildewed smells and tattered touch of a well-worn and well-loved security blanket. We went over the details of Sophie's mother's illness and death countless times, and each time there was a new piece added or expanded or remembered, until I knew it and felt it as much as Sophie. In bearing witness this way, I understood I was helping to give voice to Sophie's grief and to acknowledge her emotional pain as real. To assure her, as Shabad (1993) writes, that her "suffering was not just a figment of (her) imagination that was endured unnecessarily, but that it had a real and meaningful existence." Until this was actively witnessed, we could not even consider the possibility of Sophie moving on to a more alive way of being. So that's what we did, time and time again, in a repetitive cycle that moved bit by bit to an authentic affective experience that we could both acknowledge. These sessions were filled with an emotional heaviness that was hard to bear. "Do we really need to go there again?" Sophie would ask, knowing full well that wherever we started, that's where the material would inevitably take us. Part of what made the process so difficult for me was understanding where we were headed (where, in fact, at times I was leading her) which was closer to the emotional pain and reality of loss. The goal was to facilitate an active mourning process as opposed to a melancholic one, a distinction Freud made clear in his writings in 1917. While mourning and melancholia share significant similarities, there are fundamental differences between them. Mourning is considered a normal, healthy, and necessary response to a loss, while melancholia is seen as a pathological response, often resulting in depression and suicidal risk. In melancholia, there is no real object loss to the subject, which was certainly the case with Sophie. And even when she could fleetingly acknowledge the loss, at times she could not understand why it was so disturbing. "Is how I'm feeling really all about my mother?" she'd ask. My job, as Sophie's therapist, was to help her move out of the past, into the present, and allow her to imagine a future. Sophie's ability to do this hinged on her recognition that her mother was really gone, and that she needed to continue on without her. It felt like both a cruel and a loving task.

I am no stranger to maternal countertransference but with Sophie my feelings were immediate and stronger than usual. My identification with Sophie might have offered both "bright spots" in treatment based on my "readily available personal experience," (Goldberger, 1993) but also may have led to "blind spots," precluding full analytic exploration and sufficient distance from my strong countertransferential pulls. I had fantasies about finding Sophie a real estate broker, sending her silverware when she moved to her new place, with a note to remind her to eat, and of setting her up with a professional musician friend to help her get a more appropriate job. I had to work hard to contain my overwhelming need to be a good object for this bereft girl, to keep myself from trying too hard to repair the trauma that I knew could never be fully reparable (Harris, 2009). And to remind myself that no matter how much I identified with her, or even loved her, her experience was not the same as mine and she was not mine, and the best I could do was guide her toward finding her own way.

At the time I started working with Sophie, my own adolescent daughter was also veering between childlike neediness and pseudo-adult independence. Like Sophie, she was not quite ready to be launched into the world. At home, I felt caught in the whirl of complicated mother-daughter relationships, worried about not giving enough, and alternatively, about giving too much; about how much dependence to support and how much independence to encourage. Mothering my own teenage daughter brought me close to feeling my way into Sophie's loss. I could easily imagine how lost my own daughter would have been without me and couldn't help but think of Sophie navigating adolescence without *her* mother. My work with Sophie also heightened an awareness of my own vulnerability, as I got pulled into her family drama of fear and dying. I carried Sophie's loss with me out of the treatment room and into my private space, in a way that felt constant and intrusive at times, the indelible image of a motherless daughter etched permanently on my mind.

Curiously, one of the only times Sophie ever contacted me out of session was about a year into treatment, when I was on vacation with my husband and daughter, touring colleges for the upcoming year. In what now seems like an unnecessarily self-disclosing response to her query about where I was going, I had told Sophie what I was doing. Possibly it was an aggressive acting out on my part in reaction to feeling so drained by the work. Writing about this now, I feel a sudden burst of shame for my casual reminder to Sophie that she wasn't my number one priority and wondering who took *her* around to visit schools. I remember feeling torn when Sophie called me, trying to tune in to her neediness and sense of abandonment, while my daughter stared at me with resentment for my work encroaching on our time. I reset my boundaries and got off the call, knowing there would be ruptures on both sides, but trusting that no real damage was done, and that repair was fully possible.

The particular circumstances surrounding Sophie's mother's death contributed to her difficulty letting go. After five long years of pain and suffering, with only one brief remission, Sophie's mother died at home in bed early one morning after Sophie left her side briefly to take a shower. Her father told her that her mother was "just sleeping" and sent her off to school. When she got home, her mother's body was gone. Sophie was both furious and guilt ridden because, on some level, she believed that her mother would still be alive, if she, Sophie, had not stopped to take care of herself. And the fact that she hadn't been able to say goodbye made it harder to absorb the loss, and helped to build an unconscious fantasy about what had happened to that missing body (Torok, 1968) which, in turn, made it harder to accept that her mother was really gone. Instead, it was as if she were held in a suspended state, which allowed Sophie to stay mired in the melancholic feelings that kept her internalized object alive and also held her emotionally and developmentally captive, forever a little girl in a cotton jumper with a Peter Pan collar.

The specter of death, with its melancholic anxiety, hovered over the treatment. Each break in sessions, each holiday, each vacation, brought up the fears of who would survive the separation. What if I never returned? What if she died while I was gone? And if we both made it through, then who else would have to go missing? Numerous times Sophie showed up in my waiting room while I was away. "I knew you weren't here," she would say, "but I wasn't really sure." There are many ways to understand this behavior. To touch base with my office out of some need for object constancy in my absence, to double check her own reality testing for my being away, or in some magical thinking kind of way, to remind me that she was still there, like a small child who hides inside her mother's suitcase while the parents are packing for a trip, making sure she won't be left behind. I can visualize her waiting patiently. When I asked, Sophie couldn't remember if she stayed the whole forty-five minutes or if she even checked her watch or her calendar. She just knew she had to come. I wonder if this was some reenactment of what happened with her mother. That if she didn't accept the absence, it didn't have to be real. Or was it Sophie rehearsing my inevitable loss, practicing sitting shiva in my waiting room?

For years of her childhood, starting with her mother's diagnosis when she was nine years old, Sophie had consciously practiced what her mother's death would be like for her and how she would cope. In many ways, Sophie claimed, the rehearsals were much harder than the reality of her mother's death, partially because they caused her to relive the loss repeatedly and partially because she held these fantasies privately, unwitnessed, and on her own. Ongoing anticipation of her mother's death also set the stage for Sophie living in a kind of dream state, where she wasn't certain what was real and what was pretend. This I believe was relived by me in the confusion of my opening dream, and reenacted in my waiting room so many years later. What was inside and what was outside? What was real and what was practice or pretense? And who was inside of whom? Looking back now, I realize I was pulled into Sophie's netherworld early on in treatment, where time and space were occluded, and we floated along together in a morass of melancholy. In my identification with Sophie's sensitive child, I had the tendency to feel rather than inquire, and needed to build up both of our tolerances to Sophie's pain.

In a bizarre twist of fate, when Sophie's mother actually did pass away, Sophie was scheduled to be in a school play the following night. In what I imagine was her father's attempt to support her, and move on, he brought many of the mourners from the funeral to her performance. Sophie remembers looking out at the audience and feeling that the whole experience was unreal. Most of the people would not even have been there to see her on stage if they weren't already in town for her mother's funeral. Her dad's well-intentioned but misguided decision resulted in Sophie's confusion and a conflation between her continuing life and her mother's death, and a collapse of the psychic space between the two spheres.

Three years after her mother's death, Sophie's father remarried a woman with two sons of her own. Sophie's two little brothers were young enough to bond easily with their new stepmother, but Sophie's refusal to even try left her outside the family circle. Adding to her isolation was the fact that, with his new marriage, her father suddenly cut off all contact with her mother's friends and relatives. Like an angry non-custodial parent locked into a high-conflict divorce, his action can be seen as an expression of murderous envy, symbolically killing his dead wife, once again (Donner, 2006) and killing off his own feelings of loss in the process. In later years, we understood these actions as Sophie's father's need to "circle the wagons" in an effort to keep the vultures—and his own terror, raising three young children on his own—at bay. Like Sophie, he had his own experience of blocked mourning and defense against vulnerability. Both father and daughter shared the flip sides of the same omnipotent fantasy. In Sophie's case, believing her mother could be revived if she simply refused to let her go. And, in her father's case, believing that once she was dead, he could wipe out the fact that she had ever been alive at all. Before he remarried, he threw out all of Sophie's mother's belongings, including heirloom family antiques and keepsakes she was saving for her children, into three giant dumpsters that sat on the driveway for days. What Sophie took from this, at age seventeen, was an erasure of her mother's family constellation. "It was clear we were supposed to start over," says Sophie, "as if our first family had never existed at all."

While shutting down and shutting out appeared to be Sophie's father's primary defensive style, his wife's memory was not completely erased. For years, Sophie's father ran in charity marathons in her memory. And the entire family attended church services each Christmas and donated handmade ornaments in Sophie's mother's name. But there was no sharing of memory or speaking of her absence between these isolated events; her name was never spoken out loud and there was no language or affect accessed (Gaines, 1997) to give private, interior meaning to the public family rituals. Out of emotional context, these symbolic actions offered little solace or opportunity to resolve mourning. Sophie recalled being the only one crying and how her ongoing depression wore on her siblings. Everyone else judged her failure to move on as a weakness, yet she saw it as a sign of loyalty, binding her to her mother's existence and implying that their relationship was more special than anyone else's or, at the very least, walling off her mother from her other children, and declaring her Sophie's alone.

Sophie was her mother's only daughter. They shared an artistic sensibility and spent time going to concerts and museums. But Sophie's favorite memories of her mom are of the times the two of them spent chatting every Sunday morning, after church, on a bench in a cemetery next door. " I didn't even notice the graves," she said dismissively, when she saw the surprised look on my face. I pressed further to find out what made those moments so special, and Sophie mentioned the quiet and the intimacy, perhaps in the afterglow of feelings engendered in the church services those mornings. Sophie's mom was a deeply religious woman. She taught Sunday school and often quoted favorite Bible passages to her children, stressing the importance of humility and turning the other cheek. Memorable to Sophie was her mother's strong belief in the Resurrection, that Christ returned to life on the Sunday following the Friday on which he was crucified. I wondered about the setting for those intimate talks between mother and daughter, the nonchalance of sitting amongst gravestones, which might have helped lay the groundwork for Sophie's future trouble grieving. Was Sophie holding out hope that her mother would return to life, like Christ?

Or was Sophie simply languishing in the maternal bond that had been nurtured in this melancholic setting?

Those graves were the first indication that other ghosts would be visiting the consulting room. In addition to losing her mother as an adolescent, we learned in time that Sophie was carrying her mother's many losses as well. It turns out that Sophie's mother was a doctor who worked with a geriatric population. She often grew attached to her elderly patients, going home and sharing their life stories and eventually their deaths with her emotionally attuned daughter. In addition, Sophie's mom lost her own mother in her early twenties and told Sophie many times about how much she missed her. "Young adulthood is when someone *really* needs their mother" was a line Sophie's mother often repeated. In retrospect, I wonder if this statement contributed to Sophie's shame about her childhood grief and to her crisis in her twenties, when she may have unconsciously felt some permission from her mother to finally fall apart, with grief and with rage. "How dare she do the same thing to me that her own mother did to her? How dare she not be here when I need her most?"

As details filled in, I learned that Sophie's mother had grown up in the American South, a heritage about which she felt conflicted. On the one hand, she enjoyed standing out as a proud Southerner in the small New England town she lived in, and continued to feel attached to the family's land, which she passed down to her children upon her death. But growing up in the South also meant growing up in a culture permeated by sadness and humiliation in the wake of the American Civil War. During this bloodiest war in American history, battlegrounds literally turned into makeshift graveyards overnight and it took years for bodies to be appropriately identified and buried. Southern morale suffered a lasting sense of shame, not only by losing, but by being deemed morally inferior to the North in the process. Today, one hundred and fifty years later, mourning remains unresolved, and the trauma of the Civil War is still maintained through rituals such as annual battlefield reenactments and celebrated anniversaries of southern states' dates of secession from the union. These events provide vehicles for passing the unprocessed trauma of the Civil War, both consciously and unconsciously, from generation to generation. In America, there has been little acknowledgement of how much the South had to sacrifice for the nation to stay whole, or to what extent our republic was founded on death and on suffering (Faust, 2008), much like the dynamics of Sophie's blended family, where the original loss was covered over in celebration of the new union.

Sophie, in part, has romanticized her connection to the South. She remembers visiting her grandfather's house and the rich smells of the freshly cut grass and the honeysuckle and the freedom of running through the fields. She is also pulled toward nostalgia for a simpler and more pure agrarian existence, with less commercialism and consumerism than the modern day northeastern world she had grown up in. Sophie's mother's childhood was quite different, growing up on a small family farm with no glamour and lots of hard work. I expect Sophie's fantasy is a manic defense, a girlish attempt to preserve her mother in some other time and place, before illness took hold. And a defense as well against the depression intrinsically tied up with nostalgia, which, in translation, literally means "return home" to "pain."

In a way, it was not only Sophie who remained stuck in time, but for Sophie, her mother did as well. Sophie was politically progressive and sensitive; she never glossed over the shameful aspects of the southern legacy, which she found abhorrent, but for her, the South was symbolically and emotionally attached to her mother *as a child* at least partially because she continued to see her mother through the *eyes* of a child. Her mother, she reported, was a "saint," who "never complained" about being sick and handled her situation with the utmost grace. Sophie can recall no episodes of her mother's impatience, anger, or resentment before or during her illness, though she (Sophie) does report hearing her mother quietly weeping in her bed at night. This idealized version of her mother's selflessness interfered with Sophie's ability to see her mother as a complex woman with a full range of emotions and desires, and, through this identification, Sophie had a hard time recognizing her own disavowed negative emotions and more complex desires and motivations. Over the years, Sophie did allow herself to morph into a more fully nuanced individual, but was never able to confront her mother's real life limitations, as she would have done naturally in her mid or later adolescence, had her mother survived.

I knew little about the South until I discovered the work of southern author William Faulkner in college. I was enthralled by his languid prose and drawn to his southern characters' preoccupation with their region's complicated history. My work with Sophie frequently stirred up my memories of reading Faulkner, who famously wrote of the South, "The past is never dead. It's not even past" (Faulkner, 1951). I also related personally to the burden of living with a history that was always present. While we never spoke seriously about my father's past in China, the history of anti-Semitism and the Holocaust were daily touchstones in my family life, which provided a justification for parents' clannish attitudes and distrust of all people, places and things that were not considered Jewish or even "Jewish enough." In my family, we were all taught to be on constant alert for the next anti-Semitic backlash. To be in denial about this inevitable future occurrence was thought to be dangerously naïve.

A few years into treatment, my well-learned caution crashed headlong into Sophie's Pollyannish denial, in regards to her romantic life, creating a rupture that invited her fantasies of the South into the process. Typically, Sophie had been dating damaged young men in hopes of rescuing them and bringing them back to health. But this time, she started dating a successful, self-confident young man, whose wealthy family helped support him in pursuing progressive causes. Sophie was immediately drawn in. Within a few weeks, I saw this pensive young woman turn into a giggling schoolgirl, suddenly dreaming about princess dresses and lavish lawn weddings. I questioned her about her uncharacteristic certitude and dramatic change in personality. "It's destiny," she replied. "After all, we're both from the South." My inquiry was persistent, my own intergenerational transmission of suspiciousness leading the way. I feared Sophie was being naïve and I had a hard time watching her set herself up for further pain. I could see clearly that this man, raised in a Southern but also clannish Jewish family, much like my own, would not rescue her, as she was hoping, and take her back to a simpler time, before her mother got sick and her world fell apart. Sophie, not surprisingly, experienced my line of questioning as unempathic, like someone throwing cold water on her face, and telling her it's time to grow up. In a way, that is what I was saying, that her denial was as dangerous as her despair, one setting her up for disappointment, and the other not offering any relief from the harsh realities of life. When this brief relationship ended, Sophie regained perspective and thanked me for being concerned enough to want to protect her, and for reminding her that the only direction to move in time was forward.

It was arduous work with Sophie. She would take one step forward toward embracing life, but would easily falter and fall back into depression. I don't believe I fully understood the extent of Sophie's depressive stasis until she casually mentioned that the electricity had been turned off in her apartment for weeks. She hadn't paid her bill. And she hadn't even bothered to make a call about having the electricity turned back on. She liked living in darkness, she explained, or at least liked to know that she could. There was no sense of adventure about this. Rather, it was about keeping herself in a state of limbo, not quite alive, but not quite dead either. This was both an internal experience as well as one projected to the outside world, that, as long as she was living in this suspended state, that she was not quite seeable to others either. It didn't even occur to Sophie that she was making an odd choice until she heard herself telling the story aloud in therapy. "I guess I have to decide," she said, "if I really want to enter the land of the living."

Symbolic of Sophie's identification with her dead mother was a framed series of charcoal drawings of human figures that Sophie did for her senior art project in college and that, as an adult, she kept carefully hidden in the back of her closet. Most significantly, each figure was missing an arm or a leg. Sophie says of the pictures that she wanted to "demonstrate her equally permanent internal scar in a way that people could see." But I think of these drawings as something more, as representing the psychological equivalent to a medical syndrome called phantom limb pain. In this syndrome, the limb is no longer there, but the patient is haunted by the physical pain that remains, not from the site of amputation, but from the space where the missing limb used to be, as if it were still present. This medical syndrome results in confusion between reality and fantasy—how can I possibly feel my leg hurting if it is really no longer there?—and raises questions about where the pain actually resides. In the mind? In the body? In the emotional attachment to the missing limb? In the miscommunication between the whole and intact body of the past and the damaged one in the present? This kind of haunting pain is very similar in feel to the unformulated trauma experiences that are transmitted unconsciously from generation to generation, challenging to grasp onto and too amorphous to contain, leaking from the past to the present, and from the unconscious to the conscious, and back again. Showing up in uncanny ways, like in the charcoal drawings of limbless bodies, eerily evocative of the injured soldiers hobbling home on crutches from the Civil War.

With great effort, Sophie made progress over time dealing with her many phantom feelings and family ghosts. She shored up her relationships with peers, switched to a more professional job, and returned to graduate school. She started to build tentative but authentic friendships with her stepmother and stepbrothers that did not negate her mother's existence. And, after a series of devastating relationships, she started seeing a kind and grounded young man and they became engaged. With palpable fear, she reached out to several people in her mother's family, planning on inviting them to her wedding. By being willing to engage with aging relatives, she was finally acknowledging the passage of time and getting dangerously close to shaking the intense hold that her mother's ghost had on her. "I guess all this time," she said, "I couldn't accept that she was really gone. In my head, she was here but not here, like in a coma."

Shortly afterwards, Sophie reported this dream:

"I am walking into a room to talk to my mother, alone. There is a big desk, two chairs, a couch, and a bright light behind her. She tells me that I am not her biological daughter. I hear this as her giving me permission to live; I do not have to get cancer and die young. When I think about that room now, it's similar to this room. In fact, it's the same room. You are also giving me permission to let go."

As Sophie relayed her dream, she was quite calm, but I was increasingly aware of holding back tears. At first I believed that my tears were from awe that this psychoanalytic process, which at times I have seriously doubted, can work so profoundly. But then I started to wonder. In holding back my own tears, am I replicating Sophie's historical stance (Reis, 2009) of silently holding her grief? Or modeling some new way of being, neither flooded nor repressed? Whose tears are they anyway? Mine or Sophie's or both of ours, for all of our mourned and yet to be mourned ghosts?

After analyzing the dream, Sophie offered this childhood anecdote: "As kids, I remember we used to talk about which superpowers we wished for. My friends would want the typical ones, like to fly or be invisible. But I always wished that I could stop time. Now I finally understand why."

Epilogue

Sophie had a challenging year leading up to her wedding, facing and refacing, processing and reprocessing, her mother's absence at each significant milestone in the planning, proving once again the truth of Green's words that "there is no end to the dead mother dying" (1972). The choice and wording of the invitations, which did not carry the name of her mother, negotiating with her father over the guest list to include friends and relatives from the past, wedding dress shopping with her stepmother, another reminder of her mother's absence, and finding a place for yet another mother substitute in the form of her mother-in-law to be. My place in this panoply of mothers "once removed" was as container and witness and transitional object, as Sophie learned to allow others in and continue on the road toward autonomy. It was a huge step forward for her to attend her first wedding dress fitting on her own, with my cell phone number newly re-entered in her phone contacts "just in case." And it took a lot of restraint on my part not to offer to go with her, to trust that she was finally strong enough to incorporate her mother's loss and stand on her own in the world.

Several of Sophie's mother's relatives did attend the wedding. This was the first time Sophie had seen them since her mother's death. During the rehearsal dinner, two of her maternal aunts approached her to discuss the condition of Sophie's mother's gravesite, which they had just visited for the first time since the burial. They reported that the cement bench, which Sophie had personally selected in lieu of a headstone, had been split in two by a recent storm. Again, an experience of uncanniness. As she was telling me this, I sat in anxious anticipation of Sophie's reaction. But, to my relief, Sophie experienced this news as a kind of liberation, "as if a permanent weight had been lifted off my shoulders." As other family members stepped up to symbolically share in the loss, Sophie could afford to step away. Rather than cave in when she heard that the bench split in two, Sophie's fantasy was that her mother was saying that she no longer needed her there, to sit with her in that same graveyard, as she had done since she was a small child.

For Sophie, it has been a long journey from fear and dread to what Ornstein calls the "uncertain abyss of hope" (1995). Courageously, she has shifted her identity from motherless child to young adult to recently becoming a mother herself. With her newfound faith in the future, she bought a house in the suburbs with her husband and started a family. In preparation for her move to her new home, she took the charcoal drawings out of their frames and lovingly rolled them into museum quality tubes for storage. "I don't have to look at them anymore," she explained, "but I need to know that they are there, as a testament to all I have lost." She has taken up a new instrument and is planning on planting honeysuckle this Spring.

Note

1 Natasha Trethewey, poet laureate of the United States from 2012 to 2013, won a Pulitzer Prize for *Native Guard*, a book of poetry about one of the first black regiments which served in the Civil War. The themes in her personal life, as well as in her elegiac verse, reverberate throughout this case. Like Sophie, she is haunted by the death of her mother

when she was a young girl. She is haunted as well by the many ghosts of unburied black soldiers during the war. Her work also makes reference to the ways human limbs carry the weight of a multilayered and complex intergenerational transmission of history. As she says, "In my dream,/ the ghost of history lies down beside me,/rolls over, pins me beneath a heavy arm" (Pilgrimage, *Native Guard*, p.20).

Bibliography

Apprey, M. (1999). Reinventing the Self in the Face of Received Transgenerational Hatred in the African American Community. *Journal of Applied Psychoanalytic Studies*, I (2): 131–143.

Abraham, N. & Torok, M. (1984). "The Lost Object-Me": Notes on Identification within the Crypt, *Psychoanalytic Inquiry*, 4: 221–242.

Brown, L. (2007). On Dreaming One's Patient: Reflections on an Aspect of Countertransference Dreams. *The Psychoanalytic Quarterly*, 76: 835–861.

Davoine, F. & Gaudilliere, J. (2004). *History Beyond Trauma*. New York: Other Press.

Donner, M.B. (2006). Tearing the Child Apart: The Contribution of Narcissism, Envy, and Perverse Modes of Thought to Child Custody Wars. *Psychoanalytic Psychology*, 23: 542–553.

Faimberg, H. (2005). *The Telescoping of Generations: Listening to Narcissistic Links Between Generations*. London: Routledge.

Faulkner, W. (1951). *Requiem for a Nun*. New York: Random House.

Faust, D.G. (2008). *This Republic of Suffering: Death and the American Civil War*. New York: Vintage Books.

Freud, S. (1917). *Mourning and Melancholia*, Standard Edition, XIV: 243–258.

Gaines, R. (1997). Detachment and Continuity. *Contemporary Psychoanalysis*, 33: 549–571.

Gerson, S. (2009). When the Third is Dead: Memory, Mourning and Witnessing in the Aftermath of the Holocaust, *International Journal of Psychoanalysis*, 90: 1341–1357.

Goldberger, M. (1993). Brightspot, a Variant of Blind Spot, *The Psychoanalytic Quarterly*, 62: 270–273.

Green, A. (1972). *On Private Madness*. Connecticut, CT: International University Press.

Harris, A. (2009). You Must Remember This. *Psychoanalytic Dialogues*, 19: 2–21.

Lieberman, A. Padron, E., Van Horn, P., Harris, W. (2005). Angels in the Nursery: The Intergenerational Transmission of Benevolent Parental Influences. *Infant Mental Health Journal*, 26 (6): 504–520.

Ornstein, A. (1995). Dread to Repeat and the New Beginning, *Annuals of Psychoanalysis*, 2: 231–248.

Reis, B. (2009). Performative and Enactive Features of Psychoanalytic Witnessing: the Transference as the Scene of Address. *International Journal of Psycho-analysis*, 90: 1359–1372.

Shabad, P. (1989). Vicissitudes of Psychic Loss of a Physically Present Parent. In D. Dietrich and P Shabad, (Eds), *The Problem of Loss and Mourning: Psychoanalytic Perspectives*, 101–126. CT: IUP.

Shabad, P. (1993). Repetition and Incomplete Mourning: The Intergenerational Transmission of Traumatic Themes. *Psychoanalytic Psychology*, 10: 61–75.

Trethewey, N. (2006). *Native Guard*. New York: Houghton Mifflin Company.

Torok, M. (1968). The Illness of Mourning and the Fantasy of the Exquisite Corpse, Chapter 4, *New Perspectives in Metapsychology*, 107–124.

Winnicott, D. W. (1958). The Capacity to be Alone. *The International Journal of Psycho-Analysis*, 39: 416–420.

Winnicott, D. W. (1974) Fear of Breakdown. *International Review of Psychoanalysis*, 1: 103–107.

Chapter 2

Ghostly intrusions

Unformulated trauma and its transformation in the therapeutic dyad

Heather Ferguson

> *"Although finding love can set development in motion, there is no end to the dead mother's dying, and it holds him prisoner."* (Green, 1972, p. 153)

Four years into treatment with my patient Frank, amid a deadlock of which we were only dimly aware, I had a striking dream: "*Frank is pregnant and needs an abortion. He is scared, vulnerable, and fragile. I go with him and two of his close friends to an abortion clinic. I am a therapist-like friend, not as close with Frank as the other two, with whom he does not share his secret. At the office, a clinician leads him to an operating room. After the abortion is complete, Frank sobs inconsolably. The nurse won't release him from the room until he is feels better. As he is being released, I reassure myself that his two friends will care for him in my absence and see that he is fed.*"

Upon awakening from this dream, riveted with shame, I began to ponder its double meaning: a symbol of our unspoken impasse and an unwitting intersection of our histories. Frank, now in his mid-forties, began therapy for the first time over a decade ago. In our initial meeting, Frank's bodily presence revealed the imprint of his traumatic past. With his slow and tortured movements, he communicated the weight of unprocessed pain over his mother's sudden death in his adolescence. Frank seemed frozen, his vitality and growth aborted by the catastrophic loss that he was left alone to bear. "Love was cut off when my mother died. I was alone," he deplored. For Frank, melancholia represented a foreclosed or suspended grieving because his loss, never recognized or symbolized by his family, went unwitnessed, leaving in its wake a "kind of haunting" (Harris, 2009a).

Overweight since childhood, Frank struggled with low self-esteem and lingering body shame that inhibited his freedom to pursue romantic relationships. Although Frank achieved success as a writer, in love he felt like a failure. In our early treatment, empowered to date, Frank tracked how his negative self-perception interfered with these interactions. Never making it past the first date, he felt like "sloppy seconds," humiliated by his designation, "best friend." By our third year of work, with nary a girlfriend in sight, Frank despaired his probable fate: "forty year old virgin," the ultimate failure.

Meeting his increased anger and hopelessness, I, in turn, felt inadequate and powerless. Engaged in a reverberating, reciprocal experience of helplessness and hopelessness, yet unknown to us, I felt weighty dread in anticipation of our sessions. Struggling to stay empathically engaged, my supervisory dream arrived as a shocking but welcome messenger, offering important clues about the nonconscious process between us (Blechner, 1995, 2001; Sands, 2010).

Ghostly intrusions and forestalled mourning

From Shakespeare's Hamlet to Loewald's (1960) metaphoric ghosts, we have wrestled with burying our dead. As Brothers (2008) suggests, all therapeutic relationships may be ghost stories. Spectral ties that afflict our patients similarly haunt the therapist. In this chapter, I describe the affective intersection of my history and Frank's, ghostly ties that haunted us both, illuminated by my dream, which clarified our impasse and awakened necessary mourning. Coburn's (1998) notion of "affective intersection" describes the coexistence of the patient's unconscious communication and the analyst's resonate narcissistic vulnerability. My dream alerted me to the psychic loss disavowed in my history that eclipsed my ability to fully reflect, empathize, and understand Frank.

My own unformulated loss, and its attendant shame, collided with Frank's desperate plea to be held and deeply understood in his despairing depths, for we shared a common ancestry. Like Frank, I grew up with a depressed parent; in my case, an artist father who was never able to process the tragedy of his brother's suicide, which compounded his own serious, recurrent depression. My father could not utter his brother's name for decades, frozen by this shattering loss and his own sense of failure. Similarly, Frank's mother, Eva, was despondent and enigmatic, haunted by the unacknowledged and ungrievable deaths of her sister, father, and mother.

Our mutual experience of parental absence and intangible loss left, for us both, a residue of guilt and shame. Not fully recognized, I believe Frank and I shared an internalized sense of failure over not enlivening our depressed parent. What I dreamt for both of us, what we felt somatically, we could not yet formulate consciously (Stern, 2009, 2012).

Only in retrospect would I grasp the depth of Frank's need to preserve an unblemished tie with Eva, her ghost in stasis, securing their unbreakable bond while keeping overwhelming loss at bay. By exploring the unsettling communication in my supervisory dream, a graphic illustration of vanquished childhood needs and loss—a place of intersection for us both—greater receptivity to Frank's struggle ensued, loosening our stalemate.

My intent here is to illustrate how living out non-represented feelings in the therapeutic dyad becomes a powerful form of psychoanalytic witnessing and facilitates forestalled mourning. This necessary recognition and shared process awakens unprocessed loss, for both analyst and patient, allowing previously sequestered feelings to be symbolized in a mutual exchange. In this intense, nonconscious affective interaction, the therapist becomes an alive other, capable of "living through" and containing intense negative affects in contrast to the psychically dead or absent parent (Bromberg, 2003; Shabad, 1989). In this process, the patient's solitary experience of deadness transforms into one of being an alive participant who can have a genuine impact on the therapist, shifting the analytic atmosphere (Beebe & Lachmann, 2002; Newman, 1999; Peltz, 1998; Reis, 2009; Searles, 1973). Just as Frank had wanted to protect his idealized tie with Eva, now he challenged me to experience, nonconsciously, his own helplessness and to disconfirm his expectation of abandonment.

A black hole within

Frank, the youngest child in a large family, had a strong bond with his mother, Eva, a painter from a well-to-do family. Born in the Midwest, Eva moved to the Northeast to study art and married Rafi, Frank's father, shortly after college. They both recounted a sweet camaraderie in the early years of their marriage, despite significant personal and cultural differences.

In contrast, Rafi was a poor Egyptian Jew who emigrated to America alone, at age eighteen, to improve his family's life conditions. Rafi's father, who remained in Egypt, struggled with alcoholism and lost the family business. With little formal education, Rafi established a successful business in America and generously supported relatives, many of whom he later helped resettle in the U.S.

Frank, feeling distant and disdainful, described Rafi as an "empty wallet." Rafi, blamed for the collapse of the marriage, remained a shadow parent, lost as an agentic figure. Frank's idealized identification remained tenaciously tied to Eva.

Eva's father, also alcoholic, abandoned the family when she was five years old. Later, her older sister reconnected with their father—a reunion forbidden by their mother, provoking her outrage and rejection. Eva was denied access to her father and sister, both of whom died of cancer a decade later. Once married, Eva focused exclusively on her children, devoting her energy to their creative pursuits while sublimating her own artistic aspirations.

During this time, Eva became the sole caregiver for her mother, a role she sustained until her mother died. As silent witness and observer, Frank became an appendage of Eva's unmetabolized trauma. Death and loss became the backdrop experience of his childhood. By then, Frank was eight years old, and the specter of death and the role of mothering became infused in him. As her children matured and became independent, Eva lost her sense of purpose and depression took hold.

In session, I speculated that these unacknowledged (and unmourned) multiple losses left Eva frozen, in a suspended state that contributed to her depressive withdrawal, a traumatic freeze that held intergenerationally transmitted losses, disavowed and unmetabolized (Abraham & Torok, 1984). Eva was a living ghost, an ethereal presence caught up in a bereavement that turned her gaze from her children as her depression deepened. Frank identified a suicidal quality to Eva's lack of self-care—first as she struggled with untreated depression, slipping into solitary drinking, and later as she prophesized her own death from cancer—leaving Frank a complicated amalgam of rage, helplessness, shame, and unbearable sadness. Internalizing this feeling of impending doom, young Frank remained the ever-perfect son attempting to resuscitate Eva from her own psychic deadness by staying close and distracting her with his wit and intelligence.

In a bid for what must have been an expression of buried anger and marital discord, Eva moved out of the family home when Frank was thirteen. Perhaps she too yearned to free herself from a life where she had supplicated her own needs and desires to take care of others. It is unclear if she was engaged in a love affair. Two years later, Eva, with only fourteen days left to live, heartbreakingly disclosed to her family that she had terminal cancer. Frank violently sobbed, "In both of the worst moments of my life—my parents' separation and my mother's death—I didn't have the help from the one person I counted on: my mother!" This painful lament marked Frank's double loss: Eva's slow withdrawal from the family, unarticulated and unacknowledged, compounded the catastrophe of her untimely death.

Frank's father and siblings withdrew into their own grief-ridden spheres, leaving Frank unable to bear his pain, much less ponder and communicate what was poignant—the absence of an attuned and receptive parent. He experienced "double loss" (Hagman, 1993, 1996; Shane & Shane, 1990): loss of his mother who provided vital self-object needs—comfort, validation, and affirmation—and loss of his father—perhaps the real sloppy seconds—who he found emotionally impotent tangled in his own psychic morass of confusion and pain. Without a vital witness, Frank turned his sense of helplessness inward in the form of self-denigration and self-hatred. He declared, "I feel a black hole inside, a feeling of sadness in my gut. I am reminded, over and over again, that I am a failure, a f—up."

In a poignant session with Frank and his older brother, each sibling described a different relational experience with Eva. Although Frank said, "her death was like the period at the end of a long, dark, sad story," his brother's description of Eva's alcohol abuse evoked psychic suicide. Believing, however, Eva was unfairly criticized by his siblings, Frank's allegiance to her remained unquestioned. He imagined joining Eva in a deep, authentic sadness, devoid of criticism and anger. Frank maintained a self-protective distance from his family who, he said, fell woefully short of Eva's attuned presence. In psychic retreat (Peltz, 1998, Steiner, 1993), Frank pursued a solitary intellectual path and maintained a defensive distance from his family, both in defiance and in an effort to shore up his vulnerable self (Ornstein, 2009).

Foreshadowing our impasse

Frank's sexual exploration was hijacked by the disorienting break up of his parents' marriage, leaving him with a complex mix of ambivalence and fear of his sensual desires. In one memory, a model scene (Lichtenberg, et al., 1992), Frank recounted the mortification and betrayal he felt when his mother discovered his secret *Playboy* magazine and later teased the anonymous offender at the dinner table; a chance for resolution and the emergence of healthy Oedipal strivings lost. Did his sexual aliveness, the beginning stirrings of healthy Oedipal longing, become overshadowed and sullied in the wake of his mother's felt abandonment and subsequent death? Did this evocative memory reflect his mother's real disdain or assume retroactive meaning (Faimberg, 1988), entangled with so much loss? Self-hatred, displaced on his body, carried his mother's ghostly imprint, as Frank perceived his sexual urges as "dangerous and toxic." At his most desolate, Frank wailed, "I am rotting inside. There is toxic poison inside me. My sexuality is grotesque."

Model scenes—often seminal experiences jointly discovered by analyst and patient—encapsulate, in metaphoric form, experiences that represent unconscious fantasies, pathogenic beliefs, or motivational themes (Lichtenberg, et al., 1996). Frank's last meal with Eva, saturated with psychic meaning, remained iconic: another model scene. This visit, a month before Eva died, was imbued with a sense of unspoken doom as Frank registered something gravely wrong as he choked down their favorite meal. Eva put on a brave face but remained silent about her diagnosis, the same cancer that killed her sister and father. Days later, hospitalized, Eva slipped into a coma. Frank was never alone with his mother again. He never said goodbye.

In times of acute distress or loneliness, Frank would relive this moment and the potent feeling of unnameable dread: childhood foods ingested in a desperate bid for comfort would be thrown up in a state of unbearable guilt and disgust. His self-loathing, particularly acute following romantic disappointment, led to episodic binging and, on occasion, purging, as he anesthetized and punished himself simultaneously. In one session, Frank raged, "I will just eat myself to death," signaling his helpless despair over his unmet needs, appetite, and undesirable body.

Frank's words and their affective intensity communicated the paradoxical bind I struggled to understand. "I am afraid to surrender my suffering, to lose my depression because this is the tie to my mother. I want to love a woman but she won't fill the emptiness left by my mother," he implored. If Frank moved forward, he opened up possibility of new attachment. However, this carried more dread than hope as Frank believed that anything good would inevitably collapse, leaving him crushingly alone if he relinquished his idealized union with his dead mother. If he buried his mother by changing, would he lose her forever?

Maintaining the status quo, on the other hand, was equally damning, leaving Frank in the realm of "the not quite living, and the not quite dead"

(Brothers, 2008, p. 134). Only in retrospect would I decode this frozen position as an identification with Eva and a means of memorializing her thwarted life. As Butler (1995) offers, ". . . melancholy is the refusal of grief, it is also always the incorporation of loss, the miming of the death it cannot mourn" (p. 174).

The hope for a new beginning and the dread to repeat

A few years into treatment, Frank became preoccupied with a beautiful singer, and he began a rigorous campaign of dieting and exercise. As he lost sixty pounds, he fantasized that by shedding the status of "fat, incompetent little brother," returning to the family as victor with a desirable girlfriend, he could "shove it in their face." In this potent fantasy, Frank was the vengeful victor. This reparative quest (Kaufmann, 2012; Ornstein, 1995; Shabad, 1993), with its inherent strivings, expressed the hope for a new beginning, the "dread to repeat" (Mitchell, 1993, Ornstein, 1974), and his unmetabolized and displaced rage.

It also carried the wish to undo feelings of disabling shame and inadequacy, caused by the non-recognition in his childhood, and alter the helplessness that chained him to the pain of his past. In an effort to re-make his body, Frank expressed the hope of erasing his alienation and awakening his sexual longings. Implicit, however, was another thread: a bitter sense of recompense for all that could not be recovered. An expression of vengeful justice for all that was lost. When this striving failed, Frank despaired, overlaid he said with "twenty years of baked-in rage."

At his most desolate, Frank cried, "I want to smash my head and cut off my penis." Suicidal thoughts often followed. During these months, as his pain intensified, I felt the tug of my own undertow: Would our work together offer solace and alleviate Frank's deep loneliness and self-hatred? Would my own less conscious feelings of inadequacy and powerlessness—the very emotions that tied me to our work—be ever-present ghosts haunting us in the consulting room?

The treatment crunch

For Harris (2009a), clinical stalemates invariably implicate incomplete or foreclosed mourning for both patient and analyst. My work with Frank underscored my own sense of helplessness in healing my depressed father and anger over my own frustrated dependency needs. We found ourselves in an unspoken battle to sustain hope in the face of dread, which felt evocative of the emotional climate in both our childhoods.

This "bright spot" (Goldberger, 1993)—a personally evocative and vivid intersection with Frank's history—initially impaired my ability to grasp the complexity of both presence and absence in Frank's narrative. Our impasse arose from this intersubjective disjunction (Stolorow & Atwood, 1992); that is, my assimilation of Frank's emotional material altered its meaning, thus impairing my ability to full comprehend his needs. In this way, my wish to vitalize and free Frank from his inner deadness, and dislodge his attachment to his maternal imago, collided with his need for me to recognize the breadth of his despair and comprehend the unbearability of his loss.

I now recognized that my own fear of the abyss of bleak and drowning sorrow, embodied by my father's struggle, put a protective wedge between me and the depth of Frank's suffering. In our work, I had to reflect on and repair this collision in order to reactivate Frank's derailed development and move our treatment forward (Newman, 1999; Russell, 2006; Stolorow & Atwood, 1992). This challenged our unspoken, mutual errand: healing the ghostly wounds of the previous generation.

My speculations prompted further self-analysis as I came to appreciate my struggle to remain the engaged, alive witness that Frank so desperately needed (Gerson, 2009; Orange, 1995; Poland, 2000; Reis, 2009). I began to consider my dream the emergent property of our unique dyad, an unconscious analytic third (Coburn, 1998; Davoine and Gaudilliere, 2004; Ferro, 2002; Harris, 2009b; McLaughlin, 1991; Ogden, 1997, 2004a; Stolorow and Atwood, 1992). As Ogden (2004a) suggests, ". . . in dreaming the patient's undreamt and interrupted dreams, the analyst gets to know the patient in a way and at the depth that may allow him to say something that is true to the conscious and unconscious emotional experience that is occurring in the analytic relationship at that moment" (p. 864). In this way, I "dreamt my patient" and our impasse into existence (Brown, 2007; Ogden, 2004a).

My dream illuminated my feelings of inadequacy and impotence in mobilizing Frank and the stalled labor of our treatment. My dream, perhaps, symbolized Frank's unformulated experiences (Stern, 1989): the enduring trauma of being the discarded baby and his paralyzing identification with a similar part of Eva. Did I dream up his feminine identification with his mother; pregnancy as a symbol of his adhesive maternal identification? Did it symbolize his loss as well as mine?

I reflected on the context of my dream: Newly married, I was anxiously trying to conceive. Did my desire for a family collide with Frank's need to be held in his despairing depths? Was I resonating with Frank's terror of separation and emancipation as I imagined his pull toward the safety of babyhood, representing a long lost wish and a fear of failing to embody his manhood? Absorbed in my own apparitions, was I unwittingly repeating for Frank the experience of the abandoning mother who privileged her own needs? Or, was I replicating the relational template of frustrated older sibling, impatient with his lack of growth and independence?

Now, more conscious of my own contribution to our co-constructed "treatment crunch," (Russell, 1975), I used my dream's affective communication to address our unspoken, yet palpable impasse. I acknowledged my misattunement and the implicit pressure on Frank to change that reinforced his sense of aloneness and failure. In a session shortly after the dream, I simply stated that I realized how I had not fully heard how desperate and alone Frank felt. I told him I was sorry. "Thank you" was Frank's simple response. Later, in the following sessions, we discussed the curative value of my owning my empathic failure, providing a new implicit relational experience where he could experience having genuine impact on me, something that his interaction with his parents sorely lacked (Brandchaft, 1987; Lyons-Ruth, 1998; Rustin, 1997). Rustin (1997) highlights the value in inquiring about the impact of analytic activity on the patient, which "elevates the patient's influence to center stage," (p. 50) and enhances a sense of agency.

Admitting my "blind spot" (Goldberger, 1993; McLaughlin, 1991; Orange, 1995; Shaw, 2010), seemed to liberate us from Frank's defiant protest against relinquishing his depressive stance and the stalemate that fed our dynamic. Was the admission of my fallibility a needed developmental experience, a missing link in his relationship with his mother? To help Frank, I had to be deeply affected and survive the emotional turmoil in order for both of us to grow emotionally and foster the necessary shift in our dyadic process.

As I acknowledged my limitations and offered genuine repair (Fossaghe, 1995; Lachmann & Beebe, 1996), a developmental second chance unfolded (Mitchell, 1997; Newman, 1999; Orange, 1995; Slavin & Kreigman, 1998; Stolorow & Atwood, 1992). As Slavin and Kreigman (1998) write, the past is "rediscovered" by the patient as the analyst becomes a more usable new object, through a genuine negotiation process, as the analyst becomes new to herself. I became the engaged, fallible mother/older sister who could bear witness to the catastrophe that had already happened, rendering it real, tangible and endurable (Winnicott, 1974). By providing an opportunity for previously unformulated and unsharable affects to come to the fore of our relationship, space opened for his grief (Eshel, 1998; Harris, 2009b; Socarides & Stolorow, 1984).

As we settled into a more related and genuine relationship, I became pregnant and Frank went on a sabbatical. Something ineffable emerged. I believe my introspective process allowed for greater containment of affect that implicitly altered the analytic atmosphere (Odgen, 2004b; 2012; Searles, 1959, 1973). While maintaining weekly phone sessions, Frank began to date, sharing details of his exciting sexual exploits. Did the phone allow Frank enough freedom from me, his substitute mother, to share titillating details of his amorous risk-taking? Did my pregnancy signal permission for greater emotional (and sexual) freedom? Maybe I embodied the non-collapsing, sexual, and alive mother and helped awaken Frank's dormant sexual longings, so feared and loathed? Ultimately, I believe acknowledging my limitations, implicitly and explicitly, was the mutative ingredient in our deepened trust. In loosening my own omnipotent defense, a feeling of vulnerability and uncertainty emerged, joining us in our shared human struggle.

As Frank claimed his sequestered sexuality, I delighted in his expansive sexual playfulness, providing the mirroring self-object experience (Kohut, 1977) painfully missing in his young adulthood. Soon after, Frank met his future wife and they developed a deeply meaningful relationship. During this time of blossoming for both of us, I had another evocative dream: that I gave birth to a fully-grown Egyptian-looking man! This dream, perhaps, indicated our growth—his and mine—and expressed my wish to fully actualize Frank's maturation, to make room for my own baby while securing Frank's future.

Traumatic states are lived in double time

Today, still working hard in treatment, Frank expresses gratitude for the life he has been able to create with his wife and young son. However, self-hatred remains proximate, triggered by the slightest misconstrued glance or perceived judgement from his partner. As Harris (2009b) states, "Traumatic states are lived in double time—it is as if the bad thing is about to happen . . ." (p. 12). Even though Frank's frozen grief has thawed, as more conflictual feelings have become nameable and more tolerable, traumatic states can be powerfully evoked and "freeze-framed into an eternal present" (Stolorow, 2003, p. 160). Words dry up, negative feelings overwhelm, and the ghosts re-emerge. In these moments, as Green (1972) reminds us, "there is no end to the dead mother's dying" (p. 153).

Unresolved mourning and spectral ties to the dead parent become intertwined with one's character, part of one's inner architecture. Patients reveal these absences, their objects of identification, in the form of internal imprints that leave their mark on character, defenses, and symptoms as way of memorializing and rendering as real one's suffering (Abraham & Torok, 1984; Faimberg, 1988; Shabad, 1989, 1993). As Shabad (1993) writes, "In so doing, the person can assure himself that his suffering was not just a figment of his imagination that was endured unnecessarily, but that it had a real and meaningful existence" (p. 493).

In bearing witness to Frank's disillusionment, I continue to hear his suffering plea and, in the process, hope to transform his embittered world of thwarted wishes into accepting that his childhood needs will never be fully reclaimed. This also includes reconciling that our doomed and damaged objects, so formative for us both, will never be fully repaired (Brothers, 2008; Harris, 2009a). Rey (1988) suggests that patients often bring a hidden project to treatment: a wish to repair damaged inner objects in the hope of untangling toxic identifications and emancipating the self. In this sense, Rey is addressing the need to liberate personal growth by relinquishing the need to heal our wounded loved ones, allowing necessary mourning to unfold.

In our grief work, I assume shifting roles. First, I serve as the containing mother, holding feelings of crushing despair, and sharing tears as we conjure Eva's life. As Lieberman, et al. (2005) suggest, the task is more than exorcizing ghosts but welcoming the "angels in the nursery," the loving memories that infuse our patients' often forgotten histories. Gaines (1997), similarly, stresses the importance of "creating continuity;" that is, maintaining dialogue with the deceased and repairing disruption to the inner self-other relationship, thereby awakening an inner aliveness with the dead parent. In this process, we mourn Eva's truncated life—the way her expressive freedom was eclipsed by generational, cultural, and familial demands. We also acknowledge the meaningful, celebratory moments Eva missed: Frank's creative triumphs, his marriage, and the birth of his own beloved son, creating a sense of felt continuity (Gaines, 1997).

At other times, when Frank expresses his emotional and sexual needs without being overwhelmed by a terror of abandonment, I assume the role of admiring sister. We explore his fantasy of the perfect mirroring marital relationship, in addition to the exquisitely attuned therapy relationship, and wonder if this represents the unconscious wish to revive Eva and the unconditional love he so hungers for? We name the "relational 't' trauma" (Goldner, 2014) that Frank and his spouse evoke in each other—an affective intersection of their histories creating psychic gridlocks but also deep pathways of compassion. We connect his childhood feeling of "walking on egg shells" with the recurring sense of impending doom activated in his marital relationship.

When his partner recently accused him of being a baby, he felt simultaneously enraged, falsely accused, and humiliated. We carefully unpacked all the possible resonances with his disrupted childhood: his longing to be mothered again, his deep feelings of inadequacy as a grown-up, and his appreciation of his wife's own traumatic childhood and its activation in their dynamic.

Over the last four years, both my parents died, and I came to share Frank's sense of unmoored existence far more acutely and viscerally than before. Confronted with the necessity of surviving my own intense affects, I connected, personally, to the devastating and disorganizing impact of Frank's ungrieved loss. This reciprocal process evokes Slavin's (2012) call for a "kind of radical empathy"—a willingness to engage the painful struggles in ourselves in the service of making meaning around the same human dilemmas that torment our patients—leading to a genuine sense of shared relational mourning (Harris, 2009a).

It is the nature of the intersubjective interaction that allows old themes to get reworked as ghosts emerge, genealogies get reset, and we push past our imperfections (Harris, 2009a). My journey with Frank illustrates the long shadow cast by our losses and the necessary ongoing elaboration throughout our lives. Change and growth are fraught with fear and uncertainty. Just as there is emerging faith that all has not been lost, that Frank will not be forgotten, progress can easily slip away.

As Frank's fantasy of the "exquisite corpse" (Torok, 1968)—the reunion with the perfectly attuned mother—expands and shifts, he loosens his melancholic identification, expanding his relational possibilities. In this journey, Frank's tenderness and compassion toward his father and siblings has emerged. While writing this narrative, Frank shared his own dream: "*I am eighty years old and my son, Luke, is forty. It is the end of the season and we are folding up beach chairs. This is the last time we will see this place, our last summer here. I share this realization with Luke and he starts to cry. I feel this massive sadness, so big that I can't conceive of it. I turn to him and say, "There is only one feeling that is bigger than this sadness, and that is how much love I have for you."*

Conclusion

The metaphor of ghosts is an inducement to attend to the complexity of unmetabolized intergenerational traumas and more proximate losses and absences that pervade our patients' experiences and our own. In this paper, I describe a non-linear process marked by disruption, repair, and ongoing elaboration. The task of mourning, including integrating painful, shattering affects while understanding the full complexity of one's attachment to the deceased, is an enormous emotional undertaking for patient and analyst. Surviving mourning is an impossible burden to endure alone; healing necessitates a resonant witness who is willing to engage inevitable ruptures and needed repair in order to provide hope and expand the relational possibilities. Loewald's (1960) powerful question lingers: Is it ever possible to lay our ancestors—the ghosts that reside within each of us—fully to rest? Should they?

Bibliography

Abraham, N., & Torok, M. (1984). "The Lost Object-Me": Notes On Identification within the Crypt, *Psychoanalytic Inquiry*, 4, 221–242.

Atwood, G. (2012). *The Abyss of Madness.* New York: Routledge.

Beebe, B. & Lachmann, F. (2002), *Infant Research and Adult Treatment Co-Constructing Interactions*. New Jersey, NJ: The Analytic Press.

Blechner, M. J. (1995). The Patient's Dreams and the Countertransference, *Psychoanalytic Dialogues*, 5, 1–25.

Blechner, M. (2001). *The Dream Frontier*. New Jersey, NJ: The Analytic Press.

Brandchaft, B. (1987). Bonds That Shackle, Ties that Free. In: R. Stolorwo, G. Atwood, & B. Brandchaft (Eds.), *Psychoanalytic Treatment An Intersubjective Approach*. (pp. 47–65). NJ: Analtyic Press.

Bromberg, P. (2003). One Need Not Be a House to be Haunted: On Enactment, Dissociation, and the Dread of "Not-Me"—A Case Study. *Psychoanalytic Dialogues*, 13, 689–709.

Brothers, D. (2008). *Toward a Psychology of Uncertainty*. New Jersey, NJ: The Analytic Press.

Brown, L. (2007). On Dreaming One's Patient: Reflections on an Aspect of Countertransference Dreams. *The Psychoanalytic Quarterly*. 76, 835–861.

Butler, J. (1995). Melancholy Gender—Refused Identification. *Psychoanalytic Dialogues*, 5, 165–180.

Coburn, W. (1998). Chapter 2. Patient Unconscious Communication and Analyst Narcissistic Vulnerability in the Countertransference Experience. *Progress in Self Psychology*, 14, 17–31.

Davoine, F. & Gaudilliere, J. (2004). *History Beyond Trauma*. New York: Other Press.

Eshel, O. (1998). "Black Holes", Deadness and Existing Analytically. *The International Journal of Psychoanalysis*, 79, 1115–1130.

Faimberg, H. (1988). The Telescoping of Generations: —Genealogy of Certain Identifications, *Contemporary Psychoanalysis*, 24, 99–117.

Faimberg, H. (2007). A Plea for a Broader Concept of Nachtraglichkeit, *The Psychoanalytic Quarterly*, 76, 1221–1240.

Ferro, A. (2002). *In the Analyst's Consulting Room*. New York: Taylor & Francis.

Fosshage, J.L. (1995). Interaction in Psychoanalysis A Broadening Horizon. *Psychoanalytic Dialogues*, 5, 459–478.

Gaines, R. (1997). Detachment and Continuity. *Contemporary Psychoanalysis*, 33, 549–571.

Gerson, S. (2009). When the Third Is Dead: Memory, Mourning, and Witnessing in the Aftermath of the Holocaust, *International Journal of Psychoanalysis*, 90, 1341–1357.

Goldberger, M. (1993). "Bright Spot, a Variant of Blind Spot," *The Psychoanalytic Quarterly*, 62, 270–273.

Goldner, V. (2014). Romantic Bonds, Binds, and Ruptures: Couples on the Brink, *Psychoanalytic Dialogues*, 24, 402–418.

Green, A. (1972). *On Private Madness*. Connecticut, CT: International University Press.

Hagman, G. (1993). The Psychoanalytic Understanding and Treatment of Double Parent Loss. Paper presented at the winter meeting of the American Psychoanalytic Association, NYC.

Hagman, G. (1996). The Role of the Other in Mourning. *Psychoanalytic Quarterly*, 65, 327–352.

Harris, A (2009a). *Gender as Soft Assembly*. New York: Routledge.

Harris, A. (2009b). "You Must Remember This." *Psychoanalytic Dialogues*, 19, 2–21.

Kaufmann, P. (2012). On Transforming the Reparative Quest. *International Journal of Psychoanalytic Self Psychology*, 7, 414–435.

Kohut, H. (1977). *The Restoration of the Self.* New York: International University Press.

Lachmann, F. & Beebe, B. (1996). Three Principles of Salience in the Organization of the Patient-Analyst Interaction. *Psychoanalytic Psychologist*, 13, 1–22.

Lichtenberg, J.D., Lachmann, F.M., & Fossaghe, J.L. (1992). *Self and Motivational Systems*. New Jersey, NJ: The Analytic Press.

Lichtenberg, J.D., Lachmann, F.M. & Fosshage, J.L. (1996). *The Clinical Exchange* New Jersey, NJ: The Analytic Press.

Lieberman, A., Padron, E., Van Horn, P., & Harris, W. (2005). Angels in the Nursery: The Intergenerational Transmission of Benevolent Parental Influences. *Infant Mental Health Journal,* 26(6), 504–520.

Loewald, H. (1960). On the Therapeutic Action of Psycho-Analysis, *International Journal of Psycho-Analysis*, 41, 61–35.

Lyons-Ruth, K. (1998). Implicit Relational Knowing: Its Role in Development and Psychoanalytic Treatment. *Infant Mental Health Journal*, 19(3), 282–289.

McLaughlin, J. (1991). Clinical and Theoretical Aspects of Enactment. *Journal of the American Psychoanalytic Association,* 39, 595–614.

Mitchell, S. (1993). *Hope and Dread in Psychoanalysis.* New York: Basic Books.

Mitchell, S. (1997). *Influence and Autonomy in Psychoanalysis.* New Jersey, NJ: The Analytic Press.

Newman, K. (1999). The Usable Analyst: The Role of the Affective Engagement of the Analyst in Reaching Usability, *Annual of Psychoanalysis*, 26, 175–194.

Ogden, T. (1997). *Reverie and Interpretation.* London: Karnac Books.

Ogden, T. (2004a). The Art of Psychoanalysis: Dreaming Undreamt Dreams and Interrupted Cries. *The International Journal of Psycho-Analysis*, 85, 857–877.

Ogden, T. (2004b). On Holding and Containing, Being and Dreaming. *The International Journal of Psycho-Analysis,* 85, 1349–1364.

Ogden, T. (2012). *Creative Readings: Essays on Seminal Analytic Works.* London: Routledge.

Orange, D. (1995). *Emotional Understanding, Studies in Psychoanalytic Epistemology.* New York: Guildford.

Ornstein, A. (1974). Dread to Repeat and the New Beginning. *Annuals of Psychoanalysis*, 2, 231–248.

Ornstein, A. (1995). The Fate of the Curative Fantasy in the Psychoanalytic Treatment Process. *Contemporary Psychoanalysis*, 31, 113–123.

Ornstein, A. (2009). Do Words Still Matter? Further Comments on the Interpretive Process and the Theory of Change. *International Journal of Psychoanalytic Self Psychology*, 4, 446–484.

Peltz, R. (1998). The Dialectic of Presence and Absence: Impasses and the Retrieval of Meaning States. *Psychoanalytic Dialogues*, 8, 385–409.

Poland, W. (2000). The Analyst's Witnessing and Otherness. *Journal of the American Psychoanalytic Association*, 48, 17–34.

Reis, B. (2009). Performative and Enactive Features of Psychoanalytic Witnessing: The Transference as the Scene of Address. *International Journal of Psychoanalysis*, 90, 1359–1372.

Rey, J.H. (1988). That which Patients Bring to Analysis. *International Journal of Psychoanalysis,* 69, 457–470.

Russell, P. (1975). *The Theory of the Crunch.* Unpublished manuscript.

Russell, P. (2006). Trauma, Repetition, and Affect. *Contemporary Psychoanalysis*, 42, 601–620.

Rustin, J. (1997). Infancy, Agency, and Intersubjectivity: A View of Therapeutic Action, *Psychoanalytic Dialogues*, 7, 43–62.

Sands, S. (2010). On the Royal Road Together: The Analytic Function of Dreams in Activating Dissociative Unconscious Communication. *Psychoanalytic Dialogues*, 20, 357–373.

Searles, H. (1959). Oedipal Love in the Counter Transference. *International Journal of Psycho-analysis*, 40, 180–190.

Searles, H. (1973). Concerning Therapeutic Symbiosis. *Annuals of Psychoanalysis*, 1, 247–262.

Shabad, P. (1989). Viscissitudes of Psychic Loss of a Physically Present Parent. In: D. Dietrich, & P. Shabad (Eds.), *The Problem of Loss and Mourning: Psychoanalytic Perspectives* (pp. 101–126). CT: IUP.

Shabad, P. (1993). Repetition and Incomplete Mourning: The Intergenerational Transmission of Traumatic Themes. *Psychoanalytic Psychology*, 10, 61–75.

Shane, E. & Shane, M. (1990). Object Loss and Selfobject Loss: A Consideration of Self Psychology's Contribution to Understanding Mourning and the Failure to Mourn. *The Annuals of Psychoanalysis*, 18, 115–131.

Shaw, D. (2010). Enter Ghosts: The Loss of Intersubjectivity in Clinical Work with Adult Children of Pathological Narcissists. *Psychoanalytic Dialogues*, 20, 46–59.

Slavin, M.O. & Kriegman, D. (1998). Why the Analyst Needs to Change: Toward a Theory of Conflict, Negotiation, and Mutual Influence in the Therapeutic Process. *Psychoanalytic Dialogue*, 8, 247–284.

Slavin, M.O. (2012). Lullaby on the Dark Side: Existential Anxiety, Making Meaning, and the Dialectics of Self and Other. In: L. Aron, & A. Harris (Eds.), *Relational Psychoanalysis, Expansion of Theory* (Volume 4) (pp. 391–413). New York, NY: Routledge.

Socarides, D. & Stolorow, R. (1984). Affects and Selfobjects. *The Annuals of Psychoanalysis*, 12, 105–119.

Steiner, J. (1993). *Psychic Retreats*. New York: Routledge.

Stern, D.B. (1989). The Analyst's Unformulated Experience of the Patient. *Contemporary Psychoanalysis*, 25, 1–33.

Stern, D.B. (2009). Partners in Thought: A Clinical Process Theory of Narrative, *Psychoanalytic Quarterly*, 78, 701–731.

Stern, D.B. (2012). Witnessing across Time: Accessing the Present from the Past and the Past from the Present, *Psychoanalytic Quarterly*, 81, 53–81.

Stolorow, R. & Atwood, G. (1992). *Contexts of Being. The Intersubjective Foundations of Psychological Life*. New Jersey, NJ: The Analytic Press.

Stolorow, R. (2003). Trauma and Temporality. *Psychoanalytic Psychology*, 20, 158–161.

Torok, M. (1968). The Illness of Mourning and the Fantasy of the Exquisite Corpse, Chapter 4, *New Perspectives in Metapsychology*, 107–124.

Winnicott, D. (1974). Fear of Breakdown. *International Review of Psycho-Analysis*, 1, 103–107.

Chapter 3

Travel fever

Transgenerational trauma and witnessing in analyst and analysand

Michael J. Feldman

"What haunts are not the dead but the gaps left within us by the secrets of others." Notes on the Phantom, N. Abraham (1987)

Aaron called in for a phone session from Poland. On tour with a relentless schedule and demanding director but without much money, this handsome young artist was on his own, checking trays in hotel hallways for uneaten scraps of food. Surprisingly amused, he laughed at his nightly rounds; I was startled and blurted something out. "You're a Jewish boy in Warsaw with nothing to eat, maybe feeling overwhelmed is about something else!"

Aaron didn't connect hunger or continuous travel with the flight of his father's family during the Second World War. He didn't relate a director ordering him around now with a domineering father bossing him around as a boy without protection from a depressed mother. Cutting ties to any childhood past, Aaron lived in the RIGHT here and RIGHT now. Past and future collapsed into a present and any sense of space was vast and unbounded. And it went further. Keeping out ghosts from father's childhood, Aaron kept himself in the dark from ghosts of his own, including frequent moves between parental homes tending to younger brothers and sisters. When we first met, Aaron insisted he didn't need a home, food or sleep, only his work. It shouldn't be a surprise that his main artistic theme was collapsing families.

In a state of manic denial and psychic numbness, Aaron filled every free moment developing new work. Day was structured by a strict regimen of diet and exercise. But when night fell and action failed, he was haunted. Unable to sleep, he became "porous with travel fever," (Mitchell, *Hejira*, 1976). He switched into trance-like states of movement, wandered without rest in whatever town he was in or found refuge on long-distance flights to Paris. Like his other nightly rounds, Aaron had little curiosity about these spectral experiences and laughed them off. With minimal expense, he got himself to the nearest airport and purchased a ticket using numerous frequent flyer points and considerable charm. I nearly missed it. Flight was refuge. I wasn't sure Aaron could be curious enough about his ethereal high-speed act to think about the scarier prospect of slowing down.

A central thesis of this chapter is how broad historical trauma affecting many, if not all, during the 20th century and personal experience of it, collide and create symptoms that are passed down the generations. Historical is the larger context for personal. Psychoanalysts, especially American, also descend from forbearers who survived forced or voluntary emigration, global war, and economic hardship throughout the same time period. Either or both forms of trauma, historical or personal, may be familiar and remembered or eclipsed and seemingly forgotten. The encounter between personal traumatic legacy in patient and analyst is often unrecognized.

In this case presentation, negotiating impasse first required the analyst to remember and rework his own traumatic legacy more fully. Only then, could he create space in which the patient could gradually become more aware of experienced and inherited traumatic past. Initially through enactment and physical language, which better suited his defensive structures and artistic temperament, analysand induced analyst into a joint experience of intense immersion for both to witness. That required the analyst to participate in unconventional ways before his usual role, translating action into word to create meaning, became tolerable. Common language, or its absence, proved essential in this process. Above all, this chapter is about the disorientation of secrecy and perpetual migration. I suggest, "Fasten your seatbelts it (is) going to be a bumpy night" (Mankiewicz, 1950). Keeping this in mind when reading itself feels disorienting. It is not intentional. It may be inevitable.

Gap

From the start, Aaron's nocturnal spells made me imagine father's flight from childhood home during wartime. Unprocessed traumatic affect from flight during war was unconsciously transmitted to Aaron in ways he was compulsively repeating in action. Davoine and Gaudilliere (2004) describe a type of madness in patients who experience massive historical and societal trauma. Psychic collision of time, space, and history produce symptomatic "collapses of time and . . . speech," similar to those Aaron may have inherited from his father, who didn't sleep either, even though Aaron never experienced war himself.

Legacy of historical trauma may be passed down even when traumatic experience is forgotten or disavowed. Madness, described above, is also meant to capture a confused and desperate attempt by the subject to maintain meaningful social attachment under extreme circumstances. The subject's symptoms repeat a version of "what it was necessary to do in order to survive" (Davoine & Gaudilliare, 2004, p.xxiii). I wondered if Aaron's symptoms were showing us what he, or preceding generations of family members, needed to do to maintain the crucial attachment required for psychic survival under extreme conditions.

Our unexpected interaction around searching for food in Warsaw, an uncanny collision involving inherited and experienced trauma, signaled the presence of hidden history. Faimberg (2005), who also links symptoms in the present with traumatic experience in parental past, suggests there are always at least three generations present in the consulting room: subject, parent, and grandparent. A "telescoping of generations" occurs based on the subject's unconscious identification with important ancestors who endured massive trauma. Split off in order to evade conscious memory, identification becomes detectable only at key moments in transference-countertransference interplay similar to the one between us "when the discovery of the secret history," becomes possible (Faimberg, 2005, p.8).

But Aaron's need for control left him unprepared for the ambiguities in time and space stirred up by daily life and intensified in the psychoanalytic situation. Deployment of continuous work constituted what Baranger and Baranger (2008) would call Aaron's "personal bastion," a psychic space of refuge containing reassuring and omnipotent fantasies sorely needed to ward off helplessness, vulnerability, and despair. From the subject's point of view the bastion exists in a matter of fact way to protect it from becoming a focus of analytic exploration.

When we first met, Aaron was a prodigious artist in his late 20s, cheerful, talented, and outwardly humble. But there was a tension between us. His soft whisper of a voice pulled me closer, while his abstract words pushed me away. I was working hard just to hear him, but we spoke different languages. This was the first example of language as barrier. His was fleet, ethereal, and post-modern, mine clumsy, heavy, and outdated. Aaron's body language was also disorienting. Perched forward on the edge of his chair, Aaron broke through usual spatial boundary between analysand and analyst. He was in charge and I was off balance. Setting his own control, he used his body to regulate anxiety.

Aaron's spectral presentation, calm bright eyes and quiet smile, but rigid forward leaning body, was out of his awareness but resonated with Bleger's (1967) description of the subject's "ghost world." In his words, it represents relatively primitive or psychotic parts of the subject's ego. By projecting such ghostly psychic content onto the analytic frame, the subject uses it as a site where unconscious struggle with the analyst takes place, destabilizing its usual function as stable container. Current attack by the subject originates during early preverbal development and represents an attempt to ward off fear of invasion or persecution. It is meant to control the body and mind of both patient and analyst. To that end, Baranger and Baranger (2008) advise the analyst to attend to his own bodily sensations, insofar as they alert him to "invasions" by the subject "who is placing an aspect of his personal experience inside the analyst." I thought of introjection and projection onto a depressed mother.

When affective experience of traumatic experience threatens to resurface within the analytic relationship, the subject may anticipate the internal flood all over again with renewed fears of persecution, isolation, and psychic abandonment. This is the moment Gerson (2009) describes, "when the psychic container cracks," when the witnessing third is lost, "when the third is dead." At that moment, a dead third haunts the consulting room, an absence that is present or presence that is absent. It has the power to numb and disorient analysand and analyst.

Overwhelming dissociated affect also makes itself known through noticeable gaps in narrative. Gaps prevent recall of emotional experience and construction of coherent memory or narrative in one or both clinical partners. The French analyst quoted earlier, Nicolas Abraham (1987), believes gaps represent unspeakable unknown secrets buried in the unconscious by important others. Gaps are inhabited by "phantoms" the French word for ghosts that nevertheless haunt the subject. I understood Aaron's detached lack of curiosity about crucial, but missing, details of his personal and family history as evidence of unconscious gaps. His psychic survival had required splitting off and evacuating unbearable haunting affects from unthinkable family secrets that remained buried within him. The unbearable and unthinkable traumatic past he found impossible to represent and recall symbolically, he was discharging somatically and compulsively. I registered it as so disorganizing it made staying with him even more challenging. Along with disruptions in the frame, these disorienting gaps repeatedly threatened to crack my containing mind. I came to learn this was the language of ghosts.

Aaron wasn't the only one with ghosts. Phantoms of my own were stirring from grandparents who fled Central Europe before the First World War and my father's childhood in Brooklyn during the Great Depression. My father's parents fled Russian partitioned Poland to the east and my mother's parents left Austrian partitioned Poland to the south. Usually referred to by its provincial name, Galicia, the Austrian partition had the largest Jewish population in all of Austria at that time. Aaron's joke about scavenging for food in Poland triggered an inherited fear of deprivation and violence because of the eerie way it located him in my ancestral homeland. But again, it was more complicated still. Inherited fear came to mind quickly. Even though I didn't experience those events myself they were well known through family history I'd heard many times. Personally experienced fear from my own trip to Poland decades earlier was temporarily split off and only came to mind later. When I visited Poland, then a Soviet satellite under martial law, I was so afraid of going hungry I took along a jar of peanut butter. But in the office, our bodies do the talking; inherited and experienced trauma activated inside mine, disavowed and numbing inside his. Unconscious transmission also played a role. At that stage of treatment, Aaron not I was the hungry other. In part, I may have assigned him my historical hunger and shame to avoid thinking about them. To create a live analytic third, as Gerson suggests, I had to lead the way, remembering and acknowledging my own ghosts before Aaron could begin thinking about his. Blurting out in session, followed by memory of personal fear regarding hunger and dangerous travel, was a step in that direction.

From the beginning of our work, Aaron described me as "the calm center" of his chaotic world. But as soon as we agreed to meet twice a week, he announced he was leaving on tour. Surprised, I suggested exploring his feelings about our dilemma. Instead of curiosity he called up his bastion and doubted whether I truly understood him and the demands of his career. Without empathy, Aaron showed me his travel schedule for the next two years in meticulous, mind-numbing detail. I was speechless. Language deserted me. Eventually, I understood our enactment as one version of internal conflict between shame and omnipotence. He evacuated shock and confusion, leaving him powerful and in control. He was the demanding and bossy director/father and I was the helpless child.

I also understood the enactment as Aaron's need to get out, just when things between us were heating up. Being together in a calm warm way was dangerous. Experience of me as attentive and accepting stirred up intolerable longing and desire or fear of destructive collapse. What he wasn't able or ready to express in words he was communicating in action. Flight was refuge. It was also a stealth attack on the frame.

One of many moments I had of profound uncertainty, I felt unable to think. When we discussed videoconferencing, I was unsure expanding the frame would contain Aaron; but without trying, the long-term treatment he needed would surely collapse. I didn't know if Aaron was leaving or staying, if the treatment was ending or surviving. Faimberg (2005) describes the analyst's need to bear the anxiety of not knowing, and sometimes not even existing in the subject's psyche, as a key task in working with these patients. I did feel pulled toward the dead third and challenged to show my capacity for rescue, a tension in the countertransference that would repeat many times. Either way, he was using his bastion to reset at a time when the intensity of our relationship unsettled him.

A dream from a videoconferencing session confirmed haunted space:

"I'm in France, on a French couch. There are 200 nude bodies in an abandoned warehouse connected by wire."

Associations followed to art installation, sex, contagion, and death. "It's a strange dream, because I feel antiseptic toward sex," as though the dream belonged to someone else. More associations with sex and death. His father, with a history of compulsive sexual behavior, was recently diagnosed with prostate cancer. In a guilty identification with the aggressor, Aaron was preoccupied he himself was infected with a sexually transmitted virus and worried they both might die.

This was one of Aaron's first dreams. There was so much to unpack and he wasn't even in the room. It was also a transference dream and the couch was the portal through which ghostly fear came to mind. I wondered how the couch, flown to France as well, activated conflictual sexuality and guilt. Aaron tended to find older partners who were also sexually promiscuous. Eventually he admitted thinking about the Holocaust but was worried about saying so. "You're Jewish, I don't want to hurt you." Although it was his dream, and the Second World War an essential chapter in inherited family history, he located its legacy in me making him anxious and guilty. Later I learned he was assigning victim status to me, dismissing the possibility he was also a victim. Being a passive victim was intolerable. I registered unconscious uncertainty about playing dual roles in that tragedy, even though I remembered France was victim and aggressor.

Aaron also disavowed his victim status by denying his father's religious identity as Jewish. He only described him as Tunisian. Need to avoid religion altogether helped him avoid acknowledging his father was a persecuted victim during the war and a stateless refugee before migrating to Israel because of religious identity. Evacuating victim status into me made me carrier of Holocaust legacy for us both and it made him feel guilty.

Years later I would hear about father's experience in a French transit camp outside Marseilles, the required route for North African Jews emigrating to Israel. Aaron's dream originated from the unconscious transmission and fantasy about father's internment there, transit camp condensed with concentration camp. But for now what happened to him during the war, and after, was off screen. Personal traumatic experience within larger historical trauma fractured history and memory, splitting religious and national identity. Unconscious splits generated gaps inhabited by phantoms, recalling Abraham and Faimberg, creating problems in the treatment that would last for years. Instead of exploring the impact of war on his family and its meaning for Aaron, we were caught up in prolonged struggle over personal traumatic legacy. In retrospect, impasse over identity resembled attack on frame.

My paternal legacy was resonating too. With my father gravely ill, I was in a race against time to replace gaps with information about his childhood in Brooklyn during the Depression. Since his first language was Yiddish, there was always something foreign and exotic about the parts of his childhood he did speak about. But I wanted answers to replace the haunting gaps he avoided, hoping they also would explain why he often seemed so remote. When he was a young boy, his mother required an extended hospitalization. Because his father had to work during that time, he was forced to place his two young sons in a local Jewish orphanage. My father was so traumatized by this experience he never spoke about it. He preferred telling happier stories about his large extended family, turning a blind eye to the fact none of them took him in.

Gaps transmitted from my father's childhood made me assume I had special understanding of Aaron and the unspoken secret his father transmitted to him. Goldberger (1993) calls this a "bright spot," a false belief blinding me to Aaron's unique history because I assumed it was the same as mine. Both relationships were frustrating. Neither Aaron, nor my father wanted anything to do with the past. They didn't need me asking questions;

they needed me to carry the gap in a state of silent mindless loss. In both cases, family trauma was mixed up with historical trauma, from the Second World War to worldwide economic depression to the founding of the State of Israel. We were both sensitive sons haunted by gaps left within us by our fathers' secrets.

For Abraham (1987), once the secret is buried it must remain buried. Gaps and ghosts pass unconsciously from parent to child and "the special problem in these analyses lies in the (subject's) horror at violating a parental or family secret" inscribed there (p. 290). Davoine and Gaudilliere offer a description closer to the subject's conscious experience. Because descendants, like Aaron or I for that matter, didn't experience war or economic depression personally, we don't identify with it even though it's just beneath the surface.

Denying paternal Jewish identity helped Aaron disavow his connection with that trauma and any possibility of sharing buried family secrets. Aaron wanted to bring my Jewish identity into the room first, along with the ghosts haunting me. It made him feel guilty because it was just beneath the surface in him. He was testing me. By evacuating inherited shame and vulnerability, he was aggressively searching for my witnessing, containing mind, and finding it; or by collapsing it, confirming his fear of being abandoned, naked, and wired.

This time, however, I didn't stay paralyzed. As a former student of performing arts myself, my body wasn't dead and my mind wasn't numb. I was full of feeling that was physical and emotional. I was surviving Aaron's attack and reactivating my analytic mind as an embodied listener and witness (Reis 2009).

Detour

To a large extent, reactivation made me revisit my trip to Poland because it wasn't only peanut butter and hunger that came to mind but compelling excitement and fear of forbidden adventure. In many ways, Aaron and I had different strains of travel fever: his to forget, mine to remember. After college, I went to West Berlin to study German and use it as a base to explore the Eastern Bloc. Even those names conjure up a particularly traumatic, ghostly time and place, now a footnote buried in European history. Every weekend I went to the Museum of German History to absorb the complex contradiction of what took place there. When the time finally came I boarded a night train heading east. I wanted to walk the streets of

Warsaw and visit Galicia, or what was left of it, in the south. But a question kept coming up without an easy answer: why German? With whom did I imagine speaking once I got there?

My curiosity about the German language may have been another form of telescoping into me the traumatic loss and near extinction of Yiddish, my father's first language and, the language of my grandparents and generations before him. Rather than bury this loss I took up learning its modern cousin. Then I realized I wasn't just traveling, I was time traveling. Unconsciously, time collapsed. Instead of 1984, it could have been 1944 or even 1914 and language, once again, played a crucial if undefined role. When my grandparents lived in Galicia before the First World War, city names were written in three national languages—German, Polish, and Ukrainian. They could have been written in a fourth, Yiddish, even though it was not the language of an officially recognized nation. It was the language, however, of the one destined to disappear in little more than a generation like a ghost language. Galicia, at that time, was the most porous spot in Central Europe before it disappeared like a ghost altogether.

Arrival in Poland wasn't nearly as frightening as I imagined and I didn't need the peanut butter. I was jazzed up by surprise and curiosity in the faces of people I met. It was unheard of in those days for Americans, let alone young Jewish ones, to visit Poland. There weren't even hotels for foreigners. Most Poles had never met a Jewish person and without museums or education they knew few basic facts of Jewish history or the mass extermination that took place there. Being with them, with disorienting gaps of their own, came to mind later in my work with Aaron. Unaware or dismissive of traumatic past hiding in plain sight through connection with traumatizing present, they made me feel like the phantom inhabiting the gap, returning from a lost and haunting part of buried Polish history. It was collision of time and space in both directions. I was haunting them and they were haunting me. As I made my way south, this disconnection increased. My grandparents' village had disappeared too. Beneath my fear and excitement, something deeper was grounding and activating me in ways I didn't fully realize until I reached the village of Oswiecim. Austrian Galicia, home to one of the largest Jewish populations in Central Europe, became German Gailzien, site of the darkest chapter in Jewish history. During both periods, it was known by its German name, Auschwitz. My mother's parents were born less than two hours away. Her grandparents may have died there.

Without visible markers, it was difficult to process the massive scale of loss that occurred there. I felt disappointed even betrayed. West Germany built museums for its ghosts. Soviet Poland built state-sponsored amnesia. Despite photographic images, time, neglect, and deliberate destruction had erased much of the evidence leaving in its place another gap—a phantom extermination camp.

To reach some level of acceptance about what happened there, I remember repeating to myself out loud, in German and English, to steel myself in both languages in case ghosts of victims or perpetrators were listening. *Wir haben uberlebt.* We survived. I remember wanting to remind the perpetrators as well as the victims. They failed, we survived; another meaning of learning German. Looking back, I realize survival creates opportunities to witness and create narratives, transforming shame into grief and eventually mourning. Much of Aaron's struggle represented traumatic repetition in the face of massive resistance to remembering or violating family secrets. Selective identification and disavowal helped avoid remembering what didn't happen to him and affective contact with a family legacy of trauma and victimization.

The calamity of the 20th century that affected my family most was the Great Depression. With my father's health rapidly declining, I was trying to learn more about his childhood community in eastern Brooklyn, including the orphanage. By chance, I learned the name was the Brooklyn Hebrew Orphan Asylum (BHOA). When I went to scout that location, there was no menacing building only non-descript public housing. Again, what happened there had been erased. But on my second walk around the block, I noticed a statue tucked away in a corner. There was a small child crying with a plaque underneath identifying this as the site of the BHOA. It was nearly as shattering as Auschwitz. I returned to my father with documentation of my personal experience of the orphanage, sure it would move him to be more open and share more of his experience there and how he survived it. Wanting to witness with him but not for him I said, "I have something that belongs to you," handing him the photograph, "and I'm giving it back."

But he didn't want to remember and he didn't want a witness. "I know you want me to tell you something, but all I can say is this. Nothing bad happened to me there, but also nothing good." Then silence. Reflecting on this moment with my father when Aaron and I were at an impasse clarified an important point. Dismissal by Aaron created mind-numbing silence.

Tacit acknowledgment in my father's presence witnessed my experience of gaps from his traumatic history, even though he refused my wish to witness his. Sometimes filling a gap completely is impossible and part of a secret or even just a thoughtful question must be enough. My father's response wasn't as revealing as I'd hoped but it was a moment of authentic connection and largely silent possibly mutual witnessing. It remains a powerful memory.

Traumatic separation, shame, and guilt weren't my childhood experience they were telescoped into me. I had been trying to fill that gap often with unconscious fantasy. Like Aaron's dream about the transit camp in France, I had a recurrent childhood dream about being lost in an ominous institution with no room of my own. Whenever we happened to drive past an orphanage on Sunday family drives, silence made me shiver. It was the nightmare my father lived and thought he kept to himself but buried inside me unconsciously, as a "foreign body." It belonged to him not me (Abraham 1987). Acknowledging his secret history, even if it remained mostly unwritten, replaced the haunting gap with a partial answer. That, I could live with.

With a new focus on survival and memory, I returned to Aaron's symptoms of insomnia, nocturnal flight, and restless work. I returned without assumptions about the traumatic experience his family endured and knew only fragments of what they had to do in order to survive even if that meant "forgetting" as my father tried to do. Watch out, stay busy, don't sleep. If there's a ghost in your room get out. If your house is haunted, don't have one. Maybe the Holocaust could wait. Aaron took to my curiosity about survival and we began moving out of the aggressor-victim dynamic that had stalled us. I became more curious about Jewish history in French North Africa, though I kept it to myself for the time being. If war and flight were too painful to remember or imagine, I could research, even scaffold them for Aaron as I tried with my father.

History lesson

I learned a great deal about Jewish history in North Africa, especially under Fascist occupation. Much of it lies beyond the scope of this paper. Instead, I will highlight important points that relate to Aaron through family experience I did hear about or re-imagined in the context of historical source material. The legacy of French North African Jews is one of loss, dislocation, and migration spanning more than a generation. It must have overwhelmed a family of modest resources repeatedly forced to adapt to war and foreign occupation, migration, and assimilation to insure physical and psychic survival.

Aaron's father was born to a Jewish family that had lived in Tunisia for generations. During the preceding half century, the country had been a small protectorate, along with Algeria and Morocco, in what was known as French North Africa or the Maghreb. Later, scaffolding helped me learn the family migrated to Israel some time after the Second World War, not before or during, as I had imagined. In the 1960s they left for America. In Aaron's mind, further detail was mostly gap, more missing than secret or ghostly. He knew little of their emigration or his father's coming of age, even less about their experience of war and occupation.

Soon, Aaron speculated more openly about rumors of an uncle who died in Israel during military training, another who became psychotic. Ghosts were appearing directly, tied to unspoken loss that traumatized the entire family and it was in fact just beneath the surface. I was surprised as much by Aaron's lack of information as his lack of curiosity. He had even grown up on the same street as his grandparents. Then I realized that like my grandparents, they also spoke a different language; he understood even less since they only spoke it with each other. It was a North African dialect called Judeo-Arabic mixed with French and Hebrew.

The role of common language, or lack of one, reasserted a primary role in whether traumatic experience was transmitted in a more benign or malignant way. The language barrier prevented his family from sharing a coherent narrative of massive loss and dislocation with Aaron and his siblings, the third generation. In place of memory or witnessing, unconscious transmission of traumatic affect and defense occurred as buried secrets, phantoms, and physical symptoms. Our own experience speaking different languages when treatment began was a likely repetition of that barrier.

With the fall of France at the beginning of the war, French North Africa was administered by the Fascist government in Vichy. This is when Aaron's father was born. In contrast to swift and severe anti-Jewish law imposed in Europe, where my theories originated, anti-Semitic policy in the Maghreb was lax. That is until late 1942 when the German Army fully occupied Tunisia. SS units quickly began recruiting Jewish men as forced labor. Although Aaron's grandparents were surely affected by German occupation, with expectable fear of forced labor or loss of home and property, Aaron received no memory or narrative to make their experience real or understandable. Aaron's father was quite young in the war years with few ways of registering fear and helplessness beyond the somatic.

Historical record shows the German Army was quickly forced to surrender. Given the relatively brief period of occupation and war, and the absence of systematic deportation or mass extermination, it seemed plausible, as Aaron had insisted, there was no Holocaust in Tunisia, at least not like the one in Europe.

What did occur there were massive air bombardments on a nightly basis, from Allied and Axis forces, causing significant loss of life to Jewish men forced to work the German airfields. Spectral connection with Aaron's nocturnal distress did not escape my notice, and I remembered his father's insomnia also. Transmission from father to son. It felt like a potential entry point but Aaron was uninterested in exploring it further. Without more specific family history we remained stalled. In short, where was the war?

Conflictual Jewish identity also persisted. It even intensified as a new gap and family secret emerged. Aaron was time traveling also. New information, as phantom, threatened his powerful capacity to control emotion. Traveling in the Middle East, Aaron was stopped by Israeli Immigration who then separated him from his group for further questioning. For Aaron it could have been 1942 and interrogation by the SS.

It may as well have been. The authorities told him he was an Israeli citizen. Denial of Jewish identity and historical victimization collapsed. Aaron had never been more terrified. He was afraid of prolonged detention and conscription into the army. Later he learned his father had secretly made all of his children Israeli citizens years earlier. Children of Israeli citizens are automatically eligible for citizenship but only when both parents are Jewish. Aaron's father declared his mother was also Jewish when she wasn't. After all, his father laughed, her name was Rachel. But she was Protestant. His father transmitted Jewish identity to Aaron through a buried secret and the secret was a lie. Metaphor was too concrete and transference fear too intense. Conflict and confusion made compromise more brittle. Any further exploration of Jewish identity was perceived as attack motivated by my need to turn him into a passive victim. It was also intolerable. He demanded we shelve the entire topic or he else he would leave treatment.

As France withdrew from its colonies most Jews throughout the Maghreb did leave for Israel through transit camps outside Marseilles. When they finally arrived in Israel and discovered deprivation in the young State, many chose to return to North Africa. Later Aaron told me his family returned to North Africa before leaving for Israel a second time and eventually the United States. Serial dislocation and migration in parent and grandparent established travel fever in both generations directly above Aaron. His nightmare of the camp, like mine about the orphanage, derived from our fathers' traumatic experience in childhood in the context of larger historical shocks they couldn't understand or represent symbolically.

Aaron became as preoccupied with North Africa as his own lost homeland, similar to and different from my father's lifelong attachment to Brooklyn, rather than where we lived in Ohio. Tunisia as the lost homeland also denied a certain inconvenient truth of history. Jews living there were never more than second-class citizens, in fact not even citizens, any more than my ancestors were considered Austrian. No doubt my decision to learn German (before the symbolic end of childhood) was also informed by my personal choice of selective historical identity, but in addition to, rather than in place of, being Jewish. For Aaron, learning JUDEO-arabic was both impractical and intolerable. Instead, he chose French, linking him to Tunisia and France. It's no surprise that New York as a "lost" home was also telescoped into me and that to live anywhere else, except Berlin, never came to mind. Aaron's insistence, based on conscious identification and unconscious fantasy, may also have originated with his grandparents. Yet it was a place Aaron had never seen and following his experience in Israel he was determined to visit Tunisia, forget false identity, and reestablish his true one. As he allowed the unconscious gap to become a tolerable question, we began to think about ghosts originating in different parts of the Mediterranean.

With war and serial migration still off screen, we discovered a theme that did resonate with Aaron free of externally driven internal conflict. It was Exile; and it stimulated his curiosity about migration. He preferred Tunisian and French ghosts to Israeli and Jewish ones. With it came the possibility of replacing ghosts with acceptable and active ancestors.

And then my understanding of both complex relationships, with Aaron and with my father, came full circle. The impasse with my father helped me rethink the standstill with Aaron and vice versa. Separation from family coincided with my father beginning school and his formal entrance into the English-speaking world. Years later, I appreciate more deeply how traumatic but temporary separation screened off painful feelings about the permanent loss of his insular Yiddish-speaking world of childhood. He was also an exile, though that visible scar did not completely derail development.

Holding onto his first language and speaking it whenever he could provided a lasting connection. I grew up hearing him speak it all the time and remember the way his voice and personality would light up. Nothing remote.

It was painful he wasn't that lively with us but it wasn't exactly distancing. It was quirky but it was more like an interesting puzzle to figure out. Whenever friends picked up on his speech and asked if he was an immigrant it didn't embarrass me. I just laughed and said, "He's an immigrant from Brooklyn." I was born and raised in the Midwest so his language stood out. I was also referred for a speech evaluation when I began grade school. Uncanny. Diagnosis: he's fine, but is someone in your family from Brooklyn?

Now, with my newest language, psychoanalysis, I wonder if my father, who buried secrets of all kinds, also placed his love of language inside me, which I took up as a way of being closer to him. My Brooklyn accent as a child from imitating my father's accent and learning new languages ran throughout a relationship that was rarely verbal. Learning German partially bridged the barrier between us and partial connection with my father was often the most I could expect. It also created a psychic space where unspoken identification and connection could exist alongside another buried secret, loss and exile for both of us from each other.

Aaron had a different experience. His father's permanent loss of his first home, language, and security following war and emigration, preceded loss of a second homeland and language. Though he had no trouble learning English, he was unable to assimilate successfully in the third. Cumulative personal and historical trauma was divided among three languages that he wasn't able to sufficiently represent or integrate. In turn he transmitted to Aaron fragments of information, gaps filled with secret, and traumatic affects and defenses registered in his body. Aaron's grandparents also spoke a rare dialect but had fewer to speak it with and were largely unable to communicate with him. A common language—crucial to symbolize, metabolize, and share traumatic history between three generations—simply did not exist. It left Aaron in the dark and the two of us with a recurrent language barrier of our own.

Shift

Despite initial fear, videoconferencing transformed the treatment. As the frame became more flexible past struggle all but disappeared. As the new frame settled, resistance decreased and the therapeutic process began to deepen. Sessions in person combined with sessions on the Internet, set the treatment on a global migration directly tied to Aaron's travel that felt familiar and comfortable and left him in control. The new frame allowed migration to enter our dialogue, though he was not ready for me to speak other than asking him to tell me more. He remained guarded against interpretation because it pointed out experience outside his control, which to him implied criticism.

Overall, Aaron's reaction was unequivocally positive. Despite frequent changes of geographic location, he felt our connection stronger than any he had experienced before. Flight was still a refuge but no longer escape. Without interest in exploring the change, he preferred thinking about migration and it became the new organizing idea of treatment. Enactment of pulling me in to join him led to hope of my understanding him through action in ways he could not express in words. I experienced his steady stream of postcards and notices, where limited words were safe, as much more than maintaining attachment. They were love letters. Later he called this seduction but any hint of sexuality at that time was meant to control or neutralize my thinking and potential interpretation. Because the new frame was better able to contain him, it was better suited to survive aggressive attack. It even invited aggressive seduction and a wish for intimacy.

With Aaron's travel fever breaking, I was starting to sweat. Continuing to evacuate disorientation from life on the run, Aaron was placing his fever in me. To ground myself now as participant and witness, I needed to locate him in the world each session. He dismissed my questions and my disorientation. It infuriated him because it implied I was blaming him. "I'm here,' he said and that was it. He was bossy, I was helpless. It was another collision with his bastion he had no interest in exploring. Facing massive resistance, I stopped asking when I realized I had other options. By referring to our sessions as "Tuesdays and Thursdays at 5," the days and time we were together in my unchanging location, I could ground myself and reestablish an analytic attitude. He traveled and I stayed put. He could appear at my door or on my computer screen. Sometimes I wouldn't know which until the session began. Ghostly attack on the frame continued but the disorienting effect was less destructive.

Remembering I was in the same place every session was a small calibration, crucial in reducing my feverish need to locate Aaron at the beginning of each session. He could be anywhere in the world, and call in from any location—a hotel room, a studio, a theater, an airport, a private patch of grass. Unreliable Wi-Fi heightened spectral connection, as though he was contacting me from another time or place as inconsistent transmission often froze the screen or interrupted speech. Sometimes forced to find small space at the last minute, he hid himself, and us, from others nearby.

Pulling me into haunted space, that was literally long distance, he never missed a session and was rarely late. It was his ghost world and he knew how to manage this far better than I. The frame became a 21st century structure outside conventional definition of shared time and space. It was still a container, a psychic structure whose walls were supported by our joint capacity to represent them. And it was portable. Unsurprisingly, fear of collapse decreased considerably.

The longer Aaron was away, the more desire for closeness appeared in the transference. He began asking me to see his work and having dreams in which I appeared. Before I took a short vacation he told me, "I had another disturbing dream and this time you were in it." We were in my home, where Aaron secretly watched me taking care of my young son though I couldn't see him. In the basement was a swimming pool he admired where I was lifeguard. He wanted me to take him in but was afraid I didn't have time for him and would send him away, maybe to an asylum. The prospect of my leaving him, rather than his leaving me, activated an intense wish in the transference for nurturing protection and fear of abandoning rejection. Deeper exploration of internal life under my watchful eye was fraught with danger. Secretly watching my son and I together, revealed Aaron's aggressive envy and wish to take my son's place.

In fact, Aaron was the oldest of many siblings born in rapid succession. Throughout early childhood he must have watched his mother tending to them with yearning, jealousy, even resentment he needed to repress. Physical intimacy with her free from distraction of younger siblings must have been brief. Loss of her caring attention must have felt like being sent away. Ill equipped to regulate his own intense emotions and cast out into asylum-like family chaos, Aaron must have registered profound affective dysregulation throughout his body and other symptoms including insomnia. In the dream, Aaron expressed confusion: did he want to join us or have me to himself? Desire for intimacy, being internal, was confused with intrusion. He was risking rejection just when he wanted me most.

When I returned a week later, Aaron was in tears. With no money to pay the balance he was humiliated. "We have to stop. I can't let you see me like this." Fear of collapse returned more intensely than before. Our usual transaction could no longer evacuate shame or retain his omnipotence.

Need for flight returned to full consciousness. I tried pointing out our crisis was financial and emotional. "You told me your secret wish for me to take care of you and your secret fear that I won't and will send you away." With both eyes closed and face turned away, Aaron was already preparing to leave and didn't seem to hear me. Unsettled by intense and prolonged silence, one of Aaron's most disturbing phantoms, I felt an urgent need to speak and suggested decreasing to one session a week. Threatened with a new episode of travel fever, Aaron was unable to speak at all.

But now, wish for flight conflicted with a new, measurable wish to stay. Deepened attachment created a space that provided the courage to stay and begin confronting fear of limited financial resources and shameful family identification. His lip trembling, he admitted, "I am my father." He was thinking of a bankrupt theater director; I was still thinking of a Jewish boy running in the night hungry and scared somewhere in North Africa.

It was another moment of profound uncertainty, not knowing if the treatment would survive or if I understood what was happening well enough to put it in meaningful words. Looking back, hard-earned improvement in analysis contributed to this significant shift. Capacity to experience vulnerability, fear, and desire toward me increased tolerance for troubling ghosts in his internal world. Despite fear of slowing down, Aaron chose to stay without resorting to flight. Improvement left him vulnerable. Ghosts came into his mind, ready to flood it with helplessness and shame. He couldn't avoid them any longer.

Losing the second session shook the frame again, and this time Aaron too. First, he tried replacing it with more postcards and reviews that piled up in my office and inbox, assuring me of his affection and ensuring I wouldn't forget him. Aaron didn't want to explore their meaning, and with his sense of control restored he balked. "I can't put it all into words and besides there isn't enough time anyway." I registered his need to avoid further exposure and vulnerability with me. His second attempt involved his bastion more directly. He insisted I see his work and, about two years into treatment, I agreed, on the condition we talk about it afterwards.

In one performance, flight from a rejecting other shifted to connection with a containing one. Two characters inhabited a dream world but were ultimately cut off from one another. I registered frustration and despair. At one point the male character, played by Aaron, was so agitated he began punching the walls. With the set crumbling, a Stranger entered and they began picking up the pieces together. I held my breath, watching characters perform the collapse and frustration we had experienced, contained, and survived a few months earlier. Aaron had internalized new experiences with me and was expressing them in his own language on stage.

In the next session, Aaron took control right away. He wasn't interested in discussing content. He focused on his careful decision of where to seat me so he could watch me watch him. Seeing and being seen returned. If he couldn't come inside my house, he succeeded in bringing me into his. He wanted me to see feelings inside him he couldn't see himself. In the dark, womblike atmosphere of the theater, his transference wish for my omniscience felt maternal. We were enacting our own version of distraught infant and attuned caregiver. He needed me to contain, transform, and reflect his disorganizing experience, which was internal, into a form that was more manageable—representation with words. Now, when I told him what I saw he didn't turn away. He took it in, eyes wide open. Aaron was experiencing another shift from using me as receptacle for evacuated negative affect to using me as an emotionally engaged witness. Expanding the frame beyond the Internet to include theater deepened analysis even further.

In a way, we were creating a new live third. Prior struggle with words was shifting too as we started thinking about shared experience in the theater and creating new space for reflection. Aaron even began asking for help finding the words to express his feelings. Most importantly, we were doing it at a safer distance on his terms, using the Internet or stage, with me as witness in the audience. I was "becoming the analyst" he needed "unobtrusive and relational," "flexible and responsive," (Grossmark 2012). By letting Aaron set the scene, I became deeply immersed in his internal world, as he experienced it, in place of assumption. Through a largely physical language, we were starting to acknowledge the internal gap that let him feel more in control and more comfortable revealing himself in a language he spoke fluently and which I was learning to recognize and understand.

Internalizing me as meaning maker, Aaron elaborated conflict between intimacy and intrusion through spectral enactment in a dark theater. It reminded me of a subterranean pool of unconscious wishes and fears, and a growing capacity to internalize me as protective lifeguard. Expanding the search for words to express feelings and create meaning could be a matter of life or death.

Fully translating experience into words remained secondary to having a witnessing other, who was engaged and survived, but didn't rush to verbalize or symbolize at a deeper psychic level (Reis 2009). I was unsure Aaron was ready to tolerate any interpretation, let alone one where, both he and I were important. In another performance a boy is rescued when friends throw him a rope. He automatically dismissed my words; he was trying to tell me something about his childhood. "I'm talking about Childhood not my childhood." I yielded to his correction, though not without noticing he was talking about any childhood. More importantly, he had replaced barbed wire that kills with supple rope that saves.

Soon after, I learned this performance did have roots in Aaron's childhood, even though he didn't consciously connect them. He was swimming in a lake with his brothers and one of them nearly drowned. When I asked about the resemblance between that memory and his performance he was puzzled. When he dismissed me this time it was only partially. He insisted his performance had no connection with his emotional internal world at the same time insisting, "it's all in my work, that's why you have to see it." My life-saving presence was more useful seen not heard. In fact, silent witnessing was the role he cast me to play. I understood we were preparing for return of his childhood ghosts, which would appear for us to see but not comment on. Still struggling with language, struggle with one another was safely contained.

And soon narrative appeared. Aaron took his work in a new direction, drawing on themes of war, dislocation, and exile, which turned passive to active and linked him to a heroic traumatic past. To do this he reached beyond the personal and paternal past, which were shameful, to a mythic past of classical antiquity. Putting his own stamp on these myths he reversed roles and had sons rescue fathers. Still needing me as silent witness, Aaron brought the entire production to life in session, his need for omnipotent, exhibitionistic, and seductive control in full force. No element was left out, from characters to set design to lighting. It was especially important I know the young hero was also father to a son of his own. Reversal also let him identify with me as longed-for father from his dream and gratify his wish for self-repair by making himself an active rescuer, no longer passive victim of a telescoped traumatic past.

But myth isn't life and life isn't simple. On my way to the theater, Aaron called in a panic. A pipe had burst in the ceiling and water was flooding the stage. His soft controlled voice starkly contrasted with his alarming fear that water would wash out the entire production, destroying everything he had worked for. Flood in New York, air raid in North Africa, round up in Central

Europe. When news came that they had fixed the leak, Aaron was still afraid it wouldn't hold, it wasn't safe to go on. He didn't know what to do and fell silent at the other end. He was finally waiting for me to speak. Fighting off my own shock and numbness, I searched my mind for something hopeful and from somewhere I said, "It sounds like you have what you need."

Words were secondary to attachment. Reis (2009) describes how "the other who can receive this experience (the non verbal traumatic repetition) is the analyst, whose affective presence within the relationship with the patient, creates the condition for mutual experiencing of that which exists outside speech." For me, that moment on a winter night outside a theater talking by cell phone about a threatening flood was a mutual experience in which we were deeply immersed, without the words to adequately capture it. There was only the doing, and in the doing discovering trust and hope. Experiencing and witnessing that moment together would help us find the words to sort out the meaning later.

Then I saw a transcendent piece of work, deeply moving and well deserving of the critical praise it received. After the performance, Aaron quickly brought me onstage wanting me to see everything he saw, the pipe, the hole, where the water fell, and the damage that was done. It felt physical and also verbal. I felt how close to me he stood and heard his words describing the performance, thanking me again and again. I imagined an embrace, between proud, grateful son and admired, admiring father. In a way, we could have exchanged roles. Each of us knew something about fathers and sons, rescue and need to be rescued. We were still enacting the repair of a traumatic relationship with a father, something Aaron wasn't ready to analyze, at least not yet.

Ghost stories

In order to help the subject recover the ghost story, the analyst must be familiar with his own. Revisiting and coming to new terms with a ghostly past I considered worked through long ago was activated by my impasse with Aaron. Psychic reorganization of remembered and recently discovered trauma helped me become less obtrusive, remain deeply engaged, and, whenever possible, let Aaron decide how best to use me. Avoiding the rush to translate enactment into word, I became more comfortable immersed for longer periods of time in powerful, not yet symbolized experience. Another way of describing that is my evolution toward becoming a more relational analyst, whose containing and witnessing mind recovers more quickly from unavoidable cracks and who recognizes a ghost story when he hears one.

Translating a ghost story into a more workable form requires the analyst to develop fluency in its uniquely spectral language, a language that extends beyond verbal, physical, and uncanny moments in transference-countertransference to include a more nuanced vocabulary of enactment and disturbance in frame. Enactment may repeat in form but shift in meaning or function over time. Those initially intended to ward off contact, may facilitate intimacy later. Finally, understanding the meaning of alterations in frame is essential, when it is under attack or when it becomes more settled. The possibility for psychic transformation increases when analyst and analysand begin understanding each other's subjectivity and the meaning of each one's particular ghost language.

Recently, Aaron called from Europe with a new dream. "You were walking around Paris, buying food. I'm following you but you don't see me and I'm looking in garbage cans for boxes of pizza."

"I guess I'm still looking for scraps," Aaron admitted. "I'm jealous, but it's a little different. I look up to you, you can afford to buy your own food." Now we're laughing together. No longer lost or alone, more open to acknowledging hunger on many levels, Aaron is finally slowing down enough to begin thinking about ghost stories. Acknowledging the work that lies ahead to analyze and understand hidden meaning, in words rather than action, he hopes to work together for a long time. So do I.

Acknowledgments

The patient has read and given permission to publish this paper.

A shorter version of this paper was published in *Psychoanalytic Dialogues*.

I would like to thank our entire supervision group, especially Adrienne Harris, where many ideas presented here germinated and evolved. Words can't adequately express my debt and gratitude to Susan Klebanoff for her patient reading and thoughtful editing of earlier versions of this manuscript.

This paper is dedicated to the memory of Anne Alonso whose witnessing mind and soft touch continue to inspire me.

Bibliography

Abitbol, M (1989). *The Jews of North Africa during the Second World War*, Wayne State University Press, Detroit.

Abraham, N, Rand, N (1987). Notes on the Phantom: A Complement to Freud's Metapsychology, *Critical Inquiry*, Vol. 13, No. 2, The Trials of Psychoanalysis, University of Chicago Press (Winter 1987), pp. 287–292.

Akhtar, S (1999). *Immigration and Identity*, Northvale, NJ, Aronson.

Apprey, M (1993) Dreams of Urgent/Voluntary Errands and Transgenerational Haunting, in *Transsexualism, Intersubjectivity, Projective Identification and Otherness*, Duquesne University Press, Pittsburgh pp. 102–128.

________ (2004) From the Events of History to a Sense of History, in *Analysts in the Trenches: Streets, Schools, War Zones*, ed by B Sklarew, S Twemlow, and S Wilkinson, Analytic Press, Hillsdale, NJ, pp. 45–55.

Baranger, M, Baranger, W (2008) The Analytic Situation as a Dynamic Field, *International Journal of Psychoanalysis*, 89: pp. 795–826.

Bleger, J (1967) Psycho-Analysis of the Psycho-Analytic Frame. *International Journal of Psychoanalysis*, 48: pp. 511–519.

Davoine F, Gaudilliere JM (2004) *History Beyond Trauma*, Other Press, New York.

Faimberg, H (2005) The Telescoping of Generations: A Genealogy of Alienated Identifications, in *The Telescoping of Generations Listening to the Narcissistic Links between Generations*, ed by D Birksted-Breen, Routledge, New York, pp. 4–18.

_______ (2005) "Listening to Listening": An Approach to the Study of Narcissistic Resistances, in *The Telescoping of Generations*, Routledge, New York, pp. 19–30.

Ferenczi, S (1949) Confusion of the Tongues Between the Adults and the Child—(The Language of Tenderness and of Passion), *International Journal of Psychoanalysis*, 30: pp. 225–230.

Freud, S (1914) *Remembering, Repeating and Working Through*. SE 12, pp. 145–156.

Gerson, S (2009) When the Third is Dead: Memory, Mourning and Witnessing in the Aftermath of the Holocaust, *International Journal of Psychoanalysis*, 90, pp. 1341–1357.

Gerson, S (2011) Hysteria and Humiliation, *Psychoanalytic Dialogues*, 21, pp. 517–530.

Goldberger, M (1993) Bright Spot, a Variant of Blind Spot, *The Psychoanalytic Quarterly*, 62, pp. 270–273.

Grossmark, R (2012) The Unobtrusive Relational Analyst, *Psychoanalytic Dialogues*, 22, pp. 629–646.

Grotstein, J (1993) Foreword to *Intersubjectivity, Projective Identification and Otherness* by Maurice Apprey and Howard F Stein, Duquesne University Press, Pittsburgh.

Haddad, H.M. (1984) *Jews of Arab and Islamic Countries: History, Problems and Solutions*, Shengold Publishers: New York.

Kimmel, K (2011) Gerson Samuel, When the Third is Dead: Memory, Mourning and Witnessing in the Aftermath of the Holocaust, *International Journal of Psychoanalysis*, 2009, 90, pp. 1341–57, *Journal of Analytic Psychology*, 56. pp. 571–574.

Laskier, M.M. (1994) *North African Jewry in the Twentieth Century: The Jews of Morocco, Tunisia and Algeria*, New York University Press, New York.

Manekin, R (2010) *Galicia YIVO Encyclopedia of Jews in Eastern Europe*.

Mankiewicz, JL (1950) *All About Eve*, 20th Century Fox, Los Angeles.

Mitchell, J (1976) "Hejira" from Hejira, *Elektra*, Los Angeles.

Reis, B (2009) Performative and Enactive Features of Psychoanalytic Witnessing: the Transference as the Scene of Address, *International Journal of Psychoanalysis*, 90, pp. 1359–1372.

Saadoun, H. (2003) Tunisia, in *Jews of the Middle East and North Africa in Modern Times*, ed by R Simon, M Laskier, and S Reguer, Columbia University Press, New York, pp. 444–457.

Volkan, V (2004) After the Violence, in *Analysts in the Trenches: Streets, Schools, War Zones*, ed by B Sklarew, S Twemlow, and S Wilkinson, Analytic Press, Hillsdale, NJ, pp. 77–102.

Winter, J (2014). *The Great War and Jewish Memory*. London: Leo Baeck Institute.

Chapter 4

Shadows, ghosts, and Chimaeras

On some early modes of handling psycho-genetic heritage

Joshua Durban

Introduction

This chapter describes three early developmental modes of handling the individual's psycho-genetic heritage. The first one, which characterizes normal development, is called living with the shadow of one's heritage. The shadow (of history, of life and death) is a natural counterpart of the self. The second mode, which accounts for more disturbed patients, is called living under the shadows of heritage. This type is characterized by an unconscious phantasy of the person being haunted bypersecutory and vindictive ghosts instead of benign ancestors. The third mode, which might be encountered in severely disturbed patients, is being the shadow. This mode, called Chimerism, describes a confused organism, which may turn against itself as parts of it are experienced as alien. On the unconscious level this signifies a heritage which cannot be experienced or mentalized as such. Rather, it is a complete chaos, with moments where the hardly existent self is experienced as a bizarre object made up of non-combining, welded parts. These three modes will be examined with the help of material drawn from two analyses: of an autistic boy and of an adult patient who was persecuted by an unspeakable, horrific ancestral past.

Omri is a 17-year-old boy suffering from autism. He has been in a five sessions per week analysis with me since the age of three. Today, he is quite a high-functioning autistic adolescent: he is verbal, expresses a wide range of emotions and thoughts concerning himself and others, attends a special school where he has a few friends, and even participates in a basketball team. Omri did not speak at all until he was six, and his general poor condition has been described despairingly by one of his doctors as "hopeless." After much hard work done in the analysis by the two of us and outside the analysis by his devoted family, his condition has improved remarkably.

About two years ago, he suddenly looked at me and said: "Today I want to tell you my story. At first there was a white hole. It was white on white, but not the same. White was in white. White and white mixed. It was white all over, no black in the white. Eyes could not see eyes, nose could not smell nose. Then you came to help me. Then I was in the black hole, screaming and screaming but no one heard. I was screaming because black hole tried to make me black and push me back to the white hole. White hole is worse than the black hole because in the black hole there is white. I was screaming but not with my throat and tongue. I did not have them."

He was silent and became very agitated, flapping his arms and waving his head in his stereotyped movements, which have long ago disappeared from our sessions. After a while he collected himself and went on: "I was screaming 'Help me' and you heard. In the black hole there was nothing, but things were tearing and making empty. I was empty. After many years you came again and I was in a brown hole. In the brown hole things were attacking things. It was crowded, no place for me. I could not breathe. I could not move. Now we are in the green hole, covered by grass. We can run barefoot on the grass. It is soft and we do not fall."

I was stunned by this unusual monologue, which in a beautiful, precise way reviewed Omri's arduous and painful development from a horrid, undifferentiated mixture with the environment, through a painful differentiation phase which was experienced as being torn, empty, and persecuted and, finally, towards the formation of a self engulfed by a soft, flexible membrane. This movement resulted in his ability to create his own personal story of how he came to be, which he presented to me.

Oscar, a middle-aged man, presented me with his own personalized version of his history on the last year of his analysis: "When I first came to see you I was haunted by the shadows of the past and possessed by demons of hate. But what plagued me most were the unspoken, half-known secrets and horrors of my heritage. This was my legacy of cruelty, confusion and violence passed from generation to generation by my father, who collaborated with the Nazis. At least now I think I know who I am, where I came from, and what is and isn't mine."

I chose to open with Omri's and Oscar's self-expressed personal histories because they bear directly upon the topic of this chapter. I shall attempt to describe the movement from a malignant, unmentalized mixture between figure and background, self and shadow, to the "black hole" of sucking emptiness and the "brown hole" of the claustrum (Meltzer, 1992; Staehle, 1997), which serve primarily as phantasmic bodily refuges or psychic retreats, but are subsequently filled with persecution and dread, as the self is tortured and haunted by its shadows. Finally, there comes a shift toward differentiation and separateness between the person and his or her shadow. This movement is linked with the emergence of a sense of self from the matrix of its psycho-genetic heritage and with the ability to form some kind of a meaningful relationship with this heritage in unconscious phantasy.

By "psycho-genetic" heritage I refer to the idea, which is hinted at in many psychoanalytic theories, that our perinatal and postnatal physiological, mental, and historical courses of development, as well as those of our parents, are all encoded in the emerging self as unconscious phantasies. These phantasies echo not only our own unconscious narratives of becoming (bodily and mentally) but those of our significant objects. I have chosen to include both the biological-genetic aspect as well as the psycho-historical one in order to denote a process of creating a rudimentary, although fragmented and diffuse psychic experience from very early on which assumes the form of unconscious phantasies. The body remembers its history no less than the psyche and tries to process it in primitive modes of being. Furthermore, this heritage, with which we form some kind of an internal relationship, can assume many shapes and forms ranging from an undifferentiated background or part-objects to clearly definable objects. Psycho-genetic heritage—or as one child patient put it: "What makes me me"—provides an indispensable sense of continuity, of going-on-being and as such can mitigate as well as arouse various anxieties. If such a heritage cannot be contained and mentalized, illness appears.

The inability to confront such questions might cause a lot of anguish. The idea of transgenerational genetic and psychological transmission is extremely difficult, although equally fascinating, for children (and adults) to understand and to accept. The notion that we are a creation of our psychogenetic heritage, that we were projected from the past no less than we project into the present and the future, is like a double-faced Janus. It can be a comforting idea as it gives us a sense of belonging and therefore a background of continuity, security, and safety. However, its other face might be threatening as we struggle throughout life to form our own unique sense of identity against the uncanny background of being followed or, worse still, swallowed, in unconscious phantasy, by an inseparable shadow of heritage. Freud (1955) describes the way in which even our early traumas are influenced by our heritage:

> When we study the reactions to early traumas [i.e. before the fifth year], we are quite often surprised to find that they are not strictly limited to what the subject himself has really experienced but diverge from it in a way which fits in much better with the model of phylogenetic event and, in general, can only be explained by such an influence. (p. 99)

Unconscious narratives of being

In order not to become confused or mad, and in an attempt to maintain our sense of being as bounded, continuous, and unique entities, we tell ourselves conscious and unconscious stories about who we think we are, how we came to be and how we are going to end. If we cannot form such meaningful narratives of identity vis-à-vis the matrix of heritage, problems arise. It is as if we cannot think about ourselves as going-on-being and parts of us become lost or alien to ourselves. A crucial element in this formation is the attunement of the significant other as a supplier of meaning and as a bearer of memory. According to Aulagnier (2001):

> The specific factor underlying psychosis is not linked to an unconscious fantasy but arises from the consequences of an insoluble discordance between what the small child experiences somatically and psychically and the meaning imposed by the mother's discourse . . . In this way the primary delusional construction aims at creating a personal history which the child is able to invest with meaning regarding its origins, its relation to others, and the sources of pleasure and pain. (McDougall and Zaltzman, 2001, p. xxiii)

The first narratives of being in the beginning of life are sensory, perceptual, and proprioceptive ones. In that sense they are primarily bodily patterns and narratives in feelings (Isaacs, 1952). Creating a personal history thus depends initially on many innate neuro-mental potentials and functions which involve the primitive ego's sensory perception of itself and later mature, through contact with the outside world, into what may be called a Self (Tustin, 1987). Self-identity is constructed while the infant oscillates along the psycho-physiological "dual track" (Grotstein, 1980) of "flowingover-at-oneness' (Tustin, 1994) and separation. From the beginning of life there is a continuous "sorting-out" process of figure from background. In the course of development these personal proto-narratives about our origin and substance mature into signs, words, and symbols. Gampel (1998) suggests the term "protosignification" to describe that zone in which words do not exist. In a way, unconscious phantasies are a creative elaboration in a narrative form of these protosignifiers.

The intensive internal negotiations of who we are in relation to our objects are reflected in the mechanism of projective identification. Through projective identification the child also tries to form some kind of an explanatory narrative as to what are the boundaries between himself and his objects. Ignes Sodre explains this beautifully thus:

> The sense of identity stems simultaneously from the differentiation of the self from its objects and from various identifications with different aspects of the objects . . . The central characteristic of the use of 'projective identification' is the creation in the subject of a state of mind in which the boundaries between self and object have shifted. (2004, p. 54)

This shifting of boundaries assumes in unconscious phantasy quite different scripts, ranging from "becoming the object" or taking in its identity peacefully to the horror of being invaded or robbed of one's identity violently or doing the same to the object. Normal identification depends on the measure of successfully maintaining parts of the object's identity while keeping its separateness. It is interesting to note Sodre's following remark: "I must confess that I find it difficult to imagine a projection into outer space, or into something inanimate or abstract, without imagining too that whatever has been projected into has become personified in some way'' (pp. 54–5). I shall come back to this point when describing the case of Omri, and claim that, indeed, there is a pathological kind of exchange with space that precludes personification since there is still not enough of a person in the infant to form such boundaries.

Unconscious phantasies of psycho-genetic heritage

What happens when individuals cannot create such personalized histories regarding their heritage? What psychological damages are brought about when there is a pathological narrative or no narrative at all of self-identity vis-à-vis its heritage—either because it is too horrid to be told, or when there is a discordance between what was experienced and what was told or, in even more extreme cases, when there is not enough "I" or individuation to experience any differentiation between figure and background and thus no "shifting of boundaries" is possible?

I chose to use the evocative metaphor of "the shadow" in order to describe some early modes of dealing in unconscious phantasy with our genetic and historical heritage and with the inherent tension between what and who we are in relation to where we came from. I wish to propose three possible modes of dealing with the shadow of our heritage. These three modes can be described as living with a shadow, living under a shadow of a ghost, and being the shadow. Living with a shadow is our normal condition where our heritage is an inseparable counterpart of our movement through life, but one which is like a silent, unintrusive background which adds depth, volume and contrast to each and every experience. Those who live with the shadow experience good internal and external containment and the capacity to dream (to have access to alpha-function) so as to be able to transform impingement into a personal narrative that binds the anxiety (beta-element) from the impingement.

Living under a shadow implies the unconscious phantasy of being oppressed, possessed, haunted, and persecuted by the dark cloud of our shadow. This shadow is composed of hidden, insufferable elements of the child's self-experience which could not be assimilated or symbolized and were split-off and projected into the object, which becomes a ghost. This ghost consists mainly of traumatic experiences from the psycho-historical past—that of the child as well as that of his family, such as events in the external reality concerning loss, violence, and death, corresponding anxieties in the internal world associated with them and unconscious phantasies which were transmitted from one generation to the other. All these have not been effectively dealt with by the child and have not found the right words or meaning within the environment. Moreover, the child often becomes a receptacle for the environment's projections at the expense of pushing out his own budding self in favor of the ghosts of his parental heritage. This is what Fraiberg et al. (1975) described as "ghosts in the nursery." In that sense, children who live under the shadow of the ghost are often characterized by what might be called "a pipe personality." They are children who resemble an open-ended pipe or vessel which is torn open to external psychic material and resonate with it. These children could not create a coherent personal narrative supported by the object. The ghost-shadow, like the death instinct, returns repeatedly in order to have its revenge, unless it can be met with the right words, by understanding and meaning, and by recognition of the truth, of guilt and of internal responsibility. Only then can it be buried and thus change from being a fate to becoming an accompanying rather than a persecuting shadow.

The third mode, being the shadow, describes early developmental catastrophes affecting the proto-self or what Damasio also calls "core-consciousness" (Damasio, 1999). These catastrophes are mainly of a bio-physiological nature, often located in the period preceding birth or very close to it. When this proto-self is in danger while it is still in the process of becoming conscious it might be chaotically and malignantly absorbed by and welded with its surrounding. The surrounding environment cannot be experienced or introjected as a containing, narratable object about which unconscious stories are told but rather as a chaotic or diffuse mass which is malignantly absorbed into parts of the body, and thus pathologically contained. The younger the fetus or the child is, the more each impingement is registered directly in the unconscious without going through the fragile and not-yet consolidated consciousness. As a result, it can only be experienced as confused bodily sensations, leading to a confused mind. I shall refer to this phenomenon as Chimerism, borrowing the concept from bio-medicine and embryology, in order to describe the creation of a psycho-genetically deformed and confused organism which cannot identify with the object or detect what is familiar and what is alien within it, and thus it is allergic to itself and attacks itself. The Chimeric child exists in a world of non-containment, non-transformation, non-identity, non-figurability (Botella and Botella, 2005), and non-representation.

De M'Uzan (2006) first proposed the term "psychological Chimera" in order to describe the inevitable immune "anti-gene" reaction of the patient to the analyst's interpretations, which are experienced by the analysand as a monstrous, unfamiliar, and a threatening joint creation. My emphasis, however, is on the pathological, self-destroying properties of being welded, in unconscious phantasy, with alien psycho-genetic materials which are felt to be branded into the body and interfere with the evolution of the psyche. Each of these three modes refers to different levels of individuation and self-cohesion. Thus living with a shadow is the highest level and being the shadow, or psycho-genetic Chimerism, is the lowest.

Living under the shadow of ghosts

When there is a failure to tolerate internal reality, especially that of deep death anxieties, destructive phantasies, or nameless grief, and with no supportive internal or external containment, the shadow of heritage might turn in unconscious phantasy into an angry, hungry ghost. In fact, we often refer to "the shadows of the past" as psycho-historical presences of events which have not been fully exposed to the light of self-reflection and appropriate representation. As is the case with haunting ghosts, it is not fully clear whether they are part of us or alien, alive or dead. The development of speech and language, as advanced forms of representation and communication, and I would add as an identification with and recognition of our heritage, enables us to emerge as individuals with a shadow. Salomonsson (2007) has shown how the emergence of speech in a little girl was accompanied by a transformation of her fear of black holes into fear of ghosts. Loewald in his classic paper on the therapeutic nature of psychoanalysis uses the ghost-metaphor in order to describe both the pressure of the unconscious on the conscious as well the effects of transference:

> This indestructibility of unconscious mental acts is compared by Freud . . . to the ghosts in the underworld of the Odyssey—"ghosts which awoke to new life as soon as they tasted blood" (Freud, 1900, p. 553n.), the blood of conscious-preconscious life, the life of "contemporary" present-day objects . . . Those who know ghosts tell us that they long to be released from their ghost-life and led to rest as ancestors. As ancestors they live forth in the present generation, while as ghosts they are compelled to haunt the present generation with their shadow-life. Transference is pathological in so far as the unconscious is a crowd of ghosts . . . In the daylight of analysis the ghosts of the unconscious are laid and led to rest as ancestors whose power is taken over and transformed into the newer intensity of present life, of the secondary process and contemporary objects.

This process, of turning the ghosts into ancestors corresponds to the re-gathering of all the split-off parts of the self, which have been projected into the ghost–object and turned it into an angry, envious, and vindictive one, wanting the life blood and vitality of the self. The re-assimilation of all these parts creates a new balance between identity and heritage. However, when heritage is associated with extreme cruelty, violence, and death, it is extremely difficult to turn the ghosts of the past into the ancestors of today since the very fabric of psycho-historical matrix is torn and destroyed. From the vast psychoanalytic literature which deals with the effects of trauma on identification processes, identity and the development of a meaningful sense of self, several themes are particularly relevant to the present discussion. Bohleber (2002) describes how trauma leads to the loss of all good objects which give the individual empathetic meaning in the traumatic situation. This, in turn, leads to the projection of the need for empathy to the perpetrator and to its malicious introjection. Thus the malicious persecuting object takes the place of the good internal objects and determines the internal dialogue. In addition, the traumatic situation destroys the ability to symbolize it and grasp its meaning. The trauma then becomes the "black hole" within the psychic structure. "Unintegrated trauma-fragments later break into consciousness again and overwhelm the ego, which, however, cannot structure and integrate these fragments. They cannot be incorporated into a super-ordinate meaningful narrative without help. Since the traumatic experience disrupts the network of meanings for a human being . . . . the traumatic experience cannot be 'contained'. In order to describe this psychologically, we have to resort to metaphors" (Bohleber, 2002, p. 220). He mentions some of the most frequently used metaphors such as a foreign body, a hole, a gap in the psychic texture, a crypt, or the empty circle. Abraham and Torok (1984), who suggested the metaphor of the "crypt" relate the ghosts or "phantoms" which haunt both the patient's and the analyst's unconscious to the child's early relationship with his parents' unconscious:

> Should the child have parents 'with secrets', parents whose speech in not exactly complementary to their unstated repressions, he will receive from them a gap in the unconscious, an unknown, unrecognized knowledge, a nescience, subjected to a form of 'repression' before the fact. The buried speech of the parent becomes (a) dead (gap), without a burial place in the child. This unknown phantom comes back to haunt from the unconscious and leads to phobias, madness and obsessions. Its effect can persist through several generations and determine the fate of an entire family line. (pp. 223–4)

They go on to describe how this situation leads to the establishment of a closed-off place within the ego, a crypt which blocks out introjections and serves as a cocoon-like inclusion. The traumatic transmission of ghost-like material from generation to generation has led to some important theoretical formulations. Faimberg (1988) has coined the term "the telescoping of generations" in order to describe a special identification process, which has far-reaching implications on the transference and countertransference and which carries the following features. The patient's identifications are split-off and thus cannot be heard by the analyst. They can only begin to appear at a key moment in the transference with the discovery of a secret history of the patient. Faimberg claims that in this kind of identification process a history is condensed which, at least partially, does not necessarily belong to the patient's generation.

This condensation of generations is what she calls "telescoping of generations." Barrows (1999) describes a patient whose fear of her parents' internal objects, which were experienced by her as vengeful ghosts who were preventing her from developing her own personality, and with whom she was identified, led to a split between idealized and persecutory objects and between material and psychic modes of functioning. Gampel (1993, 1996) uses the term "radioactive identification" or "radioactive nucleus" to describe phenomena "that are comprised of unapproachable, non-representable remnants of the memories of social violence that remain 'radioactive,' and under whose influence other, related and sometimes non-related material, is also rendered radioactive and un-representable" (Gampel, 1998, p. 362). These radioactive elements are hidden in images, nightmares, and symptoms through which, however, they are detectable.

Oscar's shadow-ghosts

In order to illustrate the shift from living under the ghost-shadow of heritage to living with a shadow, I wish to consider material drawn from from the five-year-long, five sessions per week analysis of Oscar. He sought analysis due to great distress, depression (sometimes replaced by feelings of persecution, compulsive behaviour, and obsessive thinking), and general unhappiness in his marriage and in his relationship with his children. When I first met him I was struck by his unusual appearance. He was short and stocky, dark skinned, his brown hair was brushed to one side and he had a short, clipped moustache. I had a fleeting thought that he rather resembled Hitler. However, I pushed this thought away quickly, attributing it to my own ghosts of heritage. Oscar described his life as a nightmare. He said he was haunted by anxieties and worries of an indefinite sort. He felt he was being followed by someone, had quite a lot of paranoid thoughts concerning his colleagues, and a general mistrust of people. More consciously, he was especially worried about his son being taken as a prisoner of war, tortured, and murdered sadistically. In order to relieve these anxieties he spent hours arranging, re-arranging, and polishing shoes, washing dirty laundry, arranging it in piles, and cleaning compulsively. He complained that he found it difficult to think. He said: "Things either pass through me or get stuck inside my head." He felt possessed by terrible constant thoughts of death and catastrophes but also "by love." He fell in love with a friend of the family, who was a professional physiotherapist. Most of his childhood and adolescence he felt dirty, deformed, and unlovable. Before he got married he often used to go to prostitutes whom he called "shadow women." Oscar was married to an Israeli girl who epitomized for him the ideal vision of "the brave, new Jew."

At the beginning of his analysis he wanted to leave his family for his lover, whom he also mistrusted and suspected of being a spy. More particularly, he mentioned two events that eventually drove him to seek analytic help. The first was an accident in which he was involved causing a woman to lose her baby. The second event was when he realized, based on vague childhood memories he was not sure were his own, and through conversations with relatives, that his deceased father had probably collaborated with the Nazis in the death camps.

Oscar's father left Europe after the end of World War II and moved to another continent. There he married Oscar's mother who had grown up as an orphan. Oscar was their third child. Two older brothers had immigrated to Israel as adolescents and became ultra-orthodox. Oscar's younger brother was a sickly child who died when he was five of tuberculosis. His nickname was "Kaporeh" which in Yiddish means atonement. Oscar had always been afraid of his father whom he portrayed as a silent, ominous, ill-tempered, and sometimes violent man. The father refused to discuss his past and, after making a fortune as an agent of German products, the family moved to an upper-class suburb which, as Oscar described it, "was clean of Jews". Oscar remembered very little of his childhood except for the vivid feeling of being terrified all the time of people and especially of ghosts and shadows. He had vague memories of German voices in the middle of the night, coming to see his father, trading documents, and disappearing silently into the night. After about a year into his analysis I noticed a peculiar phenomenon which I privately called "his watery speech." Oscar would talk and I would feel as if I was slowly drowning in water. It was not like falling asleep but rather a lulling, wavy feeling, the room spinning and Oscar's words becoming shapeless and meaningless. One day I shared this feeling with Oscar. He did not respond but a week afterwards produced a clear memory from the age of six. One night the cellar where his father kept his equipment and documents was flooded. They had to leave the house. Another memory which surfaced suddenly was of his coming home from his summer vacation and being told by his mother that his brother had died. In his shock and grief he remembered thinking: "Surely father must have killed him." In Hebrew it sounded like: "Surely father must have killed Jews." When I pointed this out to him, he told me how he found out the truth about his father. It happened after he moved to Israel, following his father's death. A distant relative met him and told him that, in order to survive, his father had become the Capo of his Block in the concentration camp. Oscar heard what was said but managed to block this information out of his consciousness. "For many years," he said, "I thought it was some kind of a nightmare I've had. Not real." However, the story of his unthinkable heritage took a double form: that of a watery, undifferentiated matter and that of a more distinct narrative revealed by his persecuting internal objects and by his symptoms. In fact, his daily obsessive-compulsive routine was made out of the daily forced labour of the camp prisoners—arranging the murdered victims' shoes and clothes.

Oscar ostensibly tried to repair himself and his father in his unconscious phantasies, while in the same manner his older brothers tried to atone for their father's sins and make "Kaporeh" by turning to religion and finding a new Jewish God-father. But this reparation relied on manic, omnipotent, and obsessive mechanisms and therefore failed and was experienced as devoid of real meaning. Oscar's childhood had been a cruel sequence of empathetic failures, secrets, and lies. He was surrounded by shadows and ghosts of a mixed sort—perpetrators mixed with victims and dead children.

All this was projected into me in the transference. At times it seemed that my very presence beside him endangered him in some way. I became a threatening, deadly father, a damaged child, and an idealized Israeli all put into one in a confused way. At such moments the possibility of acquiring a solid, non-watery, and distinct identity in contrast to his menacing and confusing heritage and reaching any sort of reparation in the analysis seemed impossible to both of us.

Being the shadow: Chimaera

I wish to draw attention now to the shadow-less "white holes" described by Omri, which antedate the "black holes" or "brown holes" where ghosts and shadows might already reside. It is beyond the scope of this chapter to discuss in detail the various meanings attached to the psychoanalytic usage of the term "black holes." These generally refer to descriptive formulations regarding the nature of early infantile traumatizations of bodily separateness from the primal mother, which result in primitive mental disturbances (Bion, 1970; Eshel, 1998; Grotstein, 1990a, 1990b, 1990c, 1993; Tustin, 1972, 1981, 1987, 1990). I would like to go back to Omri, the autistic boy, and to his description of the "white hole," in order to discuss the third mode of dealing in unconscious phantasy with the shadow of heritage. This mode is the most pathological and developmentally earliest one of the three. I chose to call this mode "Chimerism—a term inspired by both the mythological combined figure of Chimaera as well as the genetic abnormality of Chimerism. The term thus incorporates two sources, mythological and biological, which reflect both the phantasmic as well as the bio-psychological aspects. In Greek mythology, Chimaera is a combined monster which has the head of a lion, the body of a goat and the tail of a dragon. In other descriptions it has the beautiful upper body of a young nymph and the repulsive lower body of a huge snake. From its mouth it could throw huge flames, which burnt everything in its way. It was one of the wind monsters who personified the fiery storm winds described by Homer as "pouncing suddenly on the darkened waves, unleashed the raging tempest to destroy man." Its father was Typhon, the son of Typhoeus. Chimaera's brother was Cerberus, the dog of Hades the god of the dead, whose job it was to accompany the dead to the underworld and to prevent their escape (Guirand, 1993, p. 146). In the English language, Chimaera's name is used to describe every bizarre, diabolical object as well as wild, foolish and improbable ideas.

Chimerism is a rare medical phenomenon which sometimes occurs as a result of the implantation of multiple embryos following IVF or other fertility treatment. As a result of being glued together in the crowded womb, one embryo might be absorbed into the other. In genetic medicine, a chimera is an organism that has two or more different populations of genetically distinct cells that originated in different zygotes. Chimeras are formed from four parent cells (from two fertilized eggs or from early embryos which fuse together) or from three parent cells (a fertilized egg is fused with an unfertilized egg or a fertilized egg is fused with an extra sperm). Each population of cells keeps its own character and the resulting organism is a mixture of mis-matched parts. In its pathological bio-psychological phantasmic manifestation, Chimerism describes a confused organism which may turn against itself as parts of it are experienced as alien and are attacked by the immune system (Ainsworth, 2003; Appel, 2007; Nelson, 2008). On the unconscious level this signifies a heritage which cannot be experienced or mentalized as such (one that normally is a mixture of both me and not-me elements coexisting). Rather, it is a complete chaos with moments where the hardly existent self is experienced at the most as a bizarre object made up of non-combining, welded parts residing in the body and later in a fusion of body-mind. Chimerical children are confused since parts of their bodies are experienced as dangerous and allergenic. They are an alien presence to themselves, or, as Omri used to call himself, "Shugormi"—a mixture of his name and mine.

The "pipe-child" who is a host to ghosts, as described in the case of Oscar, has succeeded in constructing a definable membrane or psychic skin, which massive projections have perforated so that his insides have been overpowered and overpopulated by shadow-ghosts. The chimerical child has a patch-like psychic skin which resembles a bizarre jigsaw puzzle. The pipe-child can detect the shadow as an incorporated alien presence within the self, whereas the chimerical child has fragments of self which are alien and malignant to themselves. He becomes a shadow of a child.

Omri's white hole

I first met Omri when he was three. He was referred to analysis by his pediatrician who described him as "a hopeless case of severe Autism, one of the worst I've ever seen." I met a mute, utterly withdrawn and bizarre child. However, there was something untypical about his whole being which intrigued me. He was not quite the "shell-type" child nor did he resemble the "confusional child" described by Tustin. He was not entangled or entangling in any discernible way (Tustin, 1981). Nor could I detect clearly what Houzel (1985) described as "the turbulent world of the autistic child" or the "skin folding into itself" described by Anzieu (1987) as an autistic formal signifier. I could only see a random disarray of autistic symptoms and what resembled most a mad, wounded animal attacking itself and then withdrawing into blankness.

Omri alternated between complete jelly-like limpness and frozen rigidity. At other time he would have sudden convulsions accompanied by head banging, tongue biting, and tearing out pieces of skin from his hands and legs with his teeth. He scratched himself till he bled and would often need to be bandaged so as to prevent his self-inflicted wounds. He was extremely difficult with food and most things caused him an allergic reaction. Omri did not speak and only uttered strange sounds and syllables. He did not initiate eye-contact and avoided touching or being touched.

It was very difficult to obtain information from the parents regarding the circumstances of his birth and early development. The parents were a nice, warm couple although clearly sad and worried about Omri's condition. The father was often away on business. Omri's mother was a highly efficient and elegant woman. She spent a lot of thought and care focusing mainly on Omri's physical handling and appearance. He would always be dressed in expensive designer clothes as if to create a false second-skin which would hide his wounded and deformed interior. Omri had older brothers who seemed to be normal and well adjusted. The mother described her pregnancy as "a little problematic," since she nearly had an abortion at the beginning but then it turned out that everything was fine: "Yes, I was anxious for some more weeks but all the tests showed that the fetus was alright so we calmed down." She somehow managed to steer the conversation away from that subject. It was only much later that I learnt what happened. This coincided with a turning point in the analysis which took place after two years, when Omri turned five.

I shall describe briefly his general behavior during sessions up to that point through the salient psychic material which repeatedly caught my attention, amidst the general chaos and bewilderment I have come upon several similar cases of Chimerism which deal with the earliest encoding of biophysiological impingements and their effect on the pathologies of the emergent self. However, I shall restrict myself to the more detailed description of Omri characteristic of that "white hole" period. The first pattern which I noticed was Omri's confusion between figure and background. I have written the following in my notes during the first year of analysis: "Almost every day I see Omri crashing into walls, desks, doors and furniture. It is as if he can't see them. Once he hits the walls he seems utterly surprised and then starts screaming and hits himself at the spot where he's been hit. I say: 'You did not see the wall. Where is the wall, where is Omri . . . is Omri the wall? Is the wall Omri? Something hurt you and you felt it was you and then you tried to hit back. How frightening it is not to see what is you and what is not. You are attacked by Omri.'" At other times he would bump into me and repeat the same pattern. My constant interpretations seemed to reduce this behavior after about a year and a half.

This non-discrimination between figure and background was accompanied by lack of differentiation between inside and outside, front and back, up and down, before and after and between animate and inanimate objects. A state of non-figurability and non-representation prevailed (Botella and Botella, 2005).

A second, parallel cluster of behaviors corresponded in part to what Meltzer described as "dismantling" (Meltzer et al., 1975). Meltzer distinguishes this process from splitting and writes: "It seems to us to occur in a passive rather than an active way, somewhat akin to allowing a brick wall to fall to pieces by the action of weather, moss, fungi and insects, through failing to point it with mortar" (1975, p. 12). The crumbling bricks in Omri's case were his sense organs. It seemed that each sense and sensory organ wassometimes encapsulated, insulated, and operating in a faulty way, independent of the rest (Anzieu, 1987). However, unlike Meltzer's description this was accompanied by anxiety. I wrote: "Omri pushes food into his ears and nose. He spits, shakes his head. He hears a loud noise and shuts his eyes tightly. I say: 'You do not know where food needs to go, which part of you eats, does nose eat? Do eyes hear noise? Where does sound come in? Where does food go? Then you want it out of you, but where from?'" After about two years Omri dares to come closer to me and starts feeling my mouth as I speak. He touches my eyes, my nose and my ears and then his own. "You want to learn through me what does what, what belongs with what. You see me, listen to me and smell me and now you can start to see you." This is the dawning of comparison, differentiation, and a united body.

The third unique phenomenon I have encountered with Omri is what I privately called "welding" followed by self-aggression. Omri, who was generally very careful not to touch me or be touched by me, would occasionally touch my hand. He then would appear to be glued or "stuck" in this touch, unable to break free, rigid and frozen. He would then start screaming terrible frightened screams at a very high pitch. After a few more seconds, which to me seemed like an eternity, he would struggle and break free and then feverishly bite his hands, as if wanting to remove bits of skin. I called this "being glued" or "welding" since I felt that Omri could not tolerate the feeling that my skin and his have been welded. It was a recurrent theme in our sessions and happened mainly with me but also with the table, wall, and sometimes the carpet.

I was very puzzled and perturbed by this behavior. At first I tried to understand it bearing in mind Tustin's description of the premature tearing apart of the infant from the breast, where parts of the infant are felt to be in the mother and parts of her in him (Tustin, 1990, 1994). However, the interpretations along this line had no effect. When I met the parents I described it to them and said: "It seems to me he's trying to convey something to us—something that might have happened very early in his development on an almost molecular level. It is as if something got stuck to him, got into him or absorbed into his very skin that he's trying to get rid of. It's like some kind of allergy. He experiences this something as dangerous, life threatening."

The mother became pale as I was speaking and clasped her husband's hand tightly. She then burst out crying. She said that during pregnancy, approaching mid-term, she began to bleed and thought she had lost Omri. It turned out that there was another undeveloped fetus that died. The doctors said that there was nothing to be done since the dead fetus would probably be absorbed into the living one, and no one would notice it afterwards since it was "an internal thing," as they put it. The mother drove this piece of information out of her mind. "I was so happy that Omri was saved. And besides, thinking about this monstrous creature inside my womb made me sick. I tried very hard to envisage a different baby." This dramatic story was never discussed again between her and Omri's father. The danger, loss, and subsequent un-mourned grief were all aborted and then "absorbed" into Omri.

Conclusion

One of the main differences between Oscar and Omri lies in the fact that Oscar could compose a personalized version of his history relatively easily. Although the shadowy, ghastly reality of his heritage was extremely difficult to assimilate as part of his own personality, the world around him knew and told the story. The Shoa was a clear historical fact with which he could begin to negotiate in some way. Object-relations and culture provided him with enough representations, collective symbols, and historical narratives which served as powerful containers, with the help of which he could find internal meaning. At the same time, there was enough "I" to behold himself in relation to his shadow. The Shoa was in him but it was not him, only in parts. In Omri's case there was a double catastrophe. As a fetus, he had not enough "I" which could mentalize the destruction of his genetic barriers, and thus he became the shadow. In addition, the parental environment was too traumatized to form even a rudimentary narrative concerning his origins which he might have used unconsciously. As a consequence, the formation of autism seems to have been Omri's way of protecting himself against the nameless dread and nameless grief of chimerism. In addition, autism served as a primitive form of a reparative delusion where objects, movement, life, and forms were held frozen and thus rendered harmless. In Chimerism, the idea of interpreting the past in the present (Malcolm, 1986) is somewhat problematic. There is no differentiation between the self and background and in addition the "I-not-I" is composed of non-integrative welded bits and pieces. One must first identify and create this "I" via the relationship with the analyst and the analytic environment, before a clear transference situation, followed later by historical and psychological reconstruction, can be achieved. While transference interpretations and historical reconstructions prove beneficial in cases who are under the shadow or haunted by ghosts, the chimeric child needs the presence of the analyst as a bodily beacon with the help of which he may create a discernible membrane. Using another medical metaphor, one may say that in these cases analysis aims at "object or self transplant" through a total kind of interpretation which includes not only the mind-presence of the analyst but also his bodily presence. As in the case of any organ transplant, this might lead to an unavoidable rejection. In this situation it is mainly the principles of constant verbalization, personification, detecting, and linking body parts with appropriate functions and respective emotions and, finally, the principle of reparation in action or actively "reclaiming" the split-off, lost and frozen parts of the personality (Alvarez, 1999) that prove beneficial. In all cases of the shadow, the traumatic event was not assimilated or experienced fully at the time. To be traumatized, therefore, was precisely to be possessed. To work through the trauma meant to possess the event or, in other words, to re-own one's shadow.

Bibliography

Abraham N, Torok M (1984). 'The lost object–me': Notes on identification within the crypt. *Psychoanal Inq*, 4:221–42.

Alvarez A (1999). *Live company*. London: Routledge.

Ainsworth C (2003). The stranger within. *New Scientist*, 15 November.

Anzieu D (1985). *Le moi-peau*. Paris: Dunod.

Anzieu D (1987). Les signifiants formels et le moi-peau. In Anzieu D, editor. *Les enveloppes psychiques*, 1–22. Paris: Dunod.

Appel JM (2007). The monster's law. *Genewatch*, 19:12–16.

Aulagnier P (2001). *The violence of interpretation*. London: Routledge. (The New Library of Psychoanalysis.)

Barrows K (1999). Ghosts in the swamp: Some aspects of splitting and their relationship to parental losses. *Int J Psychoanal*, 80:549–61.

Bick E (1968). The experience of skin in early object relations. *Int J Psychoanal*, 49:484–6.

Bion WR (1967). The imaginary twin. In *Second thoughts*, 3–22. London: Heinemann.

Bion WR (1970). *Attention and interpretation*. London: Tavistock.

Bion WR (1989). *Two papers: The grid and caesura*. London: Karnac.

Bion WR (1987). *Clinical seminars and four papers*. Oxford: Fleetwood.

Bohleber W (2002). The development of trauma theory in psychoanalysis. In: Varvin S, Stajner-Popovic T, editors. *Upheaval: Psychoanalytic perspectives on trauma*, 207–34. Belgrade: International Aid Network.

Botella C, Botella S (2005). *The work of psychic figurability*. Hove: Routledge. (The New Library of Psychoanalysis.)

Bronstein C (2001). What are internal objects? In: Bronstein C, editor. *Kleinian theory: A contemporary perspective*, 108–25. London, Philadelphia, PA: Whurr.

Bullock A, Stallybrass O (1977). Genetic memory. In: *The Harper dictionary of modern thought*, 258. New York, NY: Harper & Row.

Chang GCC (1992). *The Buddhist teaching of totality: The philosophy of Hwa Yen Buddhism*. Delhi: Motilal Banarsidass.

Damasio A (1999). *The feeling of what happens: Body and emotion in the making of consciousness*. San Diego, CA: Harcourt.

De M'Uzan M (2006). *Invitation to frequent the shadows*. Paper presented at the EPF conference, Athens.

Eshel O (1998). 'Black holes', deadness and existing analytically. *Int J Psychoanal*, 79:1115–30.

Faimberg H (1988). The telescoping of generations: Genealogy of certain identifications. *Contemp Psychoanal*, 24:99–117.

Fraiberg S, et al. (1975). Ghost in the nursery: A psychoanalytic approach to the problems of impaired infant–mother relationship. *Psychoanal Q*, 45:651.

Freud S (1900). *The interpretation of dreams*. SE 5:339–626.

Freud S (1916–17). *Introductory lectures on psychoanalysis*. SE 15, 16.

Freud S (1917). *Mourning and melancholia*. SE 14:237–59.

Freud S (1918). *From the history of an infantile neurosis*. SE 17:3–125.

Freud S (1919). *The 'uncanny'*. SE 17:217–53.

Freud S (1921). *Group psychology and the analysis of the ego*. SE 18:65–145.

Freud S (1923). *The ego and the id*. SE 19:3–63.

Freud S (1926). *Inhibitions, symptoms and anxiety*. SE 20:77–175.

Freud S (1955). Some thoughts on trauma In *Final contributions to the methods and problems of psycho-analysis*. SE 23, 99.

Gampel Y (1993). From the thing in itself by modeling through transformation by narration in the therapeutic space. *Br J Psychother*, 19:280–90.

Gampel Y (1996). The interminable uncanny. In: Rangell L, Moses-Hrushovski R, editors. *Psychoanalysis at the political border*, 85–95. Madison, CT: International UP.

Gampel Y (1998). Reflections on countertransference in psychoanalytic work with child survivors of the Shoa. *J Am Acad Psychoanal*, 26:343–68.

Grotstein J (1980). Primitive mental states. *Contemp Psychoanal*, 16:479–546.

Grotstein J (1990a). 'Black hole' as the basic psychotic experience: Some newer psychoanalytic and neuroscience perspectives on psychosis. *J Am Acad Psychoanal*, 18:29–46.

Grotstein J (1990b). Nothingness, meaninglessness, chaos and 'black hole'. I: The importance of nothingness, meaninglessness, and chaos in psychoanalysis. *Contemp Psychoanal*, 26:257–91.

Grotstein J (1990c). Nothingness, meaninglessness, chaos and 'black hole'. II: The black hole. *Contemp Psychoanal*, 26:377–407.

Grotstein J (1993). Boundary difficulties in borderline patients. In Boyer LB, Giovacchini PL, editors. *Master clinicians on treating the regressed patient*, vol. 2, 107–42. Northvale, NJ: Aronson.

Guirand F (1993). *New Larousse encyclopedia of mythology*. London: Hamlyn.

Houzel, D. (1985). *Le monde toubillonnaire de l'autisme*, 3, 169–183.

Isaacs S (1952). The nature and function of phantasy. In: Klein M, Heimann P, Isaacs S, Riviere J, editors. *Developments in psycho-analysis*, 67–121. London: Hogarth.

King P, Steiner R (1991). *The Freud-Klein controversies 1941–1945*. London: Routledge.

Klein M (1944). The emotional life and the ego development of the infant, with special reference to the depressive position. In King P, Steiner R, editors. *The Freud–Klein controversies 1941–1945*, 730–52. London: Routledge, 1991.

Klein M (1963). On the sense of loneliness. In Money-Kyrle, R, Joseph, B, O'Shaughnessy, E, Segal, H. editors. *Envy and gratitude and other works 1946–1963*, 300–14. London: Hogarth, 1984.

Lacan J (1977). The mirror stage as formative of the function of the I. In *Ecrits a selection*, Sheridan I, translator, 1–8. New York, NY: Norton.

Laplanche J, Pontalis JB (1988). *The language of psychoanalysis*. London: Karnac.

Loewald HW (1960). On the therapeutic action of psychoanalysis. *Int J Psychoanal*, 41:16–33.

Malcolm RR (1986). Interpretation: The past in the present. *Int Rev Psychoanal*, 13:433–43.

McDougall J, Zaltzman N (2001). Preface. In Aulagnier P. *The violence of interpretation: From pictogram to statement*, xvi–xxxi. London: Routledge. (The New Library of Psychoanalysis.)

Meltzer D (1992). *The claustrum*. Strath Tay: Clunie.

Melzer D, et al. (1975). *Explorations in autism*. Strath Tay: Clunie.

Nelson JL (2008). Your cells are my cells. *Scientific American*, February.

Palgi P, Durban J (1995). The role and function of collective representations for the individual during the mourning process: The case of a war orphaned boy in Israel. *Ethos*, 23:223–43.

Salomonsson B (2007). *The breast, the hole, and the ghost: The transition to verbal symbolic functioning*. Paper presented at the symposium "Psychoanalysis in phases of developmental transition," IPA Congress, Berlin, July 2007.

Segal H (1991). *Dream, phantasy and art.* London: Routledge.
Sodré I (2004). Who's who? Notes on pathological identifications. In Hargraves E, Varchevker A, editors. *In pursuit of psychic change: The Betty Joseph workshop,* p. 53–69. London: Karnac Books. (The New Library of Psychoanalysis.)
Staehle A (1997). *Life in the compartments of the internal mother and the emergence from the claustrum.* Paper presented to a conference in honor of D. Meltzer, Florence, 1997.
Steiner R (2003). *Unconscious phantasy.* London: Karnac Books.
Tustin F (1972). *Autism and childhood psychosis.* London: Hogarth.
Tustin F (1981). *Autistic states in children.* London, Boston, MA: Routledge.
Tustin F (1987). *Autistic barriers in neurotic patients.* London: Karnac Books.
Tustin F (1990). *The protective shell in children and adults.* London: Karnac Books.
Tustin F (1994). The perpetuation of an error. *J Child Psychother*, 20:13–23.

Chapter 5

Vaginal ghosts

Memorializing the disappeared

Sue Grand

In psychoanalysis, we have arrived at this awakening: the wounds of others must be investigated to make meaning of our own. Our present is layered with the terrors of generations past; the terrors of the present will be layered onto succeeding generations. As the locus of unspoken dread, these borrowed wounds can become our invisible master. Un-mourned, they can occupy our individual, and communal, unconscious. In this occupation, new forms of destructiveness can gestate. If traumatic experience has not been held by conscious, empathic communion, it can seize us in a renewal of violence. The persecuted can re-create the "malignant dissociative contagion" from which they once suffered as victims (Grand, 2000). They may nominate new persecutory objects and fill them with their own "catastrophic loneliness" (Grand, 2000). Humiliated, debased, enraged, abandoned, memorializing an atrocity without witness, the victim(s) can seek self-restitution through the degradation of others. Helplessness, shame, pain, even the search for witnessing and justice: all of this finds a new figural representation. It is perhaps too simplistic, but I am tempted to say: here we have the history of violence. This history makes its appearance in our consulting rooms, and on the global stage.

Somehow, we must hold, mourn, and contain the destructive aspect of trans-generational transmission. To achieve this, we must witness abjection, and acknowledge the lust for revenge. But we must balance this effort with something else. We need to see, and honor, survivors' *enduring ethics and enduring human bonds*. Embedded in catastrophic history, there are manifestations of resourcefulness, dignity, integrity, and compassion. As it is with horror, so it is with this resilience. Strength and caritas exist, but they, too, are often sequestered from mutual knowing. When malignance has dominated the human capacity for goodness, that goodness can seem eclipsed by destruction. Nonetheless, in every history of atrocity, the abject practice resistance; they care for one another; they sustain human bonds, and *refuse* to embrace evil (Grand, 2009). In every paroxysm of destruction there are those *who do not*. Solidarity, resistance, and the ethos of care: these exist in the encounter with death. Twinned with abjection, these capacities *also* shape the lives of succeeding generations. I am in agreement with Ornstein (2004). As therapists, and as cultures, the witnessing of trauma must recognize *strengths as well as wounds*. We need to celebrate enduring love, even as we recognize the radical social break that characterizes the "empty circle" (Laub and Podell, 1995).

It takes courage to receive traumatic memory. It is easy for witnessing to collapse in one direction or the other. We can idealize the heroic as an escape from atrocity. Or we can be swallowed by atrocity, and neglect the life force. It is important, however, to seek this balance, even though it will perpetually collapse. This mission is at once political and clinical, personal and collective. If we fail to witness horror, we will be prey to its reproduction. If we fail to witness dignity, we reproduce survivors' degradation. We relinquish the force of human goodness, and render ourselves impotent in the encounter with destruction. To witness both in dialogic integrity: this is a mission of regeneration that seems to exceed human possibility. After all, *one day* of genocide would seem to take decades to tell, and many minds to hold. How can we ever hope to witness all of the pain *and all of the heroics*, around the globe? Perhaps survivors do *not* have difficulty articulating their own trauma narrative. Perhaps *we* simply do not have enough time, or enough ears. So much suffering, and we have so few rituals for accountability, grief and reparation. We have few spaces in which to honor human dignity. We are fascinated with violence and power, so uninterested in ordinary kindness. How easy to despair, to surrender to atrocity's repetitions.

To resist this surrender, we must track the trans-generational transmission of dead selves *and* alive selves; bestial gestures *and* compassion (see also Guralnik, 2014). In every clinical encounter with trauma, we try to restore the linkages (inside the mind, in human bonds) that trauma has broken. These linkages have affective, relational, *and* ethical markers. It is difficult to dwell in atrocity, to be proximal to these affects, without eradicating one of the links we are trying to restore. Each time we eradicate one of these relational/affective links, we risk some kind of ethical blindness: a failure to see destruction; an eclipse of human integrity. How do we cope with this predicament as clinicians and as citizens? Sometimes, we can learn from a great teacher. A determined and resourceful patient arrives in our office, with lost links and ethical markers inscribed on her body. She is both dead and alive; she is insistent about knowing. She speaks to the ghosts of violence, and she speaks for the ghosts of human integrity.

Embodiment, lost links, and ethical markers

When Rosa came to me, I felt I already knew her. Our memories were drawn from the same landscape. Postwar Brooklyn, the row houses of Brownsville. Stickball, in the streets. Delicatessen floors covered with sawdust, barrels full with pickles that were floating in their own brine. Grocers selling homemade pasta. The smells of mandlebrot, hot bread, sweet cannoli. Prices were always negotiable for a well-told story. And in Brooklyn, there were stories. In Russian and Polish and Yiddish. In Italian and broken English. The streets were rich with gossip, with the exchange of food and solace and unwanted advice. Couples courted and quarreled and scolded their children. Children ran free in a new world. Everything was loud and public and impassioned. Voices quieted by nightfall, erupting again as dawn struck the street.

Inside the row houses, there was a dimmer universe. There were yellowed pictures, silver candlesticks salvaged from the old country. Old things, sacred objects, heavy with grief. There were wall-to-wall carpets, furniture sealed in clear plastic, pristine rooms that could not be entered. To be impoverished and to labor, to acquire a home, and at last to buy furniture. To seal that furniture in plastic for all perpetuity: this was discipline and hope and fatigue and sadness. It was a mimicry of America and a reverence for America, a longing for assimilation and a dread of dislocation. Outside on the street, children were simply children. But within these interiors, the full weight of history was fixed upon their backs. Expansive bodies shrank in upon themselves. Children moved with caution and sobriety through dark hallways, through the narrow confines of parental memory. At every opportunity, they fled to the streets. In Spring, in Summer, in Fall. Then Winter came, and ice would descend upon Brooklyn. Exuberance would be pressed into dim quarters. When I met Rosa, I knew she was from Brooklyn. I recognized her in the way she told a story: straight-shooting, quick-witted, dark-humored, and absurd. She would have us roaring with laughter while pain sat upon our chests. She seized life in dark places. Insistent about the truth, she would look at whatever needed to be seen. She could look backward at the past and forward at the future. And she was always resolute in her intentions. She could change the endings of her stories before she had even finished telling them. She had that kind of discipline and mobility and courage. She suffered. But she always did the right thing. From the first, she looked me in the eye, and she registered me as human. There would always be something simple and warm and authentic between us, a basic human decency and a basic human trust. It would take her years to offer that kindness to herself. She hated her body. She was depressed. She was always alone. She was not really lonely, but coveted her isolation. There was a dread of invasion, an exhaustion at the prospect of any intimate contact.

She lived the changing seasons of Brownsville. Professional life was the summer street. At work, she was sharp and real and really herself. Bold and independent, confident, risk-taking. She was hard-driving and hard-working, ethical, and generous in her business encounters. There were "work friends." But evenings and weekends found her in a wintry row house. There was deadness and panic and an episodic blankness that transpired without memory. A desire to drink and a struggle to avoid drinking. And a body she never looked at or allowed to be seen. She despised her orifices, her curves, and the places she thought she was lacking in curves. To Rosa, her body was nothing but a conglomerate of deformities: small breasts, sagging belly, fat hips, legs, arms. Attractive, she moved with grace, but she could not feel herself moving. For me, there was an appealing quickness to her physicality; I thought her shape made interesting shifts between the angular and the round. I was arrested by her eyes. Face, body, mind: I responded to her as womanly whole. But to Rosa, her body was in pieces; it was loosely linked fragments united by blunt hatred. She ate compulsively and she vomited; she gained and lost weight. And she joked about aspiring to anorexia.

In the years of her alcoholic youth, there were sexual encounters. Stone drunk, she still insisted on dim lighting, heavy blankets, the concealment of clothes. There was little pleasure. But there were beatings by a drunken man who made use of her. She left him. She stopped drinking, alone, without any help or intervention. She was never beaten again. Now she lives a life in which there is no female body. Insofar as she is female, she is inspired with self-hatred. Insofar as there is no self-hatred, there is no body. Below her neck is a neutered edifice, moving parts in service to mental function. Feet transact pavement; hands operate telephones, keyboards. There is nothing much in between. She has lived most of her life in an un-conflicted celibacy. She always knew she was female. But in disembodied states, her body did not have genitals or any gender marker. Indeed, her body was often entirely without existence or sensation. Twice she had almost died because she could not experience an encroaching illness.

Still, she was exceptionally clear and cogent and related in our sessions. She knew that her childhood history was undoing her. Rosa was unsure whether she had been adopted as an infant. There were indications that she was adopted, and lies about that adoption, and no information about biological parents. She didn't know if her roots were in Italy or in Russia, or even whether "her people" were really Jewish or Catholic. She grew up with her older brother, her younger sister, her mother, her father. She did not look like them. In this house, there was real warmth with her Russian-Jewish father and strict propriety from her Italian mother. There was a brother disabled by some cognitive defect, who depleted what there was of maternal attention. There was a little sister who required Rosa's nurturant attention. If Rosa was unsure of her own origins, the mother's origins were obscured by dislocations, separations, abandonments. There were relatives missing in Turin who were subsequently restored. There were relatives missing who were never restored. There were years when the mother was missing from her own family. In the mother's own childhood, there was a "home" she was taken from and a "home" she was returned to, without knowing that she had ever been missing from home. There was an adoptive family she was left with and removed from. There was a biological family where relations were ill-defined. There were brothers who were not real brothers and real sisters who were unknown to each other until their own adulthood. There were no grandparents left alive, but there was a great-uncle who seems to have been her mother's actual father. All of this was dimly connected to the disappearance of Rosa's "real" mother, her maternal grandmother, and the great-uncle's wife.

With regard to these figures, there were false explanations and no explanations and stories that cracked under the slightest scrutiny. And there was a seamless disregard for all contradiction: they were long dead, and they were not dead. Grandmother was in an Italian sanatorium, she was in an American psychiatric institution, she was mad, she had never been mad, she had died many years ago, she had only recently died. The great-aunt was dead of a brain tumor, she had died in childbirth, she never got out of Italy, she died while emigrating to America, she had been arrested by brownshirts. No one seemed to know who or where these women were, or when and where they had last been seen, or precisely where they had been lost. With regard to Rosa's "real" mother, there was no disappearance. Rosa's mother was her real mother. But somehow, Rosa never believed it. In this family, there are lost attachments and no attachments, and there are people who do not know where they come from or to whom they belong. Some relatives are Russian, and some relatives are Italian. Some aunts cook with garlic, and some aunts cook with schmalz. There are Catholics who turn out to be converted Jews. There were no religious rituals, and there were peculiar religious rituals, and there were Catholics discovered crying in synagogue. Rosa identifies herself as Italian and as a Brooklyn Jew. She speaks some Yiddish and some Italian and has an affinity for Easter and Christmas. Although the father's family was more cohesive and intact, still, there were numerous gaps and lost relatives. Throughout all of this familial confusion, there is never any talk about what mobilized such ambiguity and dislocation: there are no Nazis or Fascist assassins.

The only relative left from the grandparent generation was the mother's "widowed" great-uncle. There are a few family stories about him from the old country: He seemed garrulous, elegant, irreligious, irreverent. Then, in America, he was absent of his wife and mute about her absence. Family gatherings found him silent. He could not or would not tell his story. He did not sit with the other immigrants. He would not raise his own voice in their communal joy and lament. He refused speech and grief and all possibility of comfort. In his silence, succeeding generations were denied the privilege of remembering. Stiff-moving, remote, he passed his days in the living room, that sacred space of old photos and new furniture. He alone was permitted access to the radio and, later, the television. Sometimes, Rosa would slip in. She was curious: the forbidden furniture, the stories on the radio, the allure of the moving image. He would not speak, meet her gaze, or shift his body; he never seemed to know that she was there. There was no evidence of life on his face. The radio, the television, the newspaper, the drone of sound, the shifting image, the black and white "snow" on the screen after programming had ceased: these were his hypnotic. Silently, she watched him listen and she watched him watching. She would slip out again, unseen. In this silence, there was a universe of untold stories. This man was the locus of familial sadness and confusion. He was pitied for a solitude that could never find its name. And so, his acts of sexual predation fell outside the family register. Rosa and her sister, all of their cousins: these children knew this man as their molester. But they obeyed the prescription about the secrecy of grief. They spoke of these violations only to one another. To the adults, they spoke of nothing. Each child had a story of being molested as she "slept." Each one had pretended to be sleeping. As adults, they discovered that none of them could sleep.

Rosa knew that incest informed the hatred of her body. Our treatment explored family mysteries and stories and violations and lies. We wondered who belonged to whom, who was missing and who was there, and she tried (and often failed) to locate family history. We continued the investigation Rosa had begun in childhood. At age 10, she discovered concealed documents. The "dead" grandmother was alive in an American psychiatric institution. She had been there for more than 20 years. In this family, there was a "dead" person who was both mad and left alive. There was an alive person who was "dead" and disappeared. Exposed documents had no impact on the family story. There was an insistence that the grandmother was long dead, until the day when this grandmother actually died. Rosa was 18. There was a recognition of familial loss and a denial of familial loss. Somehow, the grandmother's recent real death was conflated with her old, fictitious death. Truth was absorbed into falsehood. Rosa's mother did not want any real maternal story. Fiction was her constant, soothing object; it occupied the space where disintegration might have been, Despite familial collusion and resistance, Rosa kept looking and she kept asking. During her treatment, Rosa discovered the conversion of Jews Into Catholics, her mother's early adoption by a foster family, her subsequent return to a biological family that was mysteriously absent of a mother.

In the context of this family, we explored the incestuous experience. I wondered why none of the children had exposed him. She said that they had pitied him for his grief and loneliness. They knew he knew he needed something he could not have with a wife. He had aroused Rosa and he had soiled her, and she had sheltered him through her compliance. If she pitied him, so she pitied her mother. This man was her mother's only parental object. Rosa sensed that the revelation of incest would orphan a woman who had already been an abandoned child. And if Rosa was adopted, who would the mother choose? And in telling, would she expose the mother's own memory of being molested by the man who was molesting the mother's children?

Rosa's mother was decent and responsible and competent in the provision basic care. But there was something strict and dour about her, an absence of tenderness, intimacy, play, and understanding. She was peculiarly withholding and dictatorial about food consumption, inducing a sense of subtle starvation. This coldness may have led Rosa to believe that she was adopted. Perhaps the image of a missing mother was a fantasy of another, more intimate attachment. A mirror for the mother's missing mother. We would never know. But certainly, there was little strength in the mother for Rosa to rely on. The mother saw my patient's independence and decided that Rosa did not need. She saw her son's inadequacy and dependence and decided that he needed. She saw Rosa mothering the younger sister and deferred that sister to Rosa's care. When she did mother Rosa, she was cloying and anxious, controlling and intrusive, full of predictions of doom. Rosa learned not to need, and she learned not to ask. To the mother, it was Rosa who had repudiated all mothering. Injured, rejected, bewildered, she gave less, but she did not cease her intrusive commentary. Ultimately, my patient knew that there was no mother there to tell. With Rosa's father, there was a steadiness of warmth and affection. He seemed solid as a rock and just as enduring. There was shared laughter between them and an easy support for her competence and independence. But he was overworked and overtired, rarely home. One did not burden him with family matters, although undoubtedly, he would have intervened about the incest. And so, for Rosa, home meant the great-uncle, the mother, the gentle but weak older brother, the dependent younger sister. It meant invasion and compliance and isolation, the deferment of her own needs, and the derailment of her own feelings. Self-isolation was her first and only effort at self-regulation.

She feared that, like her mother, I would retaliate for her isolating maneuvers. But it was so clear that we were attached. The simplicity of our bonding seemed transacted through the father and through the shared memory of those Brooklyn streets. I was at ease with her movement in and out of connection. And so, she rarely moved out of connection. We developed a relation rooted in an understanding of her need for solitude. We knew it as a healing retreat, the first of many movements toward self-regulation. With this reframing, she embarked on the project of experiencing her own needs and feelings. And I never left her. In experiencing self-regulation in the transference, it became possible for her to read her own sensations and affects. At last, she became linked to the somatic. Suddenly, there were bodily complaints about pain and illness and hunger and over-fullness. She exercised, had massages, sought out doctors and dentists. She lost weight naturally as she engaged in conscious, healthy eating. She began to speak about feelings that were rooted in sensation, about sensations that were rooted in feelings. Where there was deadness, now, in her solitude, she alternated between quiescence and pain. She spoke of some desire for intimate human contact and a dread of relinquishing her solitude. She even imagined a renewal of sexually. Still, she felt too ugly to allow herself to be seen. In her feminine body self-hatred had softened into dislike and into a more realistic appraisal. But there was a persistent dual body experience: a maligned feminine self and an unsexed, disembodied self.

Two years passed. Suddenly, she was offered a high-level executive position in the fashion industry, which required her to travel throughout Europe. She realized that travel would interfere with her treatment, rupturing our attachment, evoking some of the depression and anxiety that comes with displacement and homelessness. And of course, the fashion industry would exacerbate the devaluation of her female body. But she was very excited about traveling, about the enhancement of her career. She felt ready to terminate "for now," knowing that more work would be needed if she wanted to pursue intimacy. In the weeks before her termination, she remembered childhood adventures disrupted by mother's anxiety. She needed to share her sadness without the diminishment of excitement. She had always been bold and risk-taking. We enjoyed that excited self. And we knew that we would miss one another. It was a sad but fulfilled parting, in which her transatlantic journey seemed to mirror other transatlantic journeys, from another time. Moving into the fashion industry, her female self seemed to register a familial lamentation.

Thingness and Thanatos: Eros surpasses lamentation

A year passes. I receive a call. She is in trouble, depressed, professionally mute, and frozen. She arranges telephone sessions while she is traveling throughout Europe. She calls me, and in these phone calls, we enter a strange new phase of treatment. I cannot see her embodied. Her missing image begins to play on me with a kind of hallucinogenic action. Her voice seems cast in strange textures. I cannot see Rosa. But I can see the telephone cable traversing frigid waters, emergent in strange cities, buried under continents, ruthless in its progress. I feel my voice emerging from my own mouth. It is like a substance poured into plastic, poured from plastic into wire, from wire into that cable which is a conduit for her fear. I wonder if she can hear me speaking. I ask if she is feeling unreal. She says yes. I ask if she can see her body. She says no. Her mind is located somewhere outside of her head. She has no head. I tell her that she seems to be imploding, not with depression, but with fear. She says that she did not know it was fear. And then she says that she has known anxiety, even panic, but this is something beyond those states. It is something crackling, unraveled, avoidant of light and sound. The warm sun of Cannes has become a terrible illumination. Objects are growing in size and in dimension. Desktops, tabletops, the cushions of chairs: the inert becomes mobile and the mobile, inert. Voices are obscured in a tinnitus of sound. There has been an alteration in the lens of her sight, a tactile shift in her relation to the ground. Her universe is electrified by the uncanny significance of things. There has been no access to words, no proximity to the symbolic. She is mute in all the places where she has always been able to speak. And she cannot speak to me in our familiar language.

There is a visual acuity to my listening that I have rarely experienced. I see her landscape, and yet, I cannot see her. My words seem to grasp the shape of persecutory scenes. Shared remoteness begins to dissolve into the mirroring of fear. Still, we are mystified by the quality of her dread. She tells me what she can. For a year, she has been an executive purveyor of the young and the beautiful. Her world is peopled by idealized constructions: men, women, tall, sculpted, thin, impeccable in every feature. I anticipate the self-hatred aroused in her by their perfection. But where there has always been self-hatred, now hatred is absent, because there is no body to hate. And then she tells me this. As her work cycles through the fashion capitals, she re-encounters figures who look as if they are themselves, and yet, they are not themselves. Alien, yet recognizable, their brown eyes have become green, become blue, become brown again. Brown hair becomes red, becomes blonde. Plastic surgery erases all evidence of human frailty. What might have become real is "beautified" and obscured. Bodies are disassembled, parts reconstructed, cut, burned, inflated. Skin is peeled and shrank and stretched, as if human skin was malleable stuff. Faces "lift" into masks, Silicone is implanted in muscle, supplanting real muscle and flesh. Souls evaporate as fat is suctioned out. Lives are lived by false copies of the real, so that there is an appearance of humanity without being human.

I think about the continuous rupture in object constancy, about the absence of any attachment. The reawakened mystery of who is where and who is missing. These are familiar conditions for her pain, but they are not the terror itself. The terror seems to reside in these peculiar bodies. As I listen, my mind seems crowded with hallucinatory scenes. I see fashion models seated in identical repose. Rosa's hand unscrewing plastic heads, revealing mechanical works where human brains should have been.

Row upon row of plastic heads filled with plastic works. Torsos severed, bloodless and immaculate. Wires, screws, computer chips, plugs emerging from white necks. Heads screwed back on and a simulation of movement. Everything but the eyes. The eyes are fixed, slow-moving glass. The eyes of dolls, the eyes of the dead. I am staring at the telephone receiver in my hand. I am riveted by the surface of hard plastic, by its alien internal mechanisms. I need to unscrew the casing of the receiver and expose that interior. To find the cable which is the conduit for our voices. Perhaps this is not Rosa's living voice, but some technological improvement on the human voice, a simulation of thought and a simulation of sound. Or her voice has been prerecorded prior to her disappearance. This voice is really the voice of a prior transmission. I have been speaking to someone who was never present. I need to see her. I cannot locate her. She is the cable, buried under continents, buried under the sea. She is inside of my receiver. Trying to get out. Embalmed in plastic and wire and cable and transmitters, no longer trying to get out.

I reawaken to a considerable silence. She has stopped speaking, when, I cannot remember. Finally I speak, and she tells me that she was afraid that I was dead. In this moment, she finds the ghostly "dead" self in the transference. But in the transference, she also awakened affect and imagination inside a "dead soul." Rosa and I are deeply attached, profoundly attuned, in a zone in which attachment seems completely ruptured. It seems that she is narrating these historic ruptures of attachment. But she also seems to be narrating another forgotten history: a history of *living minds and enduring bonds* at the epicenter of madness. I tell her about the unscrewed heads, the bloodless torsos, and the mechanical works. I say that humanity seems to have been replaced by the robotic. Humans are eradicated, and the natural world has no living matter. The landscape of Cannes is an artificial rendering. Light is the residue of nuclear radiation. The earth is populated by the mutant and the dead. When she calls me, she is calling out to some remembered universe of the human, in which there is a possibility of a living human bond. She calls in the possibility that she can be alive. She says yes. There is a flood of talk about the nuclear landscape, about the humanoids that surround her. It is not as if they were robotic, they are robots. And she was the only one who knew it, until I saw their unscrewed heads. Of course, she "knows" that they are not robots. She is no more paranoid or psychotic than I am myself. She is sane and strong and rooted in reality. But there is an alternate universe that is really populated by the mutant, the dead and the robotic. We see them and we know them. In that clarity, we feel exceptionally sane, exceptionally clear, and exceptionally mad.

Some truth is emergent in this sharing of delusion. Knowledge seems to require a breakdown into symbolic equation. There is an elasticity to our minds that anchors us in "reality," and yet, it allows us to play with a contained madness. She has opened this gateway to knowledge and will not retreat from it. Once again, she is fierce in her desire for the truth. At last, I deeply recognize her, and I almost see her as I saw her last, sitting on my couch. Human, alive, embodied. Even in this measured disintegration, there is something ironic. She tells her story, and she caricatures her story, so that the story's ending is rewritten while she is still enduring it. She doesn't lose her dark humor. She's inside terror, but she also keeps her perspective. I have rarely known someone to risk this path. I comment on her courage. She sighs. She doesn't think it is courage. But I know her to possess a remarkable curiosity and fortitude. Within a week of speaking about the robots, there is a coherence of her terror and an abatement of that terror. Over the next two weeks, she jokes about the "humanoids" and rapidly recovers her capacity for speech in professional meetings. Still, she covets human contact and cannot locate anyone who is human or alive. The world retains its peculiar cast. Fearful of light and of "robotic" encounter, she stays in her hotel room at every opportunity.

Now I realize that her great-uncle was the original humanoid. Incest did not just happen as she slept. There was another story. Every Sunday, the uncle would leave the house and not return until many hours later. Rosa discovered that he was going to the movies. She longed to see a movie, to make contact with this man who did not see her. She was about eight years old, and even then, she was resourceful. She got the money for the ticket, and she followed him. She pleaded with him, and she pestered him and he moved forward in his silence. At the ticket window, they buy their tickets. He seems to accept her presence. They take their seats, and the movie starts. Together, they fix their eyes upon the screen. She is excited. He is blank. Not a word has been spoken to her. He is oblivious to her presence. He masturbates her in the dark. He is without arousal or aggression or sadism. He makes no plea for the "tender" relief of his hunger. There are no threats, no coercion of lies. There is not any kind of human regard. He never turns his head to look at her. He does not laugh at the cartoons or respond to the film. There is only sound, flickering image, fingers moving in her vagina. Infinite hours, as the film begins and ends and begins again, a continuous cycle, at which he stares unblinking. He does not register that the film is over. His fingers move, they stop moving, they move again. For Rosa, the first moments of excitement and arousal—the stimulation of the film, the stimulation of her genitals—become deadness and imprisonment and dread. She is lost and does not know her own way home. She is too frightened to leave without him. She is hungry. She needs to urinate. She needs this thing to stop in her vagina. She tries to tell him. She tries to shake him. He is unmoving and unresponsive. She becomes mute and unmoving. At last, the last show ends; an usher makes him leave the theater. She follows her uncle home. She goes to bed, mortified in her body and stripped of all embodiment.

We have spoken of this incident before. But not in so much detail. And we have never explored the impact of his deadness, until she addressed it in me. Now, we realize that she was molested by a corpse. He was a rapist who didn't even seem to know that he was raping her; he didn't know she was there even while she was being raped. Her first passions—degradation, anxiety, anger, arousal—were inspired by a severed hand. There was no whole, living human rapist imbued with the quality of malevolence. There wasn't even a whole, dead human rapist, possessed of essential bodily coherence. There was a dismembered body part autonomous in its movements. Fingers still moving after rigor mortis had consumed the rest of the corpse. Or perhaps they were not his own fingers, but those of other, remembered hands. Moving with violence and hunger and abject supplication. The twitching of his hand inside her: did this mean that someone is still alive and that she must save him? Could her arousal be the stuff that could animate the dead? Or would rigor mortis simply trap stiffening fingers inside of her?

The cold cave of her vagina. A vagina filled with bloody body parts. A vagina filled with bloodless things. As we speak of these images, we have reached the core of her disintegration. There are pieces of dismembered corpses deposited inside of her. And there is nothingness deposited inside of her, and there is no inside of her vagina in which to deposit that nothingness. There is a vagina that is a repository for corpses. There is a warm human vagina, which is the repository for human grief. And there is a thing-vagina, a crypt constructed of mortar and stone. An evacuated no-self vagina, a blankness where a vagina should have been. An absence mirroring a series of absent female bodies: mother, grandmother, great-aunt. Through this act of incest, bodies have been registered as whole corpses and fragmented corpses, as thing like and nonhuman, as empty caskets and whole cemeteries, as the body parts of unwanted memory. Rosa's vagina was nonexistent and overcrowded. It was the repository for lost generations. It memorialized history's perversities. Insofar as she was raped by a dead thing, bodies were not bodies, and they had no sex and no gender. Genitals were absent because incest was transacted between non-human things. This non-human transaction mirrored other, inhuman transactions: forgotten women who had been treated like things. Repeating the violence of which he cannot speak, the great-uncle narrated memory through the violation of her body.

In the analysis of these fantasies, in the excavation of memory, she mentions that the fashion "humanoids" are without sensuality or eroticism. Beautiful, they do not possess or evoke desire. I ask if they have genitals, and she realizes that it is as if they do not. Big breasts, broad chests, nothing between their legs. It is true that she defensively subtracts people's genitals, for in the absence of genitals, genitals can neither violate nor be violated. This is how we had initially understood her unsexed and un-gendered self, in the first phase of her treatment. As a defense against rape, against the degradation of her own incestuous arousal. This was an understanding cast in terms of human malignance and human mortification. It was a half-truth that did not reach into her disembodied self, or narrate her ethical refusal of that malignance. For Rosa, there would be no half-truths. She must have sensed that bodies lacked genitalia because they were not human. Somewhere, there were perpetrators who were inhuman, who had treated her relatives as if they were nonhuman. Even in this crisis, Rosa never treated anyone as a thing. But she needed to convey a memory that could not be spoken in our human encounter. It had to be conveyed through somatic transfiguration. And so, she took a job devoid of real human bodies. She contrived a telephone treatment in which there was a missing human image. The absent image, the absent body: these opened into traumas in which the human were not human.

After we worked with the scene in the movie theater, our conversations lost their edge of primitive disorder. When she calls, we are simply speaking. The telephone retreats into an invisibility. Strong and no longer fearful, she transacts the "humanoids" with her old humor and vitality. She inspires respect at work for her dedication and creativity. She refuses the ruthlessness that pervades her profession. She facilitates and supports subordinates, and finds some friends who are related and authentic.

She speaks of transferring to a position where she can settle in either London or Paris. Through the "thing" testimony, familial history has been released. She doesn't want to wander, homeless, across the globe. Still, we are not going to reunite. Time and distance will continue to register grief and loss. Like the narrative of the female body, this story, too, is a lament. But for Rosa, there is always a sense of possibility, resourcefulness, aliveness. At this moment, she has an extraordinary dream. She finds herself looking at her naked body in a mirror, knowing she has never looked at it before. It is attractive, slender, voluptuous. She has the larger breasts she has always desired, the long limbs, the slender waist. And she discovers that she has a penis as well as a vagina. The penis is erect, and she masturbates it, not with arousal but with a delighted astonishment. She feels beautiful and sufficient unto herself. We speak of her having an inviolate body, a new body, unmolested, emergent from within her own mind. This is not a body conferred on her by rape. And it is not conferred on her by any form of erotic affirmation. It is an imaginary body, an undoing of time. She sees that she has everyone with her and inside of her. Both vaginas and penises: men, women, girls, and boys. Everyone from the old country. Not immobilized, vengeful, dead, or broken. They are robust, young, tumescent. Adventurous, aroused, glowing resilient, laughing at fascists, active in the resistance, outwitting war. They are rescuing friends and relatives, bringing them to a new world. They are bringing them to Brownsville and to the summer streets.

Once again, Rosa is in postwar Brooklyn. There is sun and light and air. There are no missing relatives, no stories that cannot be told. Front stoops are rowdy with immigrant speech. Open fire hydrants spray water on hot, loose-bodied children. In her imagination, the great-uncle joins in the clamor of humanity. He is seated with the grandmother and the great aunt. Finally, there are women with names and faces, who weep and laugh about history. These are women who can tell their own stories of solidarity *and* abjection. They speak about jackboots, escapes from the Brown-shirts, penniless journeys, arrivals at Ellis Island, complex cycles of loss and regeneration. In Italian and in Yiddish and in broken English. In open doorways. While the smell of the cooking wafts out. In this fantasy, Rosa has the body of an unmolested child. Moving outside to the streets, inside to the row house, she is alive amid others who are embodied and alive. In this imaginary body and sustained by an imaginary family, Rosa meets a man outside of her work and has an affair. He is warm and kind and passionate. At last, she is sexually alive, naked, and unashamed. About six months later, Rosa terminated her therapy. But we knew that nothing could separate us: not time or distance, not cruelty or "cowardice," nor any kind of transatlantic journey.

Rosa's thing-vagina was a lament. It was a grave for missing relatives and missing memories. But it also referred to creativity and fortitude in the midst of annihilation. The uncle inscribed destruction on her body. But there seemed to be other inheritances from the dead: integrity, shape-shifting, attachment, intentionality, resourcefulness, wit. The thing-self was a crypt. But it also restored a vagina to a woman who did not have one. It had the emptiness of loss. But it was also overcrowded. It became a boat to America; an open door, spilling life onto rowdy streets. Through this motif, Rosa created signs for terror and for terror's state of "catastrophic loneliness" (see Grand, 2000). She memorialized atrocity, but she also refused its reproduction. Our analytic space was fraught with primordial anxieties. But laughter kept cascading through this darkness. In extremity, Rosa kept restoring us to life and asserting the dignity of the abject. The trans-generational transmission of trauma has not reached its terminus. But perhaps we have fortified ordinary kindness, in its contest with destruction.

References

Grand, S. (2000). *The Reproduction of Evil: A Clinical and Cultural Perspective*. Hillsdale, NJ: The Analytic Press.

Grand, S. (2009). *The Hero in the Mirror: From Fear to Fortitude*. London: Routledge.

Grand, S. (2010). *The Hero in the Mirror: From Fear to Fortitude*. NY: Routledge.

Guralnik, O. (2014). The Dead Baby. *Psychoanalytic Dialogues*, 24, 129–145.

Laub, D. and Podell, D. (1995). Art and Trauma. *International Journal of Psychoanalysis*, 76, 991–1005.

Ornstein, O. (2004). *My Mother's Eyes: Holocaust Memories of a Young Girl*. Cincinnatti, OH: Emmis books.

Community & culture

Chapter 6

Ghosts in psychoanalysis

Adrienne Harris, Michael S. Roth, Jack Drescher, Daniel G. Butler, Douglas Kirsner, and Don Troise

The ghost behind the ghost

Adrienne Harris

Sabina Spielrein (1885–1942) languished in the psychoanalytic canon, for a very long time, solely as footnote in Freud's *Beyond the Pleasure Principle* (Freud, 1920), along with a brief nod to her ideas in his work on the Schreber case (Freud, 1911). In the footnote, he credits her with many of the ideas and themes of the essay. It is perhaps ironic that many commentators who came to know the work on which Freud based his footnote (only in English in 1988 and in a Jungian journal) find Freud's view of destructiveness and Spielrein's actually rather different. Her Russian colleagues Luria and Vygotsky, who write a preface to the Russian translation of *Beyond the Pleasure Principle*, neglect to mention Spielrein or Freud's acknowledgements of her influence. This is, at the very least, curious, as she would have been, at that time, not only a senior colleague but also one of two IPA sanctioned training analysts in Russia (Miller, 1998; Etkind, 1997).

Spielrein hovers nonetheless, not quite extinguished, a little spectral, and more than a little demonic. Rumored to be one of the patients Jung had an affair with, caught in a power struggle between Freud and Jung, tainted as the victim of such suspected boundary violations often are, she seems to have been ALMOST erased. In the context of this volume on ghostliness, we might see Spielrein as a dying internal object in the psychoanalytic body, one of the undead.

In the late 70s a cache of letters, diaries, essays, and personal papers is discovered. There are translations, publications, and many discussions of her relations with Jung and Freud. Biographies, films, and documentaries tumble into view. Spielrein lives as the brilliant, transgressive, hysterical young girl caught between two big Daddies (three if you count her actual violently abusive real father). Brilliant, excessive, a masochistic sex toy, then a tragic doomed figure caught and trapped in some always preordained slide down to despair and death. Seen simultaneously through the lens of perversion and brilliance, but she is still ghettoized AND UNBURIED in that characterization (Carotenuto, 1982; Kerr, 1992; Covington and Wharton, 2003).

So while many have greeted the revival of Spielrein with a strong focus on her relationships with Freud and Jung, relationships both personal and professional, the effect was still more like a ghostly haunting return than a revival. In this first appearance after the discoveries of the 1990s she is demonic, tortured, perverse. But there are hints of another figure behind the first too, a caricatured and fascinating but difficult creature. That ghost, waiting to be invited in perhaps, is serious, smart, a mix of teacher, clinician, researcher, and theorist, moving as a senior and responsible figure through two scholarly, and clinical, psychoanalytic communities, first in Geneva and then in Moscow. It turns out there are not only one or two papers by a precociously intelligent 'little girl' but close to 30 papers (and probably more that remain still spectral) by a seasoned and sophisticated thinker. It is that ghost that I want to summon (Harris, 2015).

Sometime in the 1920s she is applying for a position in Moscow and had to give an account of herself. Spielrein writes: "I think that I was born for this job, that it is my calling. My life would have no meaning without it" (Etkind, 1997). The essays published in the period 1913–1931 are confident in tone, scholarly, the product of someone who combined a wide reading in psychology and psychoanalysis with keen clinical eyes and ears.

To say that Spielrein worked first in Geneva and then in Moscow is perhaps just to speak of geography. In some of the accounts and fictional treatments of her life, it is not always clear why and how these moves occurred. Were they dictated by personal choices, by unhappiness, conflict, masochism (the usual suspects)? Rarely are these developments in her personal history seen as linked to ambition and to opportunities. How to strike a balance in thinking and writing about Spielrein that honors her difficulties and brilliance?

Spielrein is a link and a major player in two periods, one in Geneva between 1913 and 1923, and the second in Moscow from 1923 to the early 1930s These are sites of what I would call a cultural and collective synergy of ideas and work that launched theories and ways of conducting both research and clinical treatment that are still potent in both psychoanalysis and psychology, particularly developmental psychology.

Another way to think about these two sites and the communities of scholars and psychoanalysts who worked in these worlds, including Spielrein, is to see the ideas and themes and projects arising in Geneva and in Moscow as elements in what Freud considered an important theoretical task: the creation and demonstration of psychoanalysis within theories of general psychology.

I am going just to summarize what I find are the key elements that Spielrein worked on in these two periods.

First, the method of observation, which she develops in the context of child analytic work. Hug-Hellmuth in her seminal book on the mental life of the child, appearing first in 1912 and then in English in 1919, notes the origins of child psychoanalysis in analysts' observations of their own children. Spielrein in 1913 published a paper on children's playful and erotic investment in speech games through observations of her first daughter Renate. In the early 1920s both she and Piaget in Geneva utilized this method in their work on the interweaving of thought and speech. From child analysis. Actually Spielrein's language observation projects predate the work Piaget initiates in Geneva in the early 1920s. There seems to me to be a line tying together Hug-Hellmuth (1912) (another lost soul), Piaget, and Spielrein, all of whom significantly carried out observations on their own children (in Hug-Hellmuth's case a nephew). Clinical methodology launches child experimental psych. What is always characteristic of Spielrein in some contrast to Piaget and later Vygotsky is her focus on the unconscious archaic elements in speech and thought, the powerful bodily registers of speech in orality and the excitements and aggressions carried in increasingly complex representations (Harris, 2015).

Second, Spielrein is working on models of developmental process, mutative action, and change. Projection/introjection; assimilation and accommodation, these are genetic epistemology, zone of proximal development and the dialectic of thought and speech, real models in line with her ideas about transformation. Piaget (1923, 1926) and Vygotsky (1987) were often seen as opponents but a reading of Piaget that stresses genetic epistemology (his term) as a model of cognitive change has very close links to Vygotsky's dialectical model of the co-evolution of speaking and thinking. Vygotsky's dialectical model of the interpenetration of language and thought: all these developmental models of mutative action share a common process. The transactions that transform internal experience through action/thought/fantasy that transforms the external world. Change arises through disequlibration and reintegration (Ferenczi 1924). Spielrein is somewhere a contributor and interlocutor in this mix. Her 1912 paper on destruction and creativity is steeped in ideas about development. Transformation, she believed, was at the heart of her ideas about sexuality in which creation and destruction moved in a dialectic tension. Destruction and creation are not instincts in opposition but mutually co-constructing. Building begins with undoing, even doing away with. Experiences and their mental and embodied representations emerge out of the necessary interplay of creation and destruction, shame and excitement, penetration and introjection that are not simply encompassed as passive and active.

Third, Spielrein from about 1913 on is developing ideas about the unfolding and dynamically transforming stages of the development of speech and thought in children. This work includes looking as stages of language and cognitive development, the move from private to social, and from egocentric (autistic) to representational) speech. From her arrival in Geneva in 1920, her research work turned towards children's speech and thinking, even as her pedagogic and clinical work turned towards work with children.

Fourth, Spielrein worked on several long papers and some shorter contributions on the development of consciousness in children, linked to developments in abilities to track causation and intention and to the child's sensitivity to elements of time and temporality. These are interests that were present even in her first more widely know paper on creativity and destruction.

Finally, and here Spielrein has some serious reputation, there is her work on female sexuality. In her great paper—or the greatest we in the English-speaking west know of—explores mind through exploring sexuality and vice versa. Strikingly, Spielrein speaks of the sexual body in a more experience-near way than our current preoccupations with attachment sometimes lead us to believe. The attachment literature involves us in the very nuanced experiences of the distal senses—vision, sound patterns, and vocal rhythm matching. Spielrein returns our attention to the sexual body, to touch, penetration, and excess and to speech and symbolization simmering with desire and bodily excitements (Dimen, 2003; Saketopoulou, 2015).

What happened? There is no dearth of candidate explanations. Gender must be at play here. And as a number of people have suggested, she may have paid a price for finding herself caught in a many-faceted conflict between Freud and Jung, although Freud continued to be supportive, to suggest that she undertake organization work in Geneva and to appreciate her potential to play a role in Russia where she was one of only two IPA sanctioned training analysts. Where is character in this, interwoven with gender and early trauma? But, we need to remember also that there is the heavy hand of history: the collapse of psychoanalysis in the Soviet Union, the destruction of Spielrein, her family (brothers and children) and community, the double force of Hitler and Stalin.

As I have tried to argue, a ghost and a ghost behind a ghost gradually come into view. Benign and not malign forces arise from an approach to her history and her work. My project is Loewaldian to turn a ghost into an ancestor, to restore a genealogy, to place Spielrein in the sequences of names.

Bibliography

Carotenuto, A. (1982). *A Secret Symmetry: Sabina Spilerein between Jung and Freud*, transl. A. Pomerans. New York: Pantheon Books.

Covington, C., & Wharton, B., eds. (2003). *Sabina Spielrein: Forgotten Pioneer of Psychoanalysis*. New York: Brunner-Routledge.

Dimen, M. (2003). *Sexuality, Intimacy, Power*. Hillsdale, NJ: Analytic Press.

Etkind, A. (1997). *Eros of the Impossible.: The History of Psychoanalysis in Russia*. New York: Westview Press.

Ferenczi, S. (1989). *Thalassa: A Theory of Genitality*. London: Karnac Books.

Freud, S. (1911). Psycho-analytic notes upon an autobiographical account of paranoia (dementia paranoids). *Standard Edition*. 12:9–79.

Freud, S. (1920). Beyond the pleasure principle. *Standard Edition*. 18:7–64.

Harris, A. (2015), Language is there to bewilder itself and others: The clinical and theoretical contributions of Sabina Spielrein. *J. American Psychoanal. Assoc*. 3, 727–768.

Hug-Hellmuth, H. (1912). *A Study of the Mental Life of the Child*, transl. J.J. Putnam & M. Stevens. Washington: Nervous & Mental Disease Publishing, 1919.

Kerr, J. (1994). *A Most Dangerous Method: Freud, Jung, and Sabina Spielrein*. New York: Knopf.

Loewald, H.W. (1978). Primary process, secondary process, and language. In *Papers on Psychoanalysis*. New Haven, CT: Yale University Press, 1980, 178–208.

Miller, M. (1998). *Freud and the Bolsheviks: Psychoanalysis in Imperial Russia and in the Soviet Union*. New Haven, CT: Yale University Press.

Piaget, J. (1923). La pensée symbolique et la pensée de l'enfant. *Archives de psychologie* 18(72):273–303 (Geneva).

Piaget, J. (1926). *The Language and Thought of the Child*. New York: Harcourt Brace.

Saketopoulou, A. (2015). On sexual perversions' potential to act as portal to unformulated mental states. In *Sexualities: Contemporary Psychoanalytic Perspectives*, ed. A. Lemma & P.E. Lynch. New York: Routledge, 205–218.

Spielrein, S. (1911). Uber den psychologischen Inhalt eienes Falles von Schizophrenie (Dementia Praecox). *Jahrbuch für psychoanalytische and psychopathologische Forschungen* 3:329–400.
Spielrein, S. (1912a). Contributions to an understanding of the child's mind (in German). *Zentralblatt für Psychoanalyse & Psychotherapie* 3:57–72.
Spielrein, S. (1912b). Destruction as cause of becoming, transl. S.K. Witt. *Psychoanalysis & Contemporary Thought* 18: 85–118, 1995. [AU: AND/OR: Destruction as the cause of coming into being. *Journal of Analytical Psychology* 39:155–186, 1994.].
Vygotsky, L. (1987). *The Collected Works of Lev Vygotsky: Vol 1. Problems of General Psychology*. New York: Plenum Press.

Why Freud still haunts us

Michael S. Roth

For those of us prone to commemorations, it is a rich season. The beginning of the Great War 100 years ago, 70 years since the Normandy invasion, and several major events in the American struggle for civil rights marking their 50th anniversary. September 23 marks 75 years since the death of Sigmund Freud.

Should we care? In many respects, Freud seems to be from another world. We know so much more now. Psychotropic medications are big business and prescribed to ever-growing numbers of the "worried well," while psychoanalysis and psychodynamic psychotherapy are more of a rarity than ever.

And then there is all that embarrassing stuff about sex and penises, about inescapable aggression and guilt. And mothers. All of that is from another time, isn't it?

After all, now we know that women are equal to men, even if we scratch our heads when trying to explain how patriarchy gets reproduced generation after generation despite our professed ethics. Now we know that sex must be not only deeply consensual, but that it should be really healthy—so safe that it is, well, less than desirable. Freud taught that we could never be sure about our own "consent" let alone another's (that's why we're turning to new laws to demand that only "yes really means yes"). He insisted that the sexual relation was the discord among fantasies and therefore rarely a terrain of great safety.

Yet Freud haunts us. He keeps popping up in places he has no business being. Just when we succeeded in pushing him out of medicine because his brand of the talking cure was inconvenient for insurance and drug companies, he began appearing in college humanities programs, theater, novels, television. A generation ago, he animated Woody Allen's jokes; more recently we could find him in *The Sopranos*, and today he is all over *Mad Men*. And just when it seems that we can dismiss him (with a laugh) from overly theoretical work by jargon-laden literary scholars, nostalgic noise arises from the psychiatric profession complaining about meds without baseline evaluations, insurance-driven mental-health treatment, and the need for patients to make meaning.

Freud may have been dead these 75 years, yet there he sits, behind us. As the old man himself noted in *The Psychopathology of Everyday Life*:

> When a member of my family complains to me of having bitten his tongue, pinched a finger, or the like, he does not get the sympathy he hopes for, but instead the question: "Why did you do that?" I myself once gave my thumb a most painful pinch when a youthful patient told me during the hour of his treatment of his intention . . . to marry my eldest daughter.
>
> Freud pinched himself, and we bite our tongues looking for sympathy. In a story about being picked on by a friend, a wife, or a sibling, for example, to be asked "What are you really getting out of this?"—that is, what are you getting out of being picked on?—is an offensive query. What desire is expressed by your injury, or in telling the story of the injury? Can we believe that this question is always merely victim blaming?

Questions about what desires are being satisfied extend from the political to the personal (and back again). What desire is the war against terrorism really satisfying? Why do police departments in small towns want to acquire big tanks? Why are some straight people so angry about some gay people embracing marriage? These questions assume that the surface answers—the reasons of which we are aware—will not get at powerful motivating factors. When asked Freudian questions, we know that the answers will be connected to desires of which we are not only unaware but about which we are likely to feel ashamed.

The answer to "What are you really getting out of X?" will always describe a kind of ambivalence. "Ambivalence" began as a technical term in psychiatry, and it came to connote a quality of all strong emotions: They give rise to and may be the product of conflict. The strongest love, for example, will always be mixed with aggression. When his sister asks

Tony Soprano, "Where does your hate for me come from?", we should know that it comes from the same place as his love for her. Love cannot be satisfied without aggression, and intense antipathy is always bound up with desire. These elements can no more be separated from one another than nourishment can be separated from digestion. There is no possibility of full, sustained satisfaction in the Freudian model because the desires one aims to gratify are contradictory.

What do we do with these conflicts? We try to forget them. Unrequited desire can hurt, and so in order to get back to work (and love), we may push it away. Frustration and the repression of frustration became central to Freud's thinking. In the 1890s, he tried to understand the phenomena of pleasure, frustration, and forgetting at the neurological level. Then he started paying attention to how we express, in disguised form, the complications of our appetites—in physical symptoms, slips of the tongue, jokes, and especially dreams. And that was the beginning of psychoanalysis.

Freud remains relevant because he provides an account of why it is so difficult to tell those stories, even why it is so difficult to gain access to our own. He called repression the cornerstone of his whole enterprise, and it has led to the staying power of his genre of questioning. No matter how much we question, we will never get to the bottom of our own motivations, let alone those of other people. Something will always remain repressed.

Sigmund became a Freudian when he created the model of an interpreter who showed how our actions and words indirectly expressed conflicts of desire of which we were unaware. The conflicts among our desires never disappeared; they became the fuel of our histories. Making sense of those conflicts, understanding our desires, he thought, gave us an opportunity to give our stories—our histories—meaning.

No story we could possibly tell would fully overcome our repression, because repression is a necessary psychical mechanism, according to Freud. This is more than a full-employment program for therapists. It is an insistence on our incapacity for transparency even as it expresses our desire for it. If Freud were no longer haunting us, we might worry that we were repressing him or his message. Such a worry would be a form of haunting. Heads he wins, tails we lose.

Freud recognized that we are the animals that respond to our biology through memory and story telling. Psychoanalysis became a vehicle for telling those histories in ways that acknowledged our conflicting desires. Psychoanalysis isn't a methodology to discover one's true history; it is a collaboration that allows one to refashion a past with which one can live. The need to do so, and the impossibility of ever doing so definitively, has ensured the continued presence of Freud in our culture.

More than three quarters of a century years after Freud's death, we might well ask how we live with the intensity of these stories; how do we manage their meanings? Well, we now have culturally approved pharmaceuticals. The intensity and ambivalence of our desires have given rise to massive attempts to control them, and those controls have sometimes fueled these very desires. We may find that our medications create the desire for the feeling of intensity that they were supposed to protect us from.

What satisfactions are we getting out of the prohibitions against certain satisfactions? Guilt both satisfies and punishes satisfaction. Freud suggested that there isn't more satisfaction, let alone happiness, in the world because we make ourselves so miserable, and because we have created a society that, under the guise of reducing suffering, is very good at making us even more miserable. Recognizing the ways that we contribute to our own misery is a pleasure (perhaps one of the reasons we keep coming back to Freud), but psychoanalysis suggests it also gives us some possibility of changing the cycle of our self-punishment.

Despite all the cheerleading for neuroscience and its fascinating machines, our vernacular psychology remains Freudian in some fundamental sense. For no matter how critical we are of psychoanalytic influence on our culture, there seems to be no way of making Freud disappear. Our notions of childhood, memory, aggression, sexuality, and, most generally, of meaning have been shaped in relation to—and often in opposition to—Freud's legacy. Although today his explanations of psychopathology, like his interpretations of specific dreams, inspire neither shock nor agreement, Freud continues to haunt our culture because his genre of questioning remains tied to our desire for meaning.

As a pragmatic theorist, Freud understood that we construct meaning and direction out of our memories in order to suffer less and live more fully in the present. As a ghost worthy of commemoration, Freud's presence can undermine the conventional ways we make sense of the world while still drawing on our connections to the past.

If we become interested only in how we are put together, in how our neurology works and not in how we make meaning from our past, then Freud will have truly disappeared from our culture. But if we continue to consider the past important for giving meaning and direction to our lives, then it's a good bet that we will continue to ask and try to respond to those annoying questions that require us to find new ways to tell our stories, to better work through who we are and what we want.

Ghosts in psychoanalysis' closet

Jack Drescher

Let me tell you about some ghosts in psychoanalysis' closet.

Psychiatrist Bertram Schafner's analyst encouraged him to enter an implausible heterosexual marriage (Goldman, 1995). He left her. Music critic Paul Moor (2001) felt painfully gaslighted by his analyst's failed efforts to change his sexual orientation. He left him. Child psychiatrist Ellis Perlswig told his training analyst he was gay and was promptly asked to resign from their Institute (Blechner, 2005). Historian Martin Duberman's (1991) analyst demanded he leave a long-term male partner or have his analysis terminated. He left the partner. Psychiatrist Richard Isay (1996) underwent a ten-year analysis, often going six times a week. Despite marrying with his analyst's encouragement, his homosexuality did not abate. After coming out as gay, his analyst refused to speak to him. Psychiatrist Ralph Roughton (2002) hid his homosexuality to become an analyst, eventually becoming director of his institute. When he came out, already a grandfather, his elderly former analyst made a public personal attack on him in a psychoanalytic newsletter.

Most of these analyses took place starting in the 1940s and continued through the 1970s. Sadly, what had begun in the 19th century as a socially provocative theory of gender and sexuality eventually evolved into a rigid doctrine of "appropriate" expressions of gender and sexuality (Drescher, 2008). Freud was not entirely blameless. Although he did not believe gays were ill, he did not see them as quite normal. They were psychosexually immature. Not *sick*, but *childish*, thank you very much.

Analysts who came after Freud were less kind. Lewes (1988) documents post-war, émigré analysts speaking disparagingly of "homosexuals" in language faintly echoing anti-Semitic diatribes of Nazi Germany. The categories analysts commonly used to describe LGB people included "sexual deviants," "sociopaths," "psychotics," and "injustice collectors." A more benign prejudice was that gay people should not become analysts because they had a "lower" psychosexual level of development than heterosexuals.

Consequently, according to analytic theory, it was not possible for gay people to treat heterosexual patients at a "higher" level of development.

Fortunately, we no longer live in an analytic world dominated by Bergler, Bieber, and Socarides. It is no longer the case that being gay is an obstacle to admission to psychoanalytic training. In the 1980s and 90s a wider range of analytic institutes began accepting openly gay candidates. Gay people no longer have to hide their sexual identities or try to change them.

Yet today's dearth of openly gay and lesbian training analysts, both within and outside the American Psychoanalytic Association, is a daily reminder of past exclusion. Anecdotally, heterosexual analysts rarely refer me heterosexual patients (although I do appreciate the gay patients referred—thank you very much!).

Further, despite a few efforts to talk about what happened, mostly by gay and lesbian analysts, on the whole there has not been much discussion about this shameful past. While it happened, few analysts spoke up to challenge those harmful, prevailing views. Yet there has been no equivalent of a Truth and Reconciliation commission or Nuremberg trial to explore and understand the damage done to an untold number of patients and analysts, most of whom did not write about their inability to conform to psychoanalysis's unproven theoretical biases. That is the specter that still haunts psychoanalysis today.

Bibliography

Blechner, M. J. (2005). The gay Harry Stack Sullivan: Interactions between his life, clinical work and theory. *Contemporary Psychoanalysis*, 45(1):1–19.

Drescher, J. (2008). A history of homosexuality and organized psychoanalysis. *J. American Academy of Psychoanalysis & Dynamic Psychiatry*, 36(3):443–460.

Duberman, M. (1991). *Cures: A Gay Man's Odyssey*. New York: Dutton.

Goldman, S. (1995). The difficulty of being a gay psychoanalyst during the last fifty years: An interview with Dr. Bertram Schaffner. In: *Disorienting Sexuality: Psychoanalytic Reappraisals of Sexual Identities*, eds. T. Domenici & R.C. Lesser. New York: Routledge, 243–254.

Isay, R.A. (1996). *Becoming Gay: The Journey to Self-Acceptance*. New York: Pantheon.

Lewes, K. (1988). *The Psychoanalytic Theory of Male Homosexuality*. New York: Simon and Schuster.

Moor, P. (2001). The view from Irving Bieber's couch: "Heads I win, tails you lose." *J. Gay & Lesbian Psychotherapy*, 5(3/4):25–36.

Roughton, R. (2002). Being gay and becoming a psychoanalyst: Across three generations. *J. Gay & Lesbian Psychotherapy*, 6(1):31–43.

The group as spectral author: Trigant Burrow's ghost

Daniel G. Butler

The group elicits a fear of becoming a phantom to oneself. It elicits a fear of becoming a no-body engulfed by the vastness of the intangible group skin. This is a fear of living death, of self-effacement, and of losing the loved, specular forms with which we identify. Bearing witness to the trauma of the group requires facing such fear—and becoming a phantom to oneself is sometimes necessary to bearing witness. Ferenczi (1949, 1995) understood this. He responded to his patients' protest by risking himself in an experiment with mutuality. And for this he became dead to a discipline that refused to bear witness as an anchoring, cultural third (Gerson, 2009). Turning a blind eye, psychoanalysis condemned Ferenczi to the traumatic absence that he confronted with his patients. Ferenczi's story has become familiar to us, but sadly less familiar is the knowledge that he was not alone in his vision for a more relational psychoanalysis. He had a transatlantic double who risked himself in silent kinship with the same pathos of mutuality. This is a double who is even more forgotten than Ferenczi—and Ferenczi is a pioneer whom many of us thought that no one could have forgotten more.

The first American-born psychoanalyst, Trigant Burrow, M.D., Ph.D. (1875–1950), admired Ferenczi from afar and while Ferenczi makes no mention of Burrow, it is reasonable to assume that he caught wind of Burrow's work (Kahn, 1996). It is unfortunate that these two men, both of whom became pariahs, were never able to befriend each other, consummating the mutuality and community ethos that both of them espouse. The essence of their work reveals two minds in sync, two spirits intertwined, together forming an unavowable identification that survives them beyond the grave.

Burrow's interest in proto-mental phenomenon ("the preconscious" or "primary matrix of consciousness") (1913/2013); the imaginary and symbolic ("social images" and the "social unconscious") (1924/2013); and true/false self experience (Burrow uncannily speaks in terms of the child's "spontaneous gesture") (1928/2013) can be said to prefigure the contributions of Bion, Lacan, and Winnicott, respectively, and his emphasis on the mother-infant relationship predates most if not all other proto-object relational theories, perhaps with the exception of Ferenczi's (1913) "Stages in the Development of the Sense of Reality," a paper Burrow (1964) extols.

Burrow's specter can also be glimpsed sans credit in the work of many post-Freudian thinkers, especially Harry Stack Sullivan and S.H. Foulkes, both voracious consumers of his early work. Although Burrow was a founder and one-time president of the American Psychoanalytic Association, his prescient and incendiary ideas—namely, his theories of group analysis and the social unconscious—led to his expulsion from APsA in 1933.

Over his 40-year-long career Burrow published seven books and approximately 70 articles, moving between psychoanalysis, group analysis, and experimental studies in neurodynamics, all the while religiously claiming his indebtedness to Freud and the basic principles of psychoanalysis. A rigorous researcher and polyglot, holding degrees in literature, psychology, and medicine, Burrow's credentials surely equal the towering stature of other pioneers in the field. But Burrow's method of psychoanalysis, which rests on a critique of individualistic, one-person psychology, ultimately alienated him from the psychoanalytic establishment. Curiously, Burrow's psychoanalysis seems to perform this very alienation, as it requires the individual's self-effacement through a critique of the ideologies upon which the self is based. Like Foucault (1982), it is as if Burrow "writes in order to have no face" (p. 17); for Burrow's author is not the face of the individual, but the specter and facelessness of the group.

Burrow refers to himself as a Freudian, yet his iconoclastic allegiance entailed an ongoing critique of Freud's project. He relentlessly deconstructs the "Freudian system," often emphasizing how it "is adequate only on the adaptive basis of normality" (p. 82). Burrow could see that when Freud claims to treat the clinical he is enacting the cultural and when he isolates the individual he commits a fallacy. "Man is not an individual," writes Burrow, "his mentation is not individualistic" (1925/2013, p. 148). For Burrow, we are always already a group, a community, a common. The neurotic individual is a neurotic society and to the extent that the individual is its *raison d'*être, psychoanalysis is a neurosis too.

Burrow's psychoanalysis is a "group" method, but as he (1927) clarifies, "group does not mean a collection of individuals. It means a phyletic principle of observation" (p. 138). Burrow's group analysis is an analysis "of the group by the group" (Galt, 1995); there are no leaders. The need for a leader is a "social image;" it is nested in the "social unconscious" that group analysis is meant to deconstruct. Affectively charged discourses saturate the social image, creating specular and psychobiological divisions within the species. Unlike Lacan, Burrow's speculum is not in the service of subject *formation* but of subject *deformation* (Lawtoo, 2013). Group analysis, then, is an attempt to bring our bio-psycho-social deformation, our division within the species, to light.

The neutral analyst is one of those social images that deform the analytic enterprise. It was his patient Clarence Shields, a working class man turned "esteemed colleague," who confronted Burrow with the traumatizing absence so often inherent in one-person psychoanalysis. Regarding Shields, Burrow (1984) writes: "I was caught up by his protest . . . though unconsciously I was still skeptical of its practical value" (p. 28). Preceding Ferenczi's foray into early relational technique, Burrow courageously undertook a mutual analysis with Shields in 1921. This was the beginning of a decades-long partnership between the two men, one that uneasily blended life, work, and group analytic principles as the code of their everyday lives.

Burrow's receptivity to the patient's protest transformed the absence of a neutral analyst into the affectively engaged presence of a like subject. Such proto-intersubjectivity was lost to a psychoanalytic community that rejected Burrow's contributions much like Ferenczi's, but it is important to remember that Burrow's theory of analytic witnessing in some ways performs this very rejection. "The psychoanalyst," in Burrow's (1927) view, "is not content but receptacle. Lacking method or design he offers nothing, but is the recipient of all there is of human experience as subjectively substantiated within himself" (p. 27). Anticipating Bion's absence of memory and desire, Burrow asserts that the psychoanalyst must empty himself. In the words of philosopher Nidesh Lawtoo, we might say that Burrow's witness is "not an ego, but a phantom of the ego" (Lawtoo, 2014). Paradoxically, it is only in this ghostly form that psychoanalysis becomes a living venture; for "life is not a technique . . . life is a subjective experience . . . a joy or a sorrow, a disappointment or an aspiration" (p. 25). Life obtains an ephemeral quality in Burrow, a quality we can only access through emptiness and the effacement of individuality. Witnessing requires that the self empathically join the other in an absence by which they are both at that moment ephemerally constituted. It is this self-effacement, this becoming of a phantom, that restores the "preconscious foundations" (Burrow, 1964) upon which all life rests.

Dating to 1913, the preconscious is perhaps Burrow's most important contribution to psychoanalysis. It denotes the earliest state of infancy in which the mother-infant pair forms a singular organism. While the preconscious is an ineffable phenomenon, it can be known through "the slow, sure rhythmic sequence of primary biological processes" (Burrow, 1937, p. 79). Foreshadowing Bion's proto-mental matrix and advances in analytic field theory, Burrow (1927) argues that the preconscious is a "kinetic dimension," one that Freud does not account for in his topographical models of the psyche. Burrow (1927) considers the movement from a Freudian, static, individual psyche to the kinetic, relational psyche as a "transition from bi-dimensional picture to tri-dimensional actuality, from contemplation of aspect to participation of function" (p. 83). Burrow's kinetic field or "laboratory method" (1925/2013) activates the analyst so that she is no longer contemplating passively but is an active participant in the co-creation of a group analytic process. To conceptualize this co-creative process Burrow turns to a wide range of thinkers, including Kurt Lewin and George Herbert Mead, and to the process philosophy of pragmatist John Dewey.

Today Burrow may be praised as a harbinger, but at the time Freud looked very unfavorably on his work. In fact, it seems that Freud could not stand Burrow, once referring to him as "a muddled babbler" (Freud in Pertegato & Pertegato, 2013, p. lxxx). Burrow went so far as to assert that Freud "willfully misunderstood" a number of his ideas, to which Freud responded: "your paper, "A Relative Concept of Consciousness," disappointed and irritated me, so that I was prejudiced against your other formulations" (Freud in Burrow, 1958, p. 98). A nationalist xenophobia may account for Freud's attitude, as he was known to be suspicious of Americans (Pertegato & Pertegato, 2013, p. lxxvii), but there is also an intellectual xenophobia in that Freud, while inclined to revise his own formulations, was impervious to revisions that came from almost anyone else. Burrow therefore posed a great difficulty. He assumed that in the spirit of scientific advance Freud would join him in paradigm-shifting revision of psychoanalysis. Burrow's assumption cost him not only Freud's affection—it cost him a place in history.

In their recent collection of his early writings, Burrow scholars Pergegato & Pertegato (2013) question why "still today one does not find, or finds so difficult to obtain, traces" of Burrow's thinking (p. lxxv). Burrow's erasure perhaps begins with Freud's distrust and almost vituperative attitude, but by 1927 Burrow's papers were routinely rejected by psychoanalytic journals. Then in 1933 he lost his university ties and was expelled from APsA. After this string of losses Burrow's absence was officially entrenched.

Consequently, he is almost entirely absent from dominant histories of psychoanalysis and yet he is present for this very reason, exemplifying the phobia of difference that mars the discipline's all too present past.

While history has not done justice to Burrow, Burrow's work is itself a commentary on a specific injustice of history, namely that the ego of the historical figure denies the group as its source and first author. Burrow's group method involves a self-effacement that is designed to make this absence present (Gurevich, 2014), thereby restoring, albeit ephemerally, the preconscious and the group as foundations of human experience. Burrow thus urges us to consider the salutary benefits of the group and its dedifferentiation. Perhaps it is only now with psychoanalysis fearing its own cultural effacement that we can consider Burrow's group without fear of engulfment. Perhaps it is only now that we can begin to imagine a dedifferentiation that binds us as one without spelling the death of our discipline. While Burrow's contemporaries could not salute his radical, group oriented, and socially conscious vision for psychoanalysis, it seems that the time for such salutations just might be among us.

Bibliography

Burrow, T. (1927). *The Social Basis of Consciousness*. New York: Harcourt.

Burrow, T. (1937). *The Biology of Human Conflict*. New York: MacMillan.

Burrow, T. (1958). *A Search for Man's Sanity: The Selected Letters of Trigant Burrow*, W.E. Galt (Ed.) New York: Oxford University Press.

Burrow, T. (1964). The strifeless phase of awareness. In: W.E. Galt (Ed.), *Preconscious Foundations of Human Experience*. New York: Basic Books.

Burrow, T. (1964). Primitive behavior, individual and generic. In: W.E. Galt (Ed.), *Preconscious Foundations of Human Experience*. New York: Basic Books.

Burrow, T. (1985). *Toward Social Sanity and Human Survival: Selections From His Writings*, A. S. Galt (Ed.) New York: Horizon.

Burrow, T. (2013). Psychoanalysis and life. In: Gatti Pertegato, E., & Pertegato, G.O. (Eds.), *From Psychoanalysis to Group Analysis: The Pioneering Work of Trigant Burrow*. London: Karnac. (Original paper presented in 1913)

Burrow, T. (2013). Social images and reality. In: Gatti Pertegato, E., & Pertegato, G.O. (Eds.), *From Psychoanalysis to Group Analysis: The Pioneering Work of Trigant Burrow*. London: Karnac. (Original paper published in 1924)

Burrow, T. (2013). A relative concept of consciousness: An analysis of consciousness in its ethnic origin. In: Gatti Pertegato, E., & Pertegato, G.O. (Eds.), *From Psychoanalysis to Group Analysis: The Pioneering Work of Trigant Burrow*. London: Karnac. (Original paper presented in 1925)

Burrow, T. (2013). The elements of group analysis. Unpublished. Cited in: Gatti Pertegato, E., & Pertegato, G.O. (Eds.), *From Psychoanalysis to Group Analysis: The Pioneering Work of Trigant Burrow*. London: Karnac. (Original paper completed in 1928)

Burrow, T. (2013). The laboratory method in psychoanalysis. In: Gatti Pertegato, E., & Pertegato, G.O. (Eds.), *From Psychoanalysis to Group Analysis: The Pioneering Work of Trigant Burrow*. London: Karnac. (Original paper published in 1925)
Ferenczi, S. (1949). Confusion of tongues between the adults and child (the language of tenderness and passion). *Int. J. Psycho-Anal.*, 30:225–230.
Ferenczi, S. (1995). *The Clinical Diary of Sandor Ferenczi*, ed. J. Dupont (trans. M. Balint & M. Z. Jackson). Cambridge, MA: Harvard University Press.
Foucault, M. (1982). *The Archaeology of Knowledge*. New York: Cornell University Press.
Galt, A. S. (1995). Trigant Burrow and the laboratory of the 'I'. *The Humanistic Psychologist*, 23(1): 19–39.
Gatti Pertegato, E., & Pertegato, G.O. (2013). Trigant Burrow's psychoanalytic and group analytic research on man's social nature through censorship and subterranean ransacking. (trans. R.M. Gatti) In: Gatti Pertegato, E., & Pertegato, G.O. (Eds.), *From Psychoanalysis to Group Analysis: The Pioneering Work of Trigant Burrow*. London: Karnac Books.
Gerson, S. (2009). When the third is dead: Memory, mourning, and witnessing in the aftermath of the holocaust. *Int. J. Psycho-Anal.*, 90:1341–1357.
Gurevich, H. (2014). Psychoanalytic mothering as making the absence present. Presented at San Francisco Center for Psychoanalysis.
Lawtoo, N. (2013). *The Phantom of the Ego: Modernism and the Mimetic Unconscious*. East Lansing: Michigan State University Press.
Kahn, S. (1996). *Ferenczi's mutual analysis: A case where the messenger was killed and his treasure buried*. Presented at the Annual Meeting of the Eastern Psychological Association, available online.

The ghost of Marilyn Monroe

Douglas Kirsner

During 1962, the momentous year of the Cuban Missile Crisis, two intertwined events occurred that were crucial steps in the journey of psychoanalysis in the US—the death of Marilyn Monroe on August 6, and the release of the last and quintessential pro-Freud movie of the Golden Era for psychoanalysis in Hollywood, John Huston's *Freud: The Secret Passion*, starring Montgomery Clift and Susannah York, on December 12.

In death as well as in life Marilyn Monroe continues to haunt American culture. As leading Los Angeles psychoanalyst Ralph Greenson's most famous patient, her suicide was a serious blow to the reputation of psychoanalysis and psychiatry, which had been held in awe. The Golden Age of psychiatry and psychoanalysis occurred during the 1950s when over half the chairs of psychiatry in the US were held by psychoanalysts, and Hollywood movies were very sympathetic to and supportive of psychoanalysis and psychiatry.

But the early 1960s saw a sudden jolt in Hollywood's attitude. The suddenness and strength of this change in attitude require some explanation. By the mid-1960s Hollywood's approach changed markedly to the point where analysts could be shown to be most unappealing psychopaths, even killers, who used their analytic or psychiatric skills for nefarious ends, abusing the confidence of their trusting patients.

As Gabbard and Gabbard (1999) note, "The swiftness and the vigor with which American movies turned against psychiatry is as remarkable as the staying power of the negative attitudes towards the profession, which have prevailed with few exceptions since the Golden Age" (p. 107). Why was this so? This sudden change was not merely because federal funding was drying up for psychiatric research and education or because it was symptomatic of the changing clinical, socioeconomic and cultural climate in which new psychotropic medications were being developed and introduced. In any case, funding dried up somewhat later in the mid-1960s. The gradual introduction of new psychoactive drugs, if anything, should have increased the allure of psychiatry, even if not of psychoanalysis. Nonetheless, from 1965, fewer medical students began to choose psychiatry as a specialty, something demonstrated to have been influenced by negative media portrayals of psychiatrists (Gabbard & Gabbard, 1999, p. 188).

One major reason for this change may well have been the reputational damage to psychiatry and psychoanalysis from Monroe's suicide. A significant part of the context was that the Freud family, from Sigmund through to Anna, were hostile to the film industry. In 1925 Freud rejected an offer from Samuel Goldwyn of $1.25 million (in today's dollars) to work on a film. Anna Freud and her US followers, especially Greenson and Kurt Eissler, strongly campaigned to stop the production of a movie directed by John Huston about the early life and work of Sigmund Freud, *Freud: The Secret Passion*. Huston had famously directed 37 feature films, including the classic *The Maltese Falcon* as well as *The Misfits*, starring Montgomery Clift and Marilyn Monroe.

On June 13, 1956, three and a half years before Monroe first consulted him, Greenson told Anna Freud that he had met with Charles Kaufman, one of the writers of the film. Greenson reported that he told Kaufman "in unmistakably clear terms that I would have nothing to do with the making of this picture, and furthermore, that I would speak to all the analysts in this area, asking them to refrain in any and every way from helping with this motion picture. He was quite shocked by my position but he did understand my point of view when I described to him your feelings in this matter" (letter to A. Freud, June 13, 1956; Greenson Papers, Department of Special Collections, UCLA). Greenson and Eissler continued their campaign by employing lawyers and by telling their colleagues not to cooperate with the making of the film.

John Huston asked Marilyn Monroe to play the part of Cecily, a hysteric who was an amalgam of one of Breuer's cases, Anna O, in *Studies on Hysteria* and Freud's Dora case. (Susannah York was ultimately cast in the part). In a letter I discovered at the Margaret Herrick Library at The Academy of Motion Picture Arts and Sciences in Beverly Hills, Marilyn Monroe wrote to Huston from the Beverly Hills Hotel on November 5, 1960:

> I have it on good authority that the Freud family does not approve of anyone making a picture of the life of Freud—so I wouldn't want to be a part of it, first because of his great contribution to humanity and secondly my personal regard for his work.
>
> Thank you for offering me the part of 'Annie O' (sic.) and I wish you all the best in this and all other endeavors.

That "good authority" was Greenson. In his memoir Huston wrote that Monroe had been the first choice to play the hysteric but "her own analyst advised against it. Not out of concern for Marilyn; he didn't believe a picture about Freud should be made at all because Freud's daughter Anna opposed the project" (1980, p. 301).

The reasons Monroe proffered only make sense as rationalizations for obeying Greenson. Her two arguments against making the film are in reality very good grounds for making it—the spread and reputation of Freud's seminal ideas. Greenson later admitted to Huston: "If he had known the type of picture it was to be, he would have recommended that Marilyn do it" (Huston, 1980, p. 301).

Would this series of events and attitudes sour the views of many in the film industry about psychoanalysis as it did more generally? At the very least, it couldn't have helped. This was a missed opportunity for a productive and effective partnership, Had the opportunity been seized rather than rejected, the spread and discussion of psychoanalytic ideas could would have been considerably assisted.

Whatever the truth about her suicide, Greenson felt deeply about Monroe who became his patient in January, 1960. He later confided in Anna Freud:

> I took over the treatment of a patient that Marianne Kris had been treating for several years, and she has turned out to be a very sick borderline paranoid addict, as well as an actress. You can imagine how terribly difficult it is to treat someone with such severe problems and who is also a great celebrity and completely alone in the world. Psychoanalysis is out of the question and I improvise, often wondering where I am going, and yet have nowhere else to turn. If I succeed, I will have learned something, but it takes a tremendous amount of time also emotion. (December 4, 1961, Anna Freud Papers, Library of Congress)

Two weeks after Monroe's death Greenson touchingly wrote to Anna Freud:

> This has been a terrible blow in many ways. I cared about her and she was my patient. She was so pathetic and she had had such a terrible life. I had hopes for her and I thought we were making progress. And now she died and I realize that all my knowledge and my desire and my strength was not enough. God knows I tried and mightily so, but I could not defeat all the destructive forces that had been stirred up in her by the terrible experiences of her past life, and even of her present life. Sometimes I feel the world wanted her to die, or at least many people in the world, particularly those who after her death so conspicuously grieved and mourned. It makes me angry. But above all I feel sad and also disappointed. It is not just a blow to my pride, although I am sure that is present, but also a blow to my science of which I consider myself a good representative. But it will take me time to get over this and I know that eventually this will only become a scar. (August 20, 1962, Anna Freud Papers, Library of Congress)

Greenson remained depressed and distraught for several months (Greenson to Anna Freud, January 20, 1963, Greenson Papers).

After discussing Monroe's life and death with Marianne Kris, Monroe's previous therapist, Anna Freud reassured Greenson, "I think noone could have held her in this life" (Anna Freud to Greenson, January 20, 1963, Greenson Papers). Whatever the case, we know that Monroe's very close involvement with Greenson (who was also linked with the events after her death) proved a very poor advertisement for psychiatry and psychoanalysis. We can only speculate as to what would have happened had Monroe starred in Huston's film, released just four months after her death. What would have been the impact of the film upon the movie industry, the fortunes of American psychoanalysis and the culture at large?

References

Gabbard, G., & Gabbard, K. (1999). *Psychiatry and the Cinema* (2nd ed.). Washington DC: American Psychiatric Press.
Hoskyns, B. (1991). *Montgomery Clift: Beautiful Loser*. London: Bloomsbury.
Huston, J. (1980). *An Open Book*. New York: Knopf.

A crucial counterfeit

Don Troise

"*. . . a ghost always has the architecture of a storm.*" (Cole Swensen)[1]

Psychoanalysis is a kind of forgery. Originally, it wanted no past other than the patient's past, no influence beyond that which patients contended with. In the incipient iterations of psychoanalysis, the story being told was thought to be exclusively the patient's, and it therefore precluded aspects of the analyst's own story. Thus, the analyst was expected to be, in a sense, without memory or desire. Unencumbered by his history, he was beyond its influence. Without a past, and, most particularly, without a traumatic past, he was free to discern and to analyze. He was free to know meaning rather than devise it. To this day, and despite the great paradigm shifts that have occurred in the field over the last thirty years or so, psychoanalysis still seems reluctant to recognize itself as a narrative practice forged from a haunted past, a notional account of personhood that has arguably been convened in the service of explaining, and enduring, trauma.

Theory is regularly written and performed in the shadow of the past. It describes experience as much as it imagines it. Much of psychoanalytic doctrine and its alterations over time can be viewed as a translation and a transformation of the traumatic past. To a great degree, theoreticians have contributed to our psychoanalytic lore by contextualizing and structuralizing that which has influenced them, by explaining themselves, and what has harmed them, *to* themselves in the guise of explaining others. At its core, psychoanalytic theory, at once a variation and an explication of that which haunts us, is experience rendered, abstracted, and universalized. But for some, in order for theory to be convincing, it can be neither personal, an emanation of lived experience, nor hallucinated. It must be objectively, demonstrably true. It must be verifiable. There will always be those who prefer that there be nothing gossamer about theory and those who believe that theory is, essentially, sheer. Whatever we judge objective truth to be, and however we attempt to measure it, the insistence of some on veridicality has gotten psychoanalysis into a lot of trouble lately. We are routinely in the position of having to describe the ghosts we're seeing. The more we try to convince others that our theories are true, not ideas but observations, or, at the least, ideas *based* on observations, the crazier we seem and the more we're marginalized by the prose sciences. Apparently, our ghosts don't haunt everyone.

Broadly speaking, there are two categorical responses to trauma that theory engages: affiliation and dissociation. The kind of response that proceeds from affiliation allows that all experience is connected and derivative; the past has happened and is, in one form or another, with us still. Responses that proceed from dissociation posit experience as essentially disconnected and prospectively imaginable; the past has *not* happened and so we can imagine it and a future free of its influence. In this context, imagination is a benign, and somewhat paradoxical, variant of dissociation, an allusive, innovative response to trauma rather than a delusive, constricted one. Affiliation permits one kind of understanding—experience is per proximity knowable—and allusive dissociation engenders another—experience is imaginable; it can be thought up. Among other things, to find meaning is not to imagine it, and to imagine is to not find meaning, i.e., to not explain. Just as there is no possibility for the elaboration of meaning without affiliation, some degree of dissociation is essential to the elaboration of imagination. How have these responses to trauma influenced the course of psychoanalysis?

The architects of psychoanalysis, Freud and Sullivan chief among them, probably developed key aspects of their psychological epistemologies consequent to their own traumatic experiences (Breger, 2000; Troise, in press). It has been argued (Breger) that Freud dissociated his significant early losses and disruptions and in the process conceived of psychoanalysis. Conversely, it would seem that Sullivan, despite dissociative tendencies of his own, nonetheless elaborated the basic principles of his interpersonal psychology from the recognition that his suffering—an acute, abiding loneliness—was affiliative, i.e., closely bound to experiences of alienation and marginalization. In a sense, Freud needed to disavow trauma to find psychoanalysis. This is, effectively, what happened when he abandoned the seduction theory,[2] a historically based understanding of neuroses, in favor of intrapsychic explanations for the same. Sullivan, on the other hand, explained "difficulties in living" not on the permutations of fantasy, but on lived experience as mediated by a range of historical, cultural, and social factors. It can be said that both men theorized their traumas from categorically opposing positions: Freud, from dissociation, and Sullivan, from affiliation. These posts create a spectrum along which most other psychoanalytic theories can be located. Taken together, as languages that carry and describe trauma, they delimit psychoanalysis. All of our psychoanalytic theories register somewhere on the continuum between those elaborated from dissociation and those elaborated from affiliation.

In the face of trauma, we hope for fantasy. What is wounding about experience, what may corrupt our reason and hurt us past what seems bearable, is that which imagination cannot modify and transfigure. All psychoanalytic theories are essentially poetics, experience transmogrified into aesthetic expression. They are perforce, imaginative constructs, mutative, and so crucial, counterfeits. Whatever we know, we know because of what we have experienced *and* what we have imagined, what we have forged. We cannot say which is more important, which better describes what it is to be sensate and alive. Imagination and experience are correspondent practices. Each needs the other to begin. If our experience has been specifically traumatic, marked by some immutable sorrow or terror, we must hope for an act of imagination to free us from the constraints of memory. But if we cannot remember, if we are, in a sense, *too* imaginative, delusive rather than allusive, then of course we are destined to repeat that which we cannot know until at last we can know it again. And then we must forget again. Psychoanalysis represents both of these responses to trauma. It is a haunted rendition of remembering and forgetting, a house apart from and a part of what we can see. If there are ghosts storming against its invisible walls, how can we say that we are not among them?

Notes

1 Cole Swensen, *Gravesend*, copyright 2012 by the Regents of the University of California. Published by the University of California Press.

2 To my knowledge, while Freud recognized the prevalence of traumatic sexualized experience, he ultimately discarded his theory that these "seductions" were etiological where neurotic suffering was concerned and replaced it with his theory of infantile sexuality. This shift from a theory rooted in traumatic *experience* to one rooted in *fantasy* was crucial to the development of psychoanalysis. Ferenczi's seminal paper *Confusion of Tongues* was originally denied publication at Freud's behest in part because it reinstated childhood sexual abuse as causal. In a letter to his daughter Anna, Freud wrote: "(Ferenczi) has completely regressed to etiological views I believed in, and gave up, 35

years ago: that the regular cause of neuroses is sexual traumas of childhood, said it virtually in the same words as I had used then!" (quoted in Gay, *Freud*, pp. 583–584). Several letters to Fleiss also reference this change of mind.

References

Breger, L. (2000). *Freud: Darkness in the Midst of Vision*. New York: John Wiley & Sons.

Gay, P. (2006). *Freud: A Life for Our Time*. New York: W.W. Norton & Co.

Troise, D. (in press). The Traumatic Field: Psychoanalysis as Trauma Translated. In: *Unknowable, Unspeakable and Unsprung: Navigating the Thrill and Danger of Living Amidst Truth, Fantasy and Privacy*.

Chapter 7

Empty arms and secret shames

Reverberations of relational trauma in the NICU

Susan Kraemer and Zina Steinberg

70 fragile newborns nested in isolettes being kept alive by advanced medical technology: that is what one sees on any given day in the neonatal intensive care unit. You will not see, but you might sense, the weighty uncertainties that haunt the corridors and shadow the faces of the parents and the staff who safeguard the babies in their care, as life and death warily circle each other. Many of these infants are born too soon; perhaps as early as 23 weeks, scary and alien looking, they are at the edge of viability. Or they might be babies born with life-threatening conditions requiring immediate surgery—often the first of many—or babies born into life with rare and frightening congenital anomalies, even fatal diagnoses. Some of these babies are "feeders and growers" just needing time and careful titrating of nutrition; their parents are able to hold and feed them almost from the beginning. Others, medical staff might refer to as "train wrecks," their despair visible as they struggle to process the limits of medicine.

Loss saturates the NICU. Many of these babies are born into or out of loss—in the aftermath of pregnancies that ended in miscarriage or stillbirth or after years of failed fertility treatments. Some are born of a multiple pregnancy where one of the babies has died in utero, others soon after a precipitous birth. Still others of these are babies born of a multiple pregnancy that entailed the difficult decision about a "selective reduction."[1]

Parents carry their own complex history, often littered with trauma and violent loss: immigration from war-torn places, childhood cancers, abject poverty, homelessness, domestic abuse, the recent death of a loved parent or partner. As all babies are imagined as a repair for old wounds, a hope for a new beginning, a balm for psychic and relational trauma, so are these critically ill babies. The NICU then is a place that holds hope but it holds hope as one holds one's breath, anxiously and vigilantly. Giving birth to a baby who is admitted to the NICU is a devastating interruption, a white-knuckled suspension of reparative fantasy, hope and reverie. Of the approximately 1000 babies admitted to the NICU each year, 5–6% will die.

In our consultations with families and with the health-care team we are alert to the many specters hovering within these spaces; Alert to those that appear, loiter, disappear, and reappear, and painfully attuned as well to the wishes, dreams and hopes that may prove only to be phantoms, permanently out of reach. There are the ghosts of the babies who have died, as well as the shadow babies who cling precariously to life. The NICU is a place of betwixt and between, where yearning, wanting, having and losing, presence and absence, empty arms and full breasts all exist simultaneously.

Harris (2007) has directed us to Davoine's likening of the analytic space to a "bridge world" (Davoine, 2007), a liminal space that is porous to the effects of trauma and unconscious process. The NICU is a particularly unique instance of a liminal space. Located in real time it resides also within a shadowy netherworld where specters of the past haunt the present and hope for the future may be too uncertain to provide an anchor. Elsewhere, we have likened the NICU to a claustrum (Steinberg & Kraemer, 2016), borrowing from Meltzer's (1992) description of a psychic world dominated by claustrophobic fear, Chaucer's use of claustrum as a synonym for womb as well as its linguistic reference to the enclosed space of a cloister (Willoughby, 2001). These multiple meanings evoke complex and divergent possibilities—a place of refuge or a space for potential growth, or, a trapped space of dread and no exit. There is little room for psychic space in this claustrum, this urgent care setting. The stakes are high, medical language and algorithmic thinking can overshadow reflection and make emotion feel shameful. Yet guilt and especially shame flourish in the cracks, intensifying trauma's attacks on linking, limiting further thought and mentalization on the part of parents, staff, and even ourselves.

It should be of no surprise that in these murky yet heightened spaces, seemingly closed-off ancient memories and feelings surface and haunt unexpectedly. As Gordon (1997) writes: "Being haunted draws us affectively, sometimes against our will and always a bit magically into the structure of feeling of a reality we come to experience, not as cold knowledge but as a transformative recognition" (p. 8). Nonetheless we have been surprised by how powerfully our own personal variously buried histories, especially those hidden in shame-filled spaces, have been evoked through our work in the NICU.

Pentimento I: Susan Kraemer

All analytic work involves a journey that is circular and recursive, moving us backwards and forwards and back again, changing our sense of the future and of the past. Sometimes we may arrive only to experience that place of beginnings, "as if for the first time" (Eliot, 1943)

One might say that no matter where you are in the narrative you are always potentially in the middle of your story, as a story about origins keeps changing shape and revealing itself in new ways (Lefkowitz, 2010, personal communication). Like a palimpsest where layers of text are scraped away, revealing other stories—"the erased, the partial, the lost and the fragmentary" (de Waal, 2010)—the stories collect, gathering new meaning. When the past is marked by hushed absence some may seek to still the silence, to fill in the blanks and make what's hidden less opaque. But in lives shadowed by loss, particularly loss dishonored by "disenfranchised grief" (Doka, 2002) memories and imagination may remain truncated, thinned by secrecy and blurred by shame. There is great pressure to leave these as empty spaces—as ghost spots—in the middle of the story. In the NICU this can be as true about stories that have yet to be written. Parents confronted with perilous uncertainty may see only "a blank where the future should be" (Alvarez, 1992, p. 175) or a phantasmagoria of dreams and illusions.

In the NICU, the tension between what can be imagined and what dare not be, what can be remembered and what must not be, is borne both by the families living these traumatic stories as well as by those who listen to them. There is so much that can only be discovered gradually, about both past and future, and this process is burdened both by fear about a terrible knowing and by shame that haunts this knowing. One particular kind of reluctance is the reluctance to stay close to the parents' experience, what I have come to regard as a fear of trespassing onto maternal (or paternal) states of mind, especially when these are darkened by shame. In what follows I will describe ways in which my personal narratives of fertility, birth, death, and loss have been re-imagined and rethought—*in uncanny ways*—as a result of my experiences in the NICU. This process of recollection has been disconcerting as it has returned me to places unknown and unremembered, as if inhabiting them only now for the very first time (Eliot, 1943).

Each time I speak or write about my work in the NICU (Kraemer, 2006) I revisit feelings of trepidation, disorientation, and otherness that still shadow me after many years of consultation. The NICU is truly a "world apart" (Cohen, 2003), an unnatural world where the beginning and end of life slam up against each other and boundaries are blurred and upended. The loss of basic assumptions threatens one's sense of self, one's place and one's role in ways both ordinary and profound. The ownership of babies, of experience and sense of purpose can feel murky and easily confused. Parents feel grievously dislocated as they leave their vulnerable infants in the care of expert others. They speak of feeling "like imposters." Nurses, even veteran souls, protest and grieve when tasked with prolonged interventions with a dying baby. A senior dedicated nurse after months of caring for an extremely premature baby despaired, "When I get to heaven I imagine finding a line of preemies saying, did you have to do all this to me? And I'll tell them, "I am wicked sorry, so sorry to do this to you but your parents asked me to do this on your behalf."[2]

For myself, it is easy to feel wrong footed, clumsy, and tentative. I circle the unit introducing myself to parents. Consultations most often occur at bedside. Spontaneous and informal, they may be brief and casual or they may evolve into something far deeper. But I am stripped of the containing supports of the consulting room which otherwise scaffold me. My agency, my authority, the questions I privilege, my ways of knowing and finding meaning all strain to accommodate to, but also to find expression in, this alien environment.

As I approach a mother sitting next to her baby's isolette, buried in her phone or prayer book, or just staring off in the distance, I find myself faltering as if on an uncertain threshold. It is not easy to step towards a mother who looks down as I come near, who offers a tight smile or a clipped retort. Or even one who is resolutely upbeat. I feel both intruder and trespasser. Will I be welcome? Does my uncertainty about what I can offer in this setting reflect the mother's helplessness, her fear of being irrelevant to her baby? Should I approach? What unknown ghosts may linger, hovering like vapor? I may have just heard about a baby's grave prognosis in a staff meeting but am uncertain if the family has been spoken to. Or perhaps, I tell myself, they have just been told and need to hold their grief close, so I dare not approach. It can be so hard to know one's way through the dark of these shattered spaces. Perhaps easier, safer, to linger on thresholds. But with time, these feelings began to make me uneasy and I started to wonder about my hesitation. What of this reluctance belonged to them, and what was mine?

Answers (at least partial ones) to these questions unfolded in unexpected ways. I made a number of Shiva visits to close friends observing the Jewish rite of mourning. Tradition directs the consoler to wait for the mourner to speak first. During those visits where the stillness felt strained I experienced a similar unease. Could it be that here, as in the NICU, I feared encroaching on these spaces of grief?

One of my earliest consultations was with Mrs. Q, mother of a very premature infant whose twin brother died within hours of birth in the middle of the night. The nurse called me over: "She is here every day at her daughter's bedside but I'm worried, she doesn't seem involved with her baby." The attending doctor expressed sharp impatience about her demands for more answers about her son's death. Invited to touch her daughter she backed away from the isolette, muttering about needing to grab the doctor in order to hear the latest lab results. Swept up in the staff's contagious anxiety I imagined her as "dispossessed of primary maternal preoccupation" (Szjer, 2005) and focused on encouraging her to hold her daughter. Through this she gradually began to form a tentative connection to her daughter and to me. But her anger and her despair—so shut down by staff and in ways, by me as well—was never fully engaged. We spoke by phone after her baby was finally discharged. From the safety of home she raged, "doesn't anyone want to know what I went through? Tell me, what kind of mother can't keep her babies alive?" I was stunned to recognize how much I had not wanted to know about the brutality of her grief and shame, how much I had overlooked her in my worry that she was overlooking her daughter.

How could I lose track of the mother in this way? Fail to stay closer to her fears about the reach of her dark feelings or her sense of illegitimacy as a mother, or better appreciate the ways in which her shame and loss and grief were at once entwined and in helpless opposition (Harris, 2009)? I became resolute about not repeating this failure. Determined to make up for my mindlessness I kept close track of all perinatal deaths (including prior losses). I began urging staff to keep these in mind as well and felt growing agitation each time they failed to remember. It struck me: when we speak of a mother having "lost" her baby it is as if we are attributing to her an unpardonable absent-mindedness (has she been careless and left it somewhere—on the windowsill perhaps, or on the bus?). I started to imagine the misplaced baby and then, I began to imagine a missing mother. Reading the medical literature, I discovered reports of obstetricians in the 1950s who acknowledged "not remembering" any details about the women who suffered stillbirths while under their care (Bourne, 1968). In his pioneering efforts to expose this conspiracy of silence, Bourne referred to these stunning lapses as "blind spots." But this seems to be yet another euphemism, one that still fails to capture the brutal bereavement that sears these deaths, or, the shameful silences that surround them (Crawford, 2008). Lost babies, lost mothers; all swaddled in a cloak of amnesia, all at risk of being lost to memory and to imagination.

Babies born of a multiple pregnancy are labeled Twin A, Twin B or Triplet A, B, and C. This label remains on the baby's isolette even if the twin or triplet subsequently dies. I learned that many NICUs have a practice of placing butterfly stickers on the nametags of surviving multiples so as to alert the team to the loss. I pursued this idea with the team, and to my dismay, could not get any traction with it. The excuses were many (e.g. who should take responsibility) and freighted with ambivalence, accentuating even more the harsh complexities of mourning these losses and of standing in the spaces with these mourners.

As I troubled over this, I came across the following cautionary words about the difficulties of mourning a tragedy when there are so few memories to process: "If mourning fails, there will be more of a desperate blocking out, a no-go area in the mind, and remembering is more of a troubled preoccupation, a haunted state of mind" (E. Lewis & Page, 1978). I then stumbled unexpectedly onto my own legacy of loss. As I walked around the unit looking out onto the same expanse of the Hudson River I saw when I gave birth in this same hospital, I began to first consider my own history in relation to these women and to others in my own family (e.g. my easy fertility, my sister's IVF—outsider, insider). I considered how fears about being envied might relate to worries about trespassing onto lives of women whose birth stories have been so unspeakably traumatic. Then, finally, my mother's first pregnancy came into focus. At seven months her baby was stillborn and clinical guidelines dictated that she carry the baby until she was induced at term. I obliged myself to contemplate this, to bring the stillborn "back to death" (Raphael-Leff, 2000). I let that grief wash over me, feeling blindsided by how out of reach this had been during these first years on the unit. I felt some shame about being so clueless and about my belated recognition. Gradually, I came to appreciate that while the fact of my mother's stillbirth was shared with me, it was not really available for shared reflection. It lingered in a place I was not free to enter. The shadow of loss that fell across my life because it fell across my mother's had not been fully nameable for me, leaving me both inside and outside of it. It sensitized me to the trauma and shame the women I work with experience, but it also intensified my concerns about intrusion and trespass.

When I met Mrs. V, a young immigrant mother of a neurologically fragile, surviving triplet I found myself preoccupied and haunted. Her doctor had urged her to reduce her pregnancy to twins and this tragically led to the death of two of the three fetuses and to the birth of the surviving triplet at 23 weeks. I learned that neither her parents nor her in-laws knew about the reduction. After weeks of polite exchanges she finally, cautiously, began to speak with me about her "negligence." Should she have agreed to the reduction? (A nurse from her country explains to me that their religion regards the body of a mother whose babies have died in utero as "a house of death.") She asked me if she made a mistake urging everything be done to save her baby; did I think he was suffering? On this particular day, we stood side by side at her baby's isolette while she reached in through the portholes to soothe her agitated son. We stood only inches from one another but she didn't meet my eyes as she confessed her doubts in a bare whisper. Her murmured words, her tone, were intimate and inviting, yet also seemed oblique, even enigmatic. Her mother with whom she had not yet shared the complexity of her pregnancy and birth story, who had travelled half way around the world to be with her, was seated only a few feet away. Speaking quietly I answered that he seemed more comfortable now that she was cradling him in her hands, but I also told her that I appreciated her concerns, and that it was incredibly difficult not to look back and question everything, as she was doing today. I then encouraged her, as I had in the past, to consider speaking with her mother about what had happened, how her doctor had urged her towards the reduction (a decision she carried with both guilt and shame). Was she now ready; might she allow herself to unburden herself, take the risk of doing so? "Perhaps," she replied.

When I returned to the unit days later her mother wasn't at the bedside but the baby's nurse, a young woman to whom she was very attached, was propping up a life-like baby doll next to the baby, joking softly about his "favorite girlfriend." The mother exclaimed, "Maybe it reminds him of his sister!" The nurse, red with shame, seemed horrified. "I'm so sorry! I didn't mean for you to think of that!" The mother quickly reassured her, "Its alright. I don't think about the past, I can't digest that. We won't tell him, it would be too much for him to bear."

Disconcerted by her quick retraction but emboldened and encouraged by her whimsy, I ventured, "You know, you have time to think about this. I know you are worried about giving him too much 'to digest', but I think that it has also been too much for you to endure—all the thoughts and feelings you have kept secret." Suddenly the nurse joined in and unexpectedly told a story about her own mother's twin pregnancy, which resulted in only one live birth, and described how her sister, who always insisted she was a twin, was finally told the story of her origins. When the nurse finished her story Mrs. V said, "maybe I will find some way to speak of it. I will think about what you have said."

Being haunted is to "live between two breaths" (de Waal, 2012) paused on a threshold, contemplating experiences at once accessible and out of reach. "Not known because not looked for, but heard, half heard, in the stillness between two waves of the sea," writes Eliot (1943). As I have become more comfortable moving between experiences that feel both alien and familiar (Hoffman, 2004) I have begun to inhabit these spaces differently, crossing from a painful sense of abjection towards a more poignant experience of belated knowing. This has enabled me to be better attuned to the unexpected collision of experiences that families and staff experience as well. The nurse's playful gesture with the doll was unexpectedly transformative for her and for the mother, reshaping their haunting and guilt stricken memories of the babies who died. When presenting at a conference on perinatal grief, where I shared some of these very stories, I had a similarly uncanny experience. Invited during an imaging exercise to contemplate my mother's lost baby, an entirely unimagined and unthought aspect of this loss unexpectedly appeared for me—an aspect of the loss more particular to me than for her—the stillborn death of *my* older brother.

Pentimento 2: Zina Steinberg

Thirty-two years ago, as an intern on a child inpatient psychiatric unit, I was uncharacteristically frozen by the admission of a four-year-old little girl. Delicate, charming and by far the youngest patient on the unit, she padded around in her footed one-piece pajamas in search of any lap that would hold her. I remember this fetching girl like I remember no other child on the unit. Her mother abandoned her and Child Protective Services was engaged. I was pregnant. I couldn't keep my eyes off her, but I didn't offer my lap. Confused for weeks by my withdrawal, in what seemed like a surprise, I remembered a family story. Hours after blowing out the candles at my fourth birthday party I was rushed to the hospital for an unexplained high fever. As I integrated my limited, haunting, and quite sketchy memories of what turned out to be three lengthy hospitalizations over the next two years, I closely watched this charming child whose family never visited and I became gradually less paralyzed. Two decades later, when I was about 50, my mother with a peculiar laugh, told of my insistent hunger strike during one of my hospitalizations and let it slip that during the many weeks of my being in the hospital she had never visited.

Six years later I launch a project to consult with families and staff in the NICU with little conscious awareness of how my medical history might be evoked. My initial reactions are passionate. While many parents sit by the isolettes, there are some babies that are noticeably alone, for what seems like days on end. I think about the babies, dream about them, but mostly I become consumed by questions about the parents. Where are many of them? Day staff says the parents come at night and night staff assumes they are there during the day. But my review of the nursing notes for certain infants reflects extremely spotty visiting, if at all. Staff expertly focus on the acute medical needs of the infant, keenly observing the infant's physical state but have an almost mindless lack of curiosity in the question that rivets me. Yes, though visiting is now allowed 24/7, there is the devastating fact of an infant alone. But in high relief for me is the shadowy image of the mother alone at home without her newborn. Yet to be linked are the shared hauntings of my three hospitalizations and these families' traumas.

Guilt and shame haunt the halls of the hospital. It is easy to hear the guilt. "Is this because I once had an abortion?" says one mother. "I got angry at the priest and stormed out of church two Sundays ago. Is this our punishment?" says a young father. Guilt, a less acute emotion, writes Helen Block Lewis (1971), can be used to bypass shame. Shame is a "sleeper" emotion, easily ignored and "the witness to it ordinarily looks the other way." It is a "ferocious attack on the self;" making us want to hide, disappear even die. (See also Kilborne, 2007.)

A NICU moment: a group of moms has been meeting regularly with me. One day K, grimacing, walks into the room. "OK, is the door closed? What happens when you pump? Do you get enough milk?" "I cover the bottle with both hands when I walk back into the unit so no one sees how little I produce. It's like I'm just an inadequate cow." A shameful secret now is shared.

I am struck by the profound embodied shame experienced by these women who, like so many NICU moms, had trouble getting pregnant and who subjected themselves to multiple trials of IVF often ending with miscarriages and even stillbirths. Now, the next maternal gift fails them too. They hook up to electric pumping machines that suction their breasts 8+ times/day and still they are not getting enough milk to nourish their infant. Stories pour out, they cry, but they also laugh. They begin to stand a bit outside themselves and find humor and comfort. It is helpful and the air feels lighter. What was dark and unspeakable now finds communal confession and symbolization (M. Lewis, 1992). "Sometimes I don't even know if my body is female! First my ovaries, then my uterus and 'incompetent cervix' and now my breasts." Others nod in recognition and more "funny" tales get told. Gender shame, I've called it: the very heart of their core gender identity is in crisis. The traumas of their reproductive history threaten to fracture their internal coherence.

We begin to speculate about the maternal (and paternal) mind in hiding, our own shames, our mothers' shames: my mother not visiting her young daughter in the hospital, my shame, her need to hide from the shame of her perceived failure and its decades long unspoken, enviously-enacted sequelae. In this liminal world of the NICU, a parent's sense of self—creative and filled with potential just a few moments earlier—is now derailed. Instead shame now lurks in the psychic spaces of their imaginations leading to dark places. Psychic equivalence reigns and the future, once peppered with hopes and dreams, is now a no-go zone. "I have become afraid of my imagination," said Susan Sontag during her last weeks of life (Rieff, 2008). So have NICU parents. Ghosts haunt.

Mrs. P, a successful lawyer, comes to the NICU most days after work, having taken much less leave than her job offers. Not engaging readily with her newborn, she comes, she asserts, "to check up on the nurses." I meet her after her baby has already been hospitalized for six weeks. Though she was initially reluctant to talk, I ask her if she would introduce me to Sylvie, her baby. We look at Sylvie's shock of dark hair and smile at how her skinny legs and arms are flung about—as if she were sunbathing. I ask her if she recalled what her daughter looked like when she was born, wondering if she could see how much she's changed. Can she find a sense of future with her baby? With posture and inflection sharp, she begins to tell me a harrowing story of the birth and not going to the hospital when her waters broke at 28 weeks. "You see I didn't want to have a child. I want to become a partner in the firm and I don't want anything to stop me. I had a deadline at work. I'm really not maternal. I tried to pump and besides not getting much milk, I hated it. My husband wanted a child. Me, I could have easily never been a mother." She then suddenly asks me about other families. Are they different? "Each has a story", I reply, "and though they are unique, there are also patterns." Mrs. P seems now almost riveted with attention, so I go on to describe how common it is for parents to feel guilt and even shame. "Shame?" She startles, grabbing my eyes. "I get furious if anyone in the immediate family tells others that Sylvie is premature. I won't send photos. I don't want anyone to see her as bad and me as bad." "Bad" hangs in the air between us and it is a few moments before she speaks again, telling me of her brother's sudden death in his sleep when she was about seven years old, something her parents would never talk about it. "My family was shattered and we still cannot mention him. I kept asking about my brother and finally my parents said that he went to a boarding school. And I, who question everything, somehow knew better than to ask ever again. Many years later I went to a funeral and saw my brother's name on a grave. I think my parents suffered profound debilitating shame. I know my father unraveled, and this too was never talked about, but oh, so obvious. Funny but I've been thinking about it all lately—a lot."[3]

Absence and silence are often centerpieces of relational trauma. "Entombed in psychic crypts" (B. Reiss, 2007), these secrets are shepherded by the ghosts that inhabit such deadened relational spaces and ensure their shame-saturated passage from one generation to the next. When the NICU consciousness expands to include more than the baby, it embraces the mother, leaving fathers in the margins. Yet, fathers too bear shame, often accompanied by a complex psychological history that becomes more visible when the couple is not communicating well; their procreative act has become destructive and fissures emerge.[4]

Ms. D gave birth to twins at 24 weeks. Days after the birth, the male baby died and about four weeks later, mom tells me that she and her husband are not talking. "He's never home, he's irritable and angry and he's not coming with me to the hospital." When I finally meet Dad he describes the day his son, William, died. "I see the doctors doing chest compressions on him and from down the hall I shout 'Stop'. He was less than one pound. They were torturing him," he cries. "But I also told them to let him die, my only son." After the birth, Ms. D was very ill and Dad thought that she might die and he'd be left with a one-pound preemie—the surviving twin girl—and their three-year-old twin daughters. "I was beside myself with anger. I thought very seriously about killing myself".

Ms. D, hardly registering a reaction, whispers, "There was a phone message from his work colleague. It was far too intimate." Dad responds, "She lost a child a few years ago and understands what I am feeling. She let me talk about our son. You've removed yourself. You are with your mom and dad and with Mary and Isabella (three-year old twins). I never hear you mention William."

I ask if she knows how worried dad was about his anger and his terror that she would die along with his son. "I didn't know how scared he was, but we have the twins and our new baby, Samantha." "But I don't have my son," he plaintively retorts. I don't know why but I ask if he's ever lost anyone else important to him and he begins a long story about his father, whom he thinks about a lot since William died. He hasn't seen him for almost 20 years, when his mother kicked his father out of the house. Talking about him was never permitted and now his ruminations feel like a betrayal of his mother. "My mother hates him. She only says, 'You were born from your father's abuse of me." He begins to weep. "I lost my son, my only son, my only chance to have a son." I quietly continue, "And your father, your only father. Your mother won't let you mention your dad and your wife won't let you mention your son." Dad murmurs through tears, "The only way I get through the day is to bury myself in work." When I then ask where William is buried, Dad says, "I can't visit Samantha in the NICU unless I visit William. He's cold and alone. I talk to him all day long, but I haven't gone to his grave." Finally mom who had been sitting stiff-jawed, speaks, "I worry about Samantha all day. For hours she's here alone. It breaks my heart. I don't want to talk about William now. I had him inside me for six months and then he was born and he was taken from me. I never held him. I keep William to myself, close to my heart—maybe it's like the only way I had William—inside of me." Dad quietly adds, "I dream about him. I imagine his skin, his eyelashes. I wonder if he's warm and comfortable. I ask him to give me strength, to guide me, to not let me give up and die."

I meet with Mr. and Ms. D about six times.[5] After the long first meeting they decide together to visit the grave and start to make it a weekly trip before coming to the hospital. At the same time, dad begins to envision finding his father, recognizing that both he and his father each lost a son. He imagines what his mother meant by saying that his father abused her and describes how shamed he has always felt thinking about his father's physical, and even sexual violence towards his mother. He felt he owed his mother so much and that his son dying was punishment for his being born in such a violent way. "I am like my father, a man who is angry and violent and doesn't deserve a son." Through relatives, he assiduously tracks down his father only to find that he died just months earlier. Samantha is soon discharged and as they live in upstate New York, I refer them to someone near their home.[6]

Ghosts of ruptured relationships thread through the D family and so many others, impeding dad from visiting his newborn daughter, threatening his relationship with his wife and causing him to obsessively and shamefully ruminate over—instead of mourn—his dead newborn only son. The connection he kept alive, though secret even to himself, was his identification with his lost angry father.

Years ago, I began a personal analysis with a dream in which someone was yelling for a gurney, though I had no conscious recollection of what a "gurney" was. When I looked it up I was surprised to learn that it was the stretcher that transports hospital patients. I was also surprised to notice, when I pressed the elevator button in my analyst's building, that the company name engraved on the brass plate was "Gurney." Thus my analysis transported me to "unthought knowns" (Bollas, 1989) of my early childhood hospitalizations, its isolation and terror and in adulthood my oft-times counterphobic pressing agency. And since working in the NICU a childhood recurrent nightmare returns to unsettle my sleep: a fetus is on the cold, 1950s linoleum floor and though I try, I can't reach it.

My work with parents in the NICU has stirred me to recognize and reflect on an aspect of hospitalizations for those babies and parents and also for myself. From these moms and dads I learned not only about the fear and guilt that they suffer, but also about the shame. And this in turn has helped me imagine the mother who couldn't be by the hospital bed, a mother unable to tolerate and regulate her feelings of failure and shame.

Final words

We have tasked ourselves with "the peculiar necessity of imagining what is in fact real" (Gourevitch, 1998) not only for families but also for staff, but as Gourevitch has also cautioned, there is "memory that we manage and memory that manages us" (*Goureritch*, 2014).

The bedside nurses who watch the babies' slow progress or decline stand at the front line, looking at the future, holding promise for themselves and the families, while managing their own personal histories and their memories of caretaking babies. Those babies who have died or who suffered much pain while in the NICU can haunt nurses. One nurse, caring for a baby at risk of dying, came to us frantic about her assignment. The father of this baby, wanting to keep his daughter alive at any cost, was frantic himself with fear, his anxiety so invasive that every staff member felt assaulted by it. The nurse couldn't tolerate his endless questions, fearing just his seeing her face betrayed what she knew, and what he couldn't bear to know. She was angry and adamant as we began to speak. But in conversation we learned that she cared deeply for this baby and understood and felt compassion for the father; she was even able to express empathy for his profound terror and agitation. She told us that usually she can gently ask parents to back off but felt so stuck with this dad at this time. We asked her if there was anything about this particular situation that might be on her mind, even if she is not fully aware of any particular thoughts. She looked up, wide eyed, and said, "I fear she will die, she is like four of my last cases and they all died. I don't want to be there when that happens, dad saw that on my face today, I don't want to have a conversation with him." We talked about the impact of these deaths, the feelings of the grieving parents. "It sounds like the dad's micromanagement is difficult, but the harder issue may be the management of your feelings of loss and helplessness. Perhaps we can talk more." She was grateful to have been offered a means of making sense of her intensely complicated reactions and felt a renewed commitment to this baby and family. (See Kraemer & Steinberg, 2006; Steinberg & Kraemer, 2010 for a fuller elaboration of our work with dissociative processes with staff.)

For 13 years we have consulted with families and staff providing space for an autobiographical narrative in a world where crisis, urgency, and bio-medical language cast a deep and long shadow, and where finding meaning can be elusive. Many have commented that the loss of meaning is similar to a traumatic assault (Ferenczi, 1949). In these places of no meaning, shame, and loss, ghosts thrive. For families of the babies and for the staff, these ghosts of past unresolved and unmourned relationships threaten to reproduce themselves in the fertile field of NICU uncertainties. By bringing the specter-like relationships to light and by readmitting and repatriating the ghosts (A. Harris, this volume) and opening up the narrative to give them substance and voice, even when painful, we see the grip of intergenerational transfer of trauma loosened.[7]

Much has been written about the importance of witnessing (Boulanger, 2007; Felman & Laub, 1992; Goodman & Meyers, 2012) to enable victims of socio-cultural and psychological trauma find personal meaning in events often too horrible to contemplate. The NICU is a polar opposite of political genocide's death machines or the humanity crushing experiences of slavery or the frightful recent tragedies of say, 9/11 or Katrina. The sole purpose of the NICU is to heal and mend the critically ill neonate. But a critical care medical staff must engage in dissociation in order to perform many of the required medical procedures. It would often be too psychologically costly to absorb and contain the parent's pain. In our work then, by being alive witnesses, sensitive to shame and interested in their often abject and unspeakable reproductive past and by listening for links to family history and appreciating deeply the power of relationships as a bulwark against further trauma (Coates, 2003), we seek to re-imagine and even transform unintegrated and under-internalized (Harris, this volume) aspects of the personal stories evoked by a complicated NICU birth. To consider ghosts in this way is to be released to new ways of thinking about remembering and forgetting, about recognition and misrecognition and about shame and loss. We did not imagine for ourselves the possibility for such subjectively and affectively intense "moments of meeting" (Stern et al., 1998) and how our own stories would thread through the rich tapestry of lives in the NICU.

Notes

1 A percentage of the babies (actual statistics are not collected) were conceived with the help of assisted reproductive technologies (ART). Multiple births are a common consequence of ART and multiples are more likely to be born prematurely. There is also data that suggests a linkage between some ART procedures and some congenital anomalies. (See Steinberg and Kraemer, 2016, for a fuller discussion of ART as experienced in the NICU.)

2 Nurses often struggle when faced with parents not ready to "give up," parents who continue to request that everything be done to prolong life even when futile.

3 A loved one "disappearing" without explanation during childhood is more common than we could have ever imagined. It also has current echoes. It is not unusual for a parent to leave the NICU at night and then return in the morning to find the baby in the next isolette to her baby not there . . . gone. And due to HIPPA regulations, no one can speak about it.

4 Male infertility often remains secret though about 40% of infertility is due to male factors.

5 It is noteworthy how in these time-limited meetings this couple could reflect on these haunting connections, yet it is not unusual. Using non-linear dynamic systems theory to tackle therapeutic action, Harris provides another lense, describing how "slight shifts in experience can give rise to change and great complexity within very short time frames" (2009). Daniel Stern in his book *The Motherhood Constellation* (1995) provides another lense, writing that the particular psychic state accompanying birth and the weeks to months after, offers a "window of altruism" on the part of the parents. Though the trauma of a NICU birth with its heightened shame and guilt threatens this altruistic state, brief and focused consultations can begin to free maternal and paternal communication and even reverie.
6 Consultations with families can feel aborted; endings premature as medical discharge criteria prevail. Further contact is usually emailed photos of the growing baby and family.
7 Good ghosts also thrive in the NICU. They may be the imagined "angel" presence of the dead twin or triplet, that parents believe will guide the surviving multiple through the NICU or the much beloved dead grandmother, who by holding out welcoming embracing arms provides a way for a parent to remove life supports and come to some peace with letting their fatally ill newborn die. (Lieberman, et al., 2005; Steinberg, 2006.)

Bibliography

Alvarez, A. (1992). *Live Company: Psychoanalytic Psychotherapy with Autistic, Borderline, Deprived and Abused Children*. London: Routledge.

Bollas, D. (1989). *The Shadow of the Object: Psychoanalysis of the Unthought Known*. New York: Columbia University Press.

Boulanger, G. (2007). *Wounded by Reality: Understanding and Treating Adult Onset Trauma*. Mahwah, NJ: Analytic Press.

Bourne, S. (1968). The psychological effects of stillbirth on women and their doctors. *Journal of the Royal College of General Practitioners*, 16: 103–112.

Coates, S., Rosenthal, J. & Schechter, D. (2003). *September 11: Trauma and Human Bonds*. Hillsdale, NJ: Analytic Press.

Cohen, M. (2003). *Sent Before My Time: A Child Psychotherapist's View of Life on a Neonatal Intensive Care Unit*. London: Karnac Books.

Crawford, A. (2008). *Born still: Euphemisms and the double taboo of women's bodies and death*. Home.chass.utoronto.ca/~percy/course/6362-CrawfordAllison.htm.

De Waal, E. (2010). My hero Cy Twombly. *The Guardian*, Dec 10, 2010.

De Waal, E. (2012). *Between two breaths*, Waddesdon Manor. www.edmundewaal.com.

Davoine, F. (2007). The characters of madness in the talking cure. *Psychoanal. Dial.*, 17(5): 627–638.

Doka, K. (2002). (ed.) *Disenfranchised Grief: New Directions, Challenges and Strategies for Practice*. Champaign, Illinois: Research Press.

Eliot, T.S. (1943). *Four Quartets*. Orlando: Harcourt Brace and Co.

Felman, S. & Laub, D. (1992). *Testimony: Crises of Witnessing in Literature, Psychoanalysis and History*. New York: Routledge.

Ferenczi, S. (1949). Confusion of the tongues between the adults and the child (the language of tenderness and passion). *Int. J. Psycho-Anal.*, 30: 225–230.

Goodman, N. & Meyers, M. (2012). *The Power of Witnessing: Reflections, Reverberations and Traces of the Holocaust: Trauma, Psychoanalysis and the Living Mind*. New York: Routledge.

Gordon, A. (1997). *Ghostly Matters: Haunting and the Sociological Imagination.* Minneapolis, MN: University of Minnesota Press.

Gourevitch, P. (1998). *We Wish To Inform You That Tomorrow We Will be Killed With Our Families: Stories from Rwanda.* New York: Picador.

Gourevtich, P. (2014). Remembering in Rwanda. *The New Yorker.* Comment, April 21, 2014.

Harris, A. (2007). Analytic work in the bridge world: Commentary on paper by Francoise Davoine. *Psychoanal. Dial.*, 17(5): 659–669.

Harris, A. (2009). "You Must Remember This". *Psychoanal. Dial.*, 19(2): 2–21.

Hoffman, E. (2004). *After Such Knowledge: Memory, History and the Legacy of the Holocaust.* New York: Public Affairs.

Kilborne,B. (2007). On shame. *Round Robin.*Vol. XX11(2), Newsletter of Section 1, Div. 39, American Psychological Ass.

Kraemer, S. (2006). So the cradle won't fall: holding the parents who hold the staff in the NICU. *Psychoanal. Dial.*, 16(2):149–164.

Kraemer, S. & Steinberg, Z. (2006). It's rarely cold in the NICU: The permeability of psychic space. *Psychoanal. Dial.*, 16(2):165–179.

Lewis, E. & Page, A. (1978). Failure to mourn a stillbirth: An overlooked catastrophe. *Brit. J. Med. Psychol.*, 51: 237–241.

Lewis, H.B. (1971). *Shame and Guilt in Neurosis.* New York: Intl. Univ. Press.

Lewis, M. (1992). *Shame: The Exposed Self.* New York: Free Press.

Lieberman, A., Padron, E., Van Horn, P., & Harris, W.W. (2005). The Intergenerational Transmission of Benevolent Parental Influences. *Inf. Mental Hlth. J.*, 26: 504–520.

Meltzer, D. (1992). *The Claustrum: An Investigation of Claustrophobic Phenomenon.* Perthshire: Clunie Press.

Raphael-Leff, J. (2000). (ed.). *'Spilt Milk': Perinatal Loss and Breakdown.* London: Institute of Psychoanalysis.

Reis, B. (2007). Witness to History: Introduction to Symposium on Transhistorical Catastrophe. *Psychoanal. Dial.*, 17:621–626.

Rieff, D. (2008). *Swimming in a Sea of Death: A Son's Memoir.* New York: Simon & Schuster.

Steinberg, Z. (2006). Pandora meets the NICU parent or whither hope? *Psychoanal. Dial.*, 16(2): 133–147.

Steinberg, Z. & Kraemer, S. (2010). Cultivating a culture of awareness: nurturing reflective practices in the NICU. *Zero to Three.* v 31, n 2, 15–21. Washington, DC.

Steinberg, Z. & Kraemer, S. (2016). The shadow side of ART. In Gentile, K. (ed). *The Business of Being Made: The temporalities of reproductive technologies, in psychoanalysis and culture.* New York: Routledge.

Stern, D. (1995). *The Motherhood Constellation: A Unified View of Parent-Infant Psychotherapy.* New York: Basic Books.

Stern, D.N., Sander, L.W., Nahum, J.P., Harrison, A.M., Lyons-Ruth, K., Morgan, A.C., Bruschwwiller-Stern, N. & Tronick, E.Z. (1998). Non-interpretive Mechanisms in Psychoanalytic Therapy: The "Something More" than Interpretation. *Int. J. Psycho-Anal.* 79: 903–921.

Szjer, M. (2005). *Talking to Babies: Healing With Words on a Maternity Ward.* Boston, MA: Beacon Press.

Willoughby, R. (2001). 'The dungeon of thyself': The claustrum as pathological container. *Int. J. Psycho-Anal.*, 82: 917–31.

Chapter 8

Mourning in the hollows of architecture and psychoanalysis

Maria McVarish and Julie Leavitt

Prologue

Friday, 13 December 2013, 8 p.m.: Making our way through an enormous gift shop—the only means of gaining entry for a tour of the Winchester Mystery House™—we find ourselves amidst a handful of teenage girls. They stalk each other with toy Winchester rifles, taking aim and pretending to shoot. Hours earlier, perhaps unbeknownst to these girls, a news story has broken about yet another school shooting in the US.[1] The irony of their play-violence at a house purportedly haunted by gun victims makes us viscerally aware of the *real* ghosts hidden behind collective denial. The same culture that fetishizes guns, ghosts, and madness (all of which are neatly consolidated in this popular tourist attraction) makes all of these an enticing barrier to shared conscience and responsibility.

Introduction

Ghosts confound our categories of experience, complicating conventional distinctions between memory, space, and emotion. On a mental level, ghosts shimmer like mirages at the horizon between unconscious memory and conscious awareness; on a sensory level, they bind psychical spaces of mourning to the physical places associated with their lives and deaths; and on an emotional level, they revive and sustain a *co-created* bond between the living and their dead, challenging survivors to account for losses and pay for them in grief.

As figures, ghosts are unstable and elusive, lacking mass, biology, or finitude in the normal sense of these words. More often than not, they are sensed as lingering absences—as, we might say, figures in the negative. Indeed, this ambiguity in relation to *presence* and *absence* is a defining characteristic of ghosts. Wanting in substance, they paradoxically give body to grief, plotting themselves into its interstices precisely so that the living may lament the unknowable status to which their dead have been relegated. They haunt places whose particular spatial features elicit the histories and relationships that concern them. We encounter the dead somewhere between the material locations marked for them by association and the hollowed out vacancies in which they, once animate, are now missing. These haunted "spaces" are peculiarly indeterminate, subsisting through entanglements of feeling and perception, self and other.

Psychoanalytically speaking, ghosts haunt individuals (and families) for particular reasons, decrying the misdeeds, traumas, and silences that belie proper genealogy. In this chapter, however, we explore how the ghosts of individuals and families *collectivize* to haunt the spatial and psychical "hollows" of popular culture more broadly. The Winchester Mystery House™, an historic residence of approximately 160 rooms located at the outskirts of San Jose, California, offers a rich case study in this regard. Whether you visit the place in person (and spend upwards of $33 for the privilege) or watch one of the many documentaries about it, you're likely to get the same explanation for its "mystery:"[2] the mansion, with its elaborately enfolded interiors, is reputed to be the haunted result of a grieving woman's madness.[3]

In preparation for a discussion of what the Winchester house could teach us about ghosts and space, the following is a selective outline of three factors shaping the Winchester "™" story: a biographical sketch of the building's designer, Sarah Winchester, based on the scant documentation about her that is publicly available;[4] a brief summary of the Winchester Mystery House™ *myth* as recited in the attraction's carefully scripted tour; and an overview of the complexly layered social context in which Mrs. Winchester lived in her own time.

Sarah Winchester

Sarah Lockwood Winchester (née Pardee) was born in New Haven, Connecticut in 1839, the fifth of seven children. Called "Sallie" within her family, she shared given names with two relatives who died before she was born: the legal name of her eldest sibling Sarah, born in 1831 and dead at one year;[5] and that of her paternal grandmother "Sally," who died just before "Sallie" (Sarah) was born. Her father, Leonard Pardee, was a third-generation master carpenter whose shop adjoined the Pardee home during Sarah's childhood.[6] Although evidently close to her immediate family members, according to her biographer Mary Jo Ignoffo, "Sarah appear[ed] to have been on a path of a loner and independent thinker before she was an adolescent" (Ignoffo, 2010, 19). She received primary school education but did not attend high school (Ignoffo, 2010, 21).[7]

In 1862, Sarah married William Wirt Winchester. The couple remained in New Haven near their families and, in 1866, bore one child. Their child, Annie,[8] died of a digestive disorder after only one month. By then, William's father, a local businessman, had founded a successful company making men's shirts, and was in the process of establishing another. The latter, which would eventually come to be called the Winchester Repeating Arms Company, would prove more enduring, and become its own legend as the maker of the "The Gun that Won the West." The father's success in enterprise helped finance a new mansion on the outskirts of New Haven, where Sarah and her husband would live with William's parents. Sarah and William actively participated in its design and construction.

In the early 1870s, William and Sarah visited San Francisco where William, heir apparent to his father's gun company, marketed his family's wares. That trip introduced Sarah to a region of the United States to which she would eventually re-locate, three years after William's death. William died of tuberculosis in 1881. His death was one of five significant losses Sarah suffered in the two decades that spanned her marriage.[9]

In 1886, after living in California for about two years, Sarah purchased a small farmhouse near San Jose, originally built over several years in the 1870s. She called the property "Llanada Villa" after an area in Spain she had visited during her travels as a new widow. Over the next 20 years—a period during which she owned and resided in several local properties concurrently—Sarah Winchester would extensively remodel and expand Llanada Villa; her efforts would transform this simple farmhouse into a "mansion," over time. Contrary to the information presented by the Mystery House™'s current owners, however, construction was *not* continuous and the work did not generally take place at night or on weekends (see Ignoffo, 2010). Sarah hired tradesmen,[10] designed the building's elaborate modifications and additions, and oversaw their construction. Work on the mansion halted suddenly in 1906 after the great San Francisco earthquake, which severely damaged whole sections of the property. Winchester elected not to continue remodeling thereafter, and ordered only those repairs necessary to stabilize the building (Ignoffo, 2010, 156).

Nearly all of what is known about Winchester's life in California comes to us from her correspondence with a few key associates: her lawyer, her sisters, and her nieces. Her letters reflect a sane, intelligent, and cordial (if socially reserved) person—someone extremely private by nature and meticulous in her business dealings. Winchester's biographer believes that Sarah's distance from the public eye was due to simple shyness, compounded, speculatively, by self-consciousness over the progression of dental caries and a disfiguring rheumatoid arthritis (Ignoffo, 2010, 144). She died on 5 September 1922 of natural causes, at the age of 83.

A year after her death, with the estate finding no immediate buyers, Llanada Villa was leased to a family who would only later come to own it.[11] This turn of events likely saved the building from demolition, since by the time they obtained title, the family—whose background lay in amusement park equipment (Ignoffo, 2010, 206–214)—had transformed the long-unoccupied dwelling into a successful tourist attraction.

The myth

In a rote script saturated with embellishment, tour guides for the Winchester Mystery House™ present Sarah Winchester's mansion as the byproduct of a ghost story. The kernels of this ghost story were actually crafted by local journalists between the years 1895 and 1911, while Winchester was still living.[12] Consolidated into the Winchester Mystery House™ tour script beginning as early as nine months after Winchester's death when it first opened as a tourist attraction, the story has framed public experience of the house ever since. The tour guides portray her as an obsessive melancholic—a guilt-ridden widow who worked on the building to assuage her grief or, alternately, to forestall her own death. In their version, during the years immediately following her husband's death, the bereft Sarah sought guidance from a Boston spiritualist. The spiritualist informed her that she would have to atone for the violence made possible by guns, as sole heir to a fortune derived from them. Specifically, if she wanted to keep the avenging spirits at bay, she would be obliged to work on a construction project in perpetuity. In this scenario, Winchester followed the advice by commanding constant (24 hours a day, seven days a week) construction on Llanada Villa, without concern for expense. This "mad" work, the guides claim, resulted in nonsensical, "bizarre" and "insane" details, like doors opening onto walls, stairs leading "nowhere," a "séance room," and several purported architectural references to the number 13.[13] Most of these "bizarre" features, however, are likely the result of Winchester's post-earthquake instructions for workers to secure and stabilize the building and then cease all construction activities beyond basic maintenance (Ignoffo, 2010, 156). Regardless, the myth of the Mystery House™ pits Mrs. Winchester squarely against the souls of those killed by Winchester guns. It goes so far as to place Sarah, at the stroke of midnight, in a small room near the present-day center of the house, claiming that she held nightly séances there in order to consult with her tormenters and receive the next day's designs.

Historical/cultural context

The ghost story behind the Winchester house belies historical fears and wishes emerging on a mass scale during Sarah Winchester's adult life—particular anxieties circulating throughout the US in response to a burgeoning expansion of gun technologies and consequent proliferation of gun violence. Her lifetime spanned not just the American Civil War and the peak and eradication of legalized slavery of Africans and African Americans in the East, but also government-endorsed attacks on Native peoples throughout the West. Across the US, deeply-embedded racist beliefs enabled oppression and aggression to be recast as *self-defense* and *inalienable rights* to land and labor. These historical conflicts tore through the aggregate racial skin of the American social psyche, leaving deep and enduring scars. Many of these beliefs and "rights" were compelled and enforced, whether directly or associatively, by guns. A collective trauma perpetuates the insidious and *societal* madness buttressing the Winchester Mystery™, and ultimately distorts our image of Sarah Winchester.

The Winchester™ ghost story also implicates Spiritualism, a movement originating in the US that rapidly gained in popularity across both the US and Europe during the 19th century.[14] Sarah Winchester lived in a time in which bereaved and displaced masses who had lost loved ones in wars around the globe were desperate to make contact with their dead.[15] The backbone of Spiritualism lay in the practice of communication between the living and their dead through spiritual mediums. For those who sought the services of these mediums, the phenomenon of communication itself provided convincing empirical evidence that deceased loved ones survived in the afterlife. There is no actual documentation suggesting, much less proving, that Sarah Winchester ever sought the guidance of a Spiritualist.

There are, however, records indicating an unprecedented rise in Spiritualist practices in both the Eastern US and in Northern California during Sarah's lifetime.[16] Such practices were not limited to marginal populations at the time. For example Faust (2008) notes that, "Mary Todd Lincoln sought regularly to communicate with her dead son Willie. She sponsored a number of séances at the White House, some of which the President himself was said to have attended" (181). In California, Leland Sr. and Jane Stanford, who founded Stanford University, visited a spiritual medium in the wake of the loss of their son, Leland Jr. (Ignoffo, 2010, 100).

Haunting vs. mourning

Writing only a few years before Sarah Winchester's Llanada Villa would be leased and re-invented as a haunted house, Sigmund Freud (1953a/1917) described the work of grieving as a fundamentally perceptual process occurring between memory and reality. In the course of carrying on after someone close has died, he said, the mourner encounters situations that remind him of the person he has lost. Memories of the lost loved one can arise with vivid, nearly hallucinatory force, elicited as if by chance through particular sensory circumstances—something as serendipitous as a play of light, a melody's refrain, an aroma passing from an open door or window. As Marcel Proust (1913) wrote during this same period, "The past is hidden somewhere outside the realm, beyond the reach of intellect, in some material object . . . which we do not suspect" (23). Memory traces of the beloved in these moments are bound up with sensory aspects of the present-tense, real world. In a manner of speaking, the dead loved one rides these sense phenomena to *return* as an object of experience, albeit fleetingly.

Yet, Freud (1953a/1917) writes, "Reality-testing has shown that the love object no longer exists" (244). The same sensations that trigger hallucinatory, ghostly experiences (those ephemeral qualities of light, familiar tunes or wafting smells) soon cleave from the reminiscence to expose the actual absence of the beloved, and the mourner is forced to acknowledge that the person who died is gone. The psychic function of a mourning process, according to Freud, is thus to detach one's living memories incrementally from the absent person, and thereby to historicize the dead as past.[17] But ghosts, by definition, withstand this incremental dissolution into memory; somehow, they manage to preserve a gestalt presence, and their presence (figurative or otherwise) *haunts*. How is this possible?

Freud insisted that the mourning process of dis-identifying takes place perceptually—between what is experienced in the temporal and environmental *present* and what is experienced virtually, in memory—as with transference to a present other. This underscores the vital relevance of the *physical context* for memory's mobilization. Haunting might thus be understood as a conjunction of what is actual and present with what is remembered from the past—with the further condition that the particular memory traces in question be both sensory in nature *and* meaningfully associated with someone who has been painfully lost. Ghosts, by this logic, need not haunt the actual places they frequented with others in life. All they require are environments that resemble—in discrete sensory ways, but also through association—the conditions they might have shared in the past with those still living. A single prompt could be enough to provoke a chain of sensory memories, and with them a feeling of ghostly presence.

All of this, we would venture, extends Freud's theories into what we might call "spatial terms," highlighting the extent to which the environment both connects us with and separates us from other individuals, at the level of sense-memory. A ghost, in this working definition, is nothing more than the residue of absence (the hollow in the real) that shared memory creates.

Space and haunting

In his account of the grieving process, Freud introduced, albeit indirectly, a critical link between sense-perception and loss. Yet his comparatively short meditations on mourning and melancholia did not lead him to develop a working theory of *how* grief permits ghosts to haunt specific places. To do this, he would have had to consider the different registers of experience that "space" entails. Most people, if they think about space at all, simply take it for granted. Space is what separates *here* from *there*: that expansive vista, or, at the limit, the "outer-space" of the stratosphere. But what if what we call "space" were really only air, land, or, at another level, a geometric measure of distance? What if, in other words, there were no such thing as "physical space," but only concrete and material things like soil, carbon, and oxygen, on the one hand, and abstract concepts like distance, measure, or "medium" on the other? Traditionally, the word "space" has encompassed all of these meanings, and more. It is important, therefore, to scrutinize the extent to which ideas about space may be connected with modes of *thinking* and *imagining*, which in turn may be reified in the environment.

In its most basic and historical sense, the word "space" has frequently been used to designate distance, a *dis*continuity which at the same time is premised on a presumption of *continuity*.[18] Space serves as a fundamental condition,[19] or tool, of thought: both a holding capacity and the ultimate limit of emptiness or no-thing. Like Immanuel Kant before him but with his own 20th century twist, Jacques Lacan (1992) linked this "no-thing" quality of space to mental functioning in general: "the fashioning of the signifier and the introduction of a gap or a hole in the real is identical" (121). In his 1960 seminar *The Ethics of Psychoanalysis* (Lacan, 1992), he called attention to the *vulnerability* that visual and architectural space introduce within the symbolic order:

> The important thing is that at a given moment ones arrives at illusion. Around it one finds a sensitive spot, a lesion, a locus of pain, a point of reversal of the whole of history . . . insofar as we are implicated in it; that point concerns the notion that the illusion of space is different from the creation of emptiness (140).

Architecture, which ostensibly concerns itself with space and spatial praxis, thus moves both toward and away from the delineation of emptiness. Each representation[20] of space, from schematic plans to construction drawings, up to and including the building itself, re-inscribes with increasing physicality a boundary in relation to which the trace of the real (as a byproduct of the limits and movement of representation) may be glimpsed.

When we construct architectural space, we delimit metric dimensions of earth, air, light, and building materials out of a polysemous contiguity. To some extent, we do this intentionally: we want protection from the elements and from undesired contact with other people. But the barriers that buildings impose can only provide protection at the expense of the contiguous real. Buildings *do* separate and contain us: they do keep others away, they do hold weather, sounds, and moonlight at bay. At the same time, however, the elements, qualities, and experiences we exclude are left to "haunt" our rooms, stairs and cabinets—just as the residua of potential meanings haunt our efforts at precise locution.[21] In positing a correspondence with reality, architecture carves a *gap* within the amorphous field of what Jacques Lacan calls the *real* (Evans, 2005, 159–161).

A further complication of space, in the everyday sense in which we use this word, is the extent to which our bodies are in and of it, reflexively. We internalize the standards of everyday architectural space to such a degree that we rarely reflect on what its walls, windows, and roofs keep from us. Through lifetimes of repeated movement, we incorporate the spatial conventions of environmental design down to their smallest and most detailed nuances: the feel, in one's feet and legs, of a stairway's standard proportion of rise to run; the sense of inside as distinct from out; a window's relationship with light, air, and view; the meaning and utility of a door, a floor, ceiling or wall; the placement of a handle on a cabinet; the "roomness" of a room, and so on. We are so habituated to each of these (and myriad other) more-or-less standardized features of environmental design that, in the course of using and moving through the built environment, any apperception of physical details remains largely unconscious.[22] Indeed, standardized units and configurations of space are fundamentally integral to our corporeal schemata.[23] We depend on them in our daily navigations of the human world.[24]

And just as conventions exist in the details of buildings, so also do they exist in the larger sense of room design, as well as in the broader *arrangement* of rooms within floor levels, or the vertical layering of a building's floor plans. In residential structures, where interiors support the most intimate and even primitive of uses ("dwelling" as a spatial reification of the originally active verb), these standards of arrangement and use are all the more charged with social mores. Indeed, it is difficult to ignore the extent to which dwellings have been organized, historically, to both enforce and reproduce social (read: patriarchal and hetero-normative) values and traditions.[25] Architectural theorist Mark Wigley traces these patterns in residential design to an historical wish to sequester women and female sexuality (Wigley, 1992, 358). He aligns this impetus with longstanding fantasies about the (architectural) meaning of sexual difference:

> The woman's body is seen as an inadequate enclosure because its boundaries are convoluted. While it is made of the same material as a man's body, it has been turned inside out. Her house has been disordered, leaving its walls full of openings. Consequently, she must always occupy a second house, a building, to protect her soul.[26]

Based on the above, one might mistakenly imagine that Sarah Winchester's sprawling mansion presented, in her time, an amplified variation on

Victorian hetero-normative space. According to historian Gwendolyn Wright, Victorian residential architecture deliberately sustained this legacy of feminine containment, translating and sublimating it within emerging ideas about privacy,[27] class,[28] and interiority[29]—as well as in, above all, ideas about the family.[30] Each of these values is reflected in the floor plans and stylistic tropes of Victorian dwellings (Wright, 1980). The sitting room, boudoir, and fainting room, as examples, were viewed as deeply feminine spaces whose names betrayed their essentially static uses. Victorian verbs associated with pregnancy and female illness—"lying in," for instance, during one's "confinement"—further underscored the extent to which women were obliged to remain indoors and inactive.[31]

Figure 8.1 Print of postcard of Winchester Mystery House before the 1906 earthquake.
Credit: Public Domain; California Room, San Jose Public Library.

Imagine, then, how people of her class and social context would have been confounded by Llanada Villa, the place where Sarah Winchester lavished by far the majority of her design attentions. As an architect, Winchester subverted many of these gender-space mores and by extension challenged the proprieties of architecture as a discipline. Most of the iconic images of the Winchester house consist of exterior photographs showing a Victorian mish-mash: jumbled and irregular turrets, balconies, dormers, and porticos, all stemming from an ever-expanding interior-scape which changed frequently over the course of two decades. It is difficult, from these images, to infer any particular hierarchy or organizational theme in the building's composition. To put this another way, if we imagine the Winchester house as a text, we must plainly confess our ignorance of its syntax. Yet to admit this ignorance is to confront directly our default expectations of hierarchy and "organization" in buildings of any type.

One might imagine that the interior spaces of the Winchester house offer a more reliable index of the building's architectural logic. In actuality, however, one's initial sense of the inside proves even less intuitive than its tumbling exteriors. Yes, the rooms and halls are constructed in the conventional ways of their time (and locale), using, for the most part, standard wood framing. Yes, the finishes—wood paneling, woven and embossed wall coverings, parquet floors, and stained glass windows—are also, by and large, common to the late Victorian era, particularly for an upscale home like this.

Nevertheless, something is decidedly *peculiar* inside the Winchester house and it is not necessarily the "bizarre" features pointed out by the tour guide. Architecturally speaking, the design of the Winchester house is distinctive in at least two significant ways: in the continuous flow of space between its rooms and halls, on the one hand, and because of the volume of daylight reaching *all* of its spaces—even its lowest, most interior parts—on the other.

We don't know, historically speaking, why Sarah Winchester chose to complicate the contours of the small farmhouse she purchased in 1886, an enigma to which we will return later. We do know, thanks to her biographer, that besides enjoying her involvement in the construction of her in-laws' substantial residence prior to moving to California, she also extensively subscribed to and read architectural journals, and in personal correspondence expressed ongoing interest in the design and furnishing of Llanada Villa (Ignoffo, 2010, 66, 67). The house itself, in its detail, demonstrates Sarah Winchester's ingenuity in solving certain kinds of architectural problems—structural ones as well as more imaginative ones, like how to use the building's roofs and gutters to capture and conserve storm water for later use in her green spaces and gardens;[32] how to let her servants know where to find her in the house; how to mediate between semi-public and deeply private uses; how to achieve thematic distinction in some areas while also maintaining stylistic consistency in room décor.[33] And so on.

Sarah Winchester's problem-solving intelligence extends to an overall logic in the house, even if its spatial priorities go against the grain of conventional residential design. Above all, an implicit sense of movement in the arrangement of its spaces confounds our habitual expectations for *stillness* in domestic interiors. The house reflects a spatiality (not a "space") that fosters a different standard for what building does or can do.

In the Winchester house, space is an effect of the fluid interplay between bodies and construction elements—not a resource to be commandeered. It takes you in but does not keep or contain you. It lets you go. Indeed, it actively ushers you through. The fixed positions recorded in photographs—iconic or otherwise—can't convey this effect; nor can the purely visual and auditory movement recorded in videos made by tourists and documentarians. Only embodied movement as such permits a full registration of the "mystery" embedded in Sarah Winchester's design. *Dwelling* in this residence does not mean staying still—nor can it mean sitting or lying down in the kinds of lady-like reposes usually associated with Victorian (with)drawing and fainting rooms. Instead, "dwelling" is a verb suggesting continuous and reflective passage: *this* space connecting with another and another; each one staking, claiming and then vacating its "roomness" to foster tentative correspondences in sense impressions: light and shadow, narrowing and widening, enclosure and expansion.

Figure 8.2 The Winchester Mystery House.

Credit: Photo by Maria McVarish.

In contradistinction to traditional homes of its time,[34] the Winchester house is, arguably, also organized around light and air. Daylight draws you in and leads you through its rooms. During waking hours, there is no need for electrical lighting or mechanical ventilation anywhere inside. Windows and skylights practically pull and bend the light to meet the needs of the building's recesses. The unlikely presence of daylight throughout the depths and layers of its rooms defies conventional architectural distinctions between inside and outside, object and space.

In these and other ways, the Winchester house obliterates the entrapping, stultifying, and normalizing functions of architecture. Indeed, winchester's work forces an awareness of two of the discipline's most basic conceits: on the one hand, architecture's presumption of a uniform, static and homogenous field of representational space; and on the other, its instrumentation of spatial experience (and, by extension, its active role in the reproduction of normative embodiment). When architectural space deviates from convention, as it does in the Winchester house, we suddenly perceive the profound and vacuous emptiness of "space" itself, as the (conceptual) absence against which substance is always posited. The Winchester house keeps asking questions about the presumptions of this kind of "*a priori*" space—licensing a renewed (or previously ill-perceived) attention to what is usually excluded and delineated by walls, floors, and ceilings. In so doing, it necessarily poses questions about the particular body, or bodily experience, of its traversers as well: are these sensations mine? Do *I* know them? Might they reflect something alien or unknown, even as I feel them? Or does having them continually re-make *me* by confronting me with a suddenly perceptible elusiveness in what I normally take for granted in the environment—thereby surprising my senses with reminders of what *isn't* there and filling me with a fleeting, tangible sense of loss? These kinds of questions might arise (even if preconsciously) in visitors to Sarah Wincheser's house, but we have no historical basis for asserting that they preoccupied its designer, or that ghosts motivated *her*.

Ghosts are the ambiguously insubstantial beings to whom we attribute our own unaccountable sensations. When we encounter them, we find ourselves, by definition, in a liminal space—a *gap*—whose apperception involves aspects of our immediate surroundings (so peculiar in the Winchester house) as well as a mnemic dimension of sensory residue, the byproduct of our long and cumulative conditioning within the built environment. Here, then, is one answer to the question of how haunting is possible: in the Winchester house, ghosts arise through Sarah Winchester's unique and unorthodox spatial aesthetic, which throws our expectations about space and dwelling into question.

The space of psychoanalytic work

We pay an unacknowledged price for the spatial claims of architecture in the form of a negative, residual spatiality—characterized here as a *gap*—which we largely ignore. In architectural and semiotic space, this gap results from the signifying gesture (of delineating rooms and walls, but equally in delineating the contours of objects and concepts through naming). In the psychoanalytic consulting room this gap is palpable not only in relation to speaking and naming, but also in a tangible form, emerging in connection with the physical and transferential setting. Here we both extend and depart from Freud's (1953b/1914) "gap" (147), a term he used at various points to characterize holes in memory left by the repression of unacknowledgeable wishes.[35] Perhaps our "gap" comes closer to what Marion Milner (2002), following art theorist Anton Ehrenzweig, called "depth mind." Depth mind performs tasks of integration through "a gap in consciousness," she writes, going on to consider "the possibility of there being something positive about emptiness, nothingness, whether empty unstructured space or the empty unstructured time that is silence" (276–77). In our use of this term, we include the "hollows in the real" of analytic space—tangibly perceived through present absences that enter and haunt the consulting room. Here, ghosts imbue the gaps between perceptual, mnemic and transferential space. The flesh-and-blood, listening presence of the analyst, combined with the physical surface of a holding environment, makes possible the visitation of losses; this "materialization" of the bond between the living and their dead is precisely what enables redress and mourning. Consequently, from this gap unfathomable dread may be glimpsed, breakdown, and madness confronted, and the "phantom's" erstwhile buried secret exhumed.[36] In psychoanalysis, Sam Gerson (2009) writes, "[w]e hope first that there is an engaged witness . . . the presence that lives in the gap, absorbs absence, and transforms our relation to loss" (1342).

In *Mourning and Melancholia*, Freud warned that the task of separation and dis-identification—facing and letting go of those who are gone, "bit by bit"—is an "extraordinarily painful" and complex process (1953a/1917, 245). Affective residua come to fill the hollows left by lost objects of the past, confounding the mourning process.[37] But clinical encounters with ghosts entail wresting the gaps, bringing these haunted spaces back into an environmental and temporal present whereby "that berserk state, in which the dead besiege the living," (Davoine and Gaudilliere, 2004, 193) may be revealed and understood, providing the conditions necessary for transformation.

The peculiar and quasi-spatial "gaps" we highlight here exist across registers of affect, memory, thought, and environment. They resemble Freud's (1953c/1919) notion of the uncanny insofar as they estrange the familiar. But Giuseppe Civitarese (2010), engaging Jose Bleger's[38] likewise pertinent notions, gets even closer to our "spatialized" gap by shifting the impetus of the *uncanny* from the internal realm of the psyche alone to its encroachment on the external "setting":

> As we know from clinical practice and from life, breaches or discontinuities in the setting give rise to disorientation and disquiet. They have the consequence of a painful sense of loss of familiarity, a form of vertigo that may descend into actual anxiety. Something alien bursts on to the scene all of a sudden. A secure place becomes unrecognizable and inhospitable. The entire fragility of the foundations of a subjectivity that cannot but discover itself to be rooted in the encounter with the other is seen to reappear (29).

The gaps we describe diverge from Freud's and even from Civitarese's depictions insofar as they really *do* originate in an extimate not-me figure (i.e. the beloved, the ghost). This is apparent in the haunting moments of recognition when emotionally-infused links forge themselves in a treatment encounter, springing from the shared unconscious to imbue the likewise shared sense-environment. What here springs forth in the consulting room resembles the hollow in the real, which makes space in the Winchester mansion feel peculiar. Just as the person of the analyst is transferentially used to elicit and hold difficult feelings, the setting (whether clinical or, in the case of the Winchester house, cultural), being "unconventional"—outside of the time and space of routine life—may be used to mediate the *past-ness* of a tangible loss. In other words, if the clinical setting is held in awareness by the analyst, it may be instrumental[ized] in confronting losses. These breaches in convention that the analytic encounter bring to bear on the analysand break through the repetition of his psychical narratives, just as Winchester's unorthodox architecture jars the lulling tendencies of spatial habituation such that—in both cases—ghosts may slip through to realms of perception, intelligibility, and emotional lucidity.

Psychical and architectural gaps like the ones we describe—between representation and real, between sense memory and environment, between secret and sadness—allow us contact with our ghosts, such that, with support, we can face them and begin to absorb the significance that their traumas bring to our lives. As Civitarese (2010) concludes regarding the risks inherent in discontinuities in the setting: "[I]t is only by exposing itself to these risks that the organism can integrate the new, can change, adapt to and learn from reality, on each occasion establishing a new equilibrium of the self" (29).

From psychical loops to cultural narratives: the ghost story

When convention dampens awareness of spatial experience, shepherding us in unconscious repetition, the gap remains obscured, just as repetition might occlude it in the aftermath of trauma. Habituation to familiar forms of experience bars contact with ghosts. The ghost story, as the traditional form in which ghost encounters are *re*-counted and exchanged, is, ironically, just such a convention and for this reason the ghost story must be distinguished from the ghost.

At its darkest, a ghost story is a self-reinforcing, reiterated narrative that fetishizes the ghost for mass consumption, striking a common nerve precisely where larger-scaled cultural losses—and the collective guilt and shame resulting from them—haunt a population. Its repetitive re-telling serves to distance listeners and story-tellers alike from the responsibilities of facing, much less mourning, these losses. The ghost story as we distinguish it enacts the same haunting as the "phantoms" that Abraham and Torok (1994) describe: "[W]hat haunts are not the dead but the gaps left within us by the secrets of others . . . the tombs of others. The phantoms in folklore merely objectify a metaphor active in the unconscious: the burial of an unspeakable fact" (172).

The ghost story is thus a trope for collective abjection: the "not-me" status of the "ghost" is forever confined to narration, bearing the emotional price of a no-space between the living and the dead. This no-space functions as a cross-temporal foreclosure, a blind madness passed from one generation to the next, obfuscating historical traumas.[39] It is in effect an aporia, mystifying facts of blatant social consequence. In this sense, it functions analogously to what Judith Butler (2010), in the context of politically sanctioned violence, calls a "frame." In wars, governments and media frame public perception of factional violence through selective imaging and reporting. Certain lives are thereby rendered recognizable and valuable and thus "grievable."[40] Those outside the frame go unrecognized and so, when killed, are left ungrieved. The alternate reification of some and omission of other lives that framing entails serves to construct for the public "a certain reality . . . through our very act of passive reception, since what we are being recruited into is . . . both its constriction and its interpretation . . ."(xii). Jingoistic framing, Butler goes on to argue, inures us to the "precariousness"[41] of *all* lives.

Framing devalues what is omitted precisely in order to valorize what it includes; in this way the ghost story bolsters and perverts the negating spatiality of consciousness that we have called the "gap." "When versions of reality are excluded or jettisoned to a domain of unreality," Butler writes, "then specters are produced that haunt the ratified version of reality, animated and de-ratified traces. In this sense the frame seeks to institute an interdiction on mourning: there is no destruction, and there is no loss" (xii–xiii).

The ghosts we seek to exhume from the Winchester ghost story exist outside the margins of what Butler calls our cultural "norms of recognition" (12). Flickering in the liminal gaps that hallow the spaces of the Winchester mansion, they ride its halls and stairs, an aggregated "remainder of 'life' – suspended and spectral – that limns and haunts every normative stance of life" (7). The Winchester "TM" myth combines their individual fates as gun victims into a more-or-less coherent and singular ghost story bound to a single (if sprawling) house. It *de-figures* their personhood within a generalizing, anesthetizing, and amnestic—if nonetheless captivating—form of entertainment.

Such de-figuration and re-framing draws a live charge from our country's ongoing debate about guns. As tour guides recount the legend of Sarah Winchester's mad constructions, their story excludes and ignores the enduring and pernicious effects of gun violence, even as thousands of people die by guns each day. Those who own and use them often claim that the deadliness of guns, the threat of violence they represent, is precisely what protects lives (and property and beliefs) from the violence of others. The implication, in this line of reasoning, is that an individual with a gun operates within his own (closed) legal and moral system.[42] The pull of a trigger reflects that person's "right" to decide whose life, property, and beliefs are recognizable. By this logic, anyone who dies at the receiving end of a gun is already judged ungrievable by the gun wielder.

In lieu of confronting the ghosts of gun violence, The Winchester Mystery House™ ghost story invents a crazy and superstitious woman who must bear the burden of atonement for violence inflicted by guns,[43] misaligning her with Spiritualism, a cultural form of grieving actually considered normal in her time. The gaps underlying the Winchester™ story cast an enduring, insidious shadow of past and present wars, vigilante murder, societal fear, and the broad violence, hatred and "ungrievability" that such fear still incites.

Conclusion

One mystery of the Winchester Mystery House may never be solved: why Sarah Winchester decided to build, and keep building, the Winchester mansion. Her story, to the extent that we can know or guess it, combines profoundly unusual and evocative features: an ironic and tragic life story survived with remarkable resilience; an enigmatic signature work in the form of the sprawling mansion-*cum*-tourist attraction; and the dramatic events and cultural shifts that shaped the world during Sarah Winchester's lifetime, leaving unspeakable marks on our own long-buried great- and great-great-grandparents.

One is compelled to fill in these gaps—to be curious about what drove Mrs. Winchester to hypothesize about her powers and her inner world. Because she was private and non-reactive in the face of negative public attention, her story was and remains vulnerable to speculation. As the flowing spaces of her house attest, however, Sarah Winchester herself is not held captive by the myths surrounding her. We are.

But there are other, more objective reasons why the Winchester house must be haunted. Her work on the mansion went against the conventions for Victorian women, even while she ostensibly worked within the Victorian architectural tradition. She had privilege and wealth, but she was female; she was female, but she was neither a wife nor a mother (the hollow space shows up here through the absence of these members of her family);[44] she was creative and productive, but she was untrained, professionally; she became empowered socially and economically, but grew physically disabled and disfigured; she was publicly visible (conducting business, litigating, purchasing, constructing or improving multiple properties, etc.) but private by nature. For these reasons, she was seen as a contradictory or eccentric public figure, fomenting projections of suspicion and antipathy.

With the sensationalist ghost story that enshrouds experience of Sarah Winchester's house, there is little room to appreciate the outstanding architectural feat she—along with many long-term, committed laborers—achieved. At the same time, the Mystery House™ story minimizes any possibility of confronting the cultural ghosts that really do linger in the aftermath of this vibrant and brutal era of US history. They rise out of 620,000 soldier deaths incurred in the Civil War[45] (Faust, 2008, xi), from the countless[46] lives lost in slavery that occasioned that war and the massive losses incurred by Native peoples in the West—of their territories and their lives—at the hands of white settlers. They rise, too, from innumerable children who succumbed to untreatable disease and countless mothers and wives lost to childbirth. The story incorporates but also obscures these many reasons why Spiritualism was needed to link survivors with the loved ones they lost.

Epilogue

After sunset, when daylight wanes, darkness gradually signals a withdrawal of space, encompassing or reigning in the flux of day. Inside the Winchester house at night, one is ensconced in layers of mediating buffers to other zones. From here, outside seems very remote—an almost negligible memory. When the lights turn out, there remains only *this* place, this room, and a series of latent elsewheres—the further afield, the less considered. Those places exist only through glass. They rest, hovering as filaments to tomorrow or from yesterday. There is, between you and there, here and then, only dark proximity.

Notes

1 http://www.cnn.com/2013/12/30/justice/colorado-school-shooting/ *accessed 13 September 2014, 9:42 PST.*

2 The Winchester house has provided the setting—physical or legendary—for countless works of popular media: television shows, feature films, video games, comic books, and theatrical performances, to name just a few. See http://en.wikipedia.org/wiki/Winchester_Mystery_House#In_popular_culture *accessed 2 January 2014, 13:26 PST.*

3 Even during Sarah Winchester's lifetime rumors about the Winchester house abounded (see footnote 12, below). The two families that have operated the property as a tourist attraction continuously since purchasing it after Sarah Winchester's death in the 1920s have doubtless had a hand in promoting and supplementing the stories that their tour guides daily present as fact. See Mary Jo Ignoffo, 2010, 114, 138, 141, 212–13, 197, 206–14.

4 Although many have written speculatively about Sarah Winchester specifically in connection with the Winchester Mystery House™, to date Mary Jo Ignoffo (2010) has

offered the most comprehensive and best-researched biography of her. Much of the biographical information for this chapter was gleaned from Ignoffo's book.

5 Likely of cholera during a seasonal epidemic (Ignoffo, 2010, 12).

6 Ignoffo, 2010, 7–9. "Undoubtedly Sarah Lockwood Pardee Winchester's lifelong appreciation of carpentry and fine woodworking was more than a little influenced by generations of Pardee joiners" (Ignoffo, 2010, 15). Her "fascination with the skill of woodworkers never waned" (Ignoffo, 2010, 19–20).

7 In this regard, Sarah Winchester was like many women of her class and time. With reference to her design of the Winchester Mystery House in particular, Sarah Winchester was not formally trained in architecture; she was, however, self-taught through experience and, in later life, also through focused reading and observation.

8 The infant Annie was named after William's beloved sister Annie Dye (Ignoffo, 2008, 36), who died in childbirth three years prior to Annie Winchester's appearance. The baby that took Annie Dye's life (and himself died 19 days later), in turn, had been named after William (Ignoffo, 2008, 35).

9 Sarah was 45 when she moved to Los Altos, California from her hometown of New Haven. By then, like many of her generation, her life was replete with losses: the deaths of her daughter (1866) and husband (1881) as previously mentioned, but also of her father (1869), mother and father-in-law (1880), and eldest sister (1884) (Ignoffo, 2008, 35–82).

10 Winchester—somewhat against the grain—also provided several of her workers accommodation in the house, along with their families (Ignoffo, 2010, 174–76).

11 At the time of Sarah Winchester's death, the house had long been in disuse. It was described in official documents of the period as "a large frame dwelling in bad state of repair and outbuilding, small pumping place and gardens" (Cited in Ignoffo, 2010, 207). The parcel included about 68 acres of land, nearly half of which were actively farmed. The land value was set at $125,000 but the house itself was considered to have no value (Ignoffo, 2010, 207). Ownership has stayed within the family that initially leased and eventually bought the property. Throughout the last century they have persistently obfuscated information regarding Sarah Winchester and the mansion (Ignoffo, 2010, 141, 207–14). See also https://answers.yahoo.com/question/index?qid=20070702152213AAnmQSP for information about the property's owners. *Accessed 1 April 2014, 16:27 PST.*

12 According to Ignoffo (2010), the first commentaries on the Winchester mansion's "unwieldy and unaccountably unfinished" appearance were published in local newspapers (namely the San Jose Mercury Herald and San Francisco Examiner) in 1895. The articles assigned a succession of motivations to the owner. "First and foremost, papers identified [Sarah Winchester] as superstitious," Ignoffo writes. "Added to that, in order, were claims that she was a snob, she was afraid of death, she felt guilty over deaths caused by Winchester guns, she was a spiritualist, and, following the 1906 earthquake, she was mad. Angry ghosts and associations with the occult appeared in articles about Winchester after the earthquake – relatively late in the complex story line" (138).

Ignoffo (2010) notes that Winchester's regard for Japanese culture and her willingness to hire Asian workers was a factor in the genesis of the Winchester ™ myth, as well. "Beginning at this time [between approximately 1906 and 1910], stories in the newspapers claimed that Sarah Winchester hosted unusual religious rituals in her home. 'One of the latest yarns is to the effect that religious services of a strange character are conducted in the house and that Orientals participate in them,' one newspaper reported" (176).

13 http://www.winchestermysteryhouse.com/thenumber13.cfm *accessed 13 September 2014, 15:54 PST.* See also Ignoffo's (2010, 209, 211) dispute with this story.

14 During this historical period pioneers of psychoanalysis, including Freud, Jung, and Ferenczi, were interested in the occult, spiritualism, and telepathy. See, for example, Massicotte (2014, 92) who suggests that interest among these early psychoanalytic thinkers mainly "focus[ed] on the unconscious conflicts expressed in spiritual communications."

15 For historical references written in the last century on Spiritualism, see Doyle, Arthur Conan (1926). *The history of spiritualism*. London: Casell and Co.; Braude, A. (1989). *Radical spirits: Spiritualism and women's rights in nineteenth-century America*. Boston: Beacon Press; Carroll, Bret (1997). *Spiritualism in antebellum America*. Bloomington, IN: Indiana University Press. Also: Massiote, Claudie (2014). Psychical transmissions: Freud, spiritualism, and the occult. *Psychoanalytic Dialogues*, 24, 88–102.

16 For example, according to documentation from the American Civil War era accumulated by Drew Gilpin Faust (2008, 181), by the outbreak of the war there were 30,000 spiritual mediums operating across the US, 30 Spiritualist groups meeting in Philadelphia, 240,000 regularly-practicing Spiritualists in New York State (6 percent of its total population), 20,000 in Louisiana, and 10,000 in Tennessee.

17 Ultimately, the work of mourning re-affirms a survivor's connection to living. The melancholic, by contrast, exists within a veritable circuit of loss—living with enduring but largely unconscious contact between memory (the trace of what is absent) and actuality. See Freud, 1953a/1917, 244–45.

18 In 1637, Réné Descartes replaced Euclid's axiomatic, logic-based geometry from the fourth century, B.C. with a graphic and notational coordinate system for representing real-number relationships. In 1687, in his *Philosophiæ Naturalis Principia Mathematica*, Sir Isaac Newton called this continuous and synchronic space "absolute." Newton further stipulated that "[a]bsolute space, in its own nature, without regard to anything external, remains always similar and immovable." Source: http://www.universetoday.com/87941/absolute-space/ acc*essed 15 March 2014, 18:14 PST.*

19 Immanuel Kant gave space an *a priori* status (Kant, I. 2005, 90 and 109).

20 "Representation" being, in a manner of speaking, the appearance or ghost of a thing: "The character of imaginary composition, of the imaginary element of the object, makes of it what one might call the substance of appearance, the material of a living lure – an apparition open to the deception of an *Erscheinung* . . .; that is to say that by means of which the appearance is sustained, but which is also at the same time an unremarkable apparition – something that creates that *Vor*, that third element, something that is produced starting from the Thing. *Vorstellung* is something that is essentially fragmented. It is that around which Western philosophy since Aristotle and *φαντασία* has always revolved.

"*Vorstellung* is understood by Freud in a radical sense, in the form in which it appears in a philosophy that is essentially marked by the theory of knowledge. And that is the remarkable thing about it. He assigned to it in an extreme form the character philosophers themselves have been unable to reduce it to, namely, that of an empty body, a ghost, a pale incubus of the relation to the world, an enfeebled *jouissance* . . ." (Lacan, 1992, 60–61).

21 See, for example, Ferdinand de Saussure's chapters on "Linguistic value" and "Syntagmatic relations and associative relations" in *Course in General Linguistics* (Saussure, 2000, 110–120).

22 The environment, by this definition, is already haunted—a manifest accretion of different embodied ideas about space.

23 See Elizabeth Grosz's (2002, 3–47) chapters, "Embodying Space: An Interview" and "Lived Spatiality (The Spaces of Corporeal Desire)." Also, "Body Images: Neurophysiology and Corporeal Mappings" and "Lived Bodies: Phenomenology of the Flesh" (Grosz, 1994, 62–111).

24 So much so that it is considered reasonable to bring suit against the designer of any building that departs from the Uniform Building Code in which these standards are codified. The legality of such a lawsuits is predicated on the general understanding that the more we become habituated to particular conventions of space, the more likely it will be that the subtlest deviations in measure or proportion may lead a careless occupant to significant injury.

25 Many of these standards, in Western countries, were laid out in Leon Battista Alberti's 1452 treatises on residential design and have hardly changed since (Wigley, 1992).
26 Wigley draws direct relationships between the arrangement of domestic spaces and Enlightenment values and effects: "It is this exposure by a system of classification, rather than a simple enclosure by walls, that entraps her. Just as the gap between spaces, the divisions of the house, represent both the order and that which is ordered" (Wigley, 1992, 341).
27 "Places for privacy in a middle-class home were the smallest and least visible of spaces, but they were carefully defined and, in general, well situated" (Wright, 1980, 39–40). Wright studies gender and power roles in Victorian dwellings by tracing their expression through standardized floor plans of the era. Mark Wigley, for his part, connects the history of domestic privacy to a broader cultural elaboration of social forms: "Each shift in the emergence of private space involves transformations of such systems (private correspondence, portraits, the bellcord, the diary, the corridor, the novel, the cabinet). The house is never a self-sufficient spatial device" (Wigley, 1992, 350).
28 "*The Theory of the Leisure Class* [by Thorstein Veblen], published in 1899, documented the ways in which 'conspicuous consumption' was replacing conspicuous leisure as the most visible means for demonstrating an individual's cultural reputation. And architecture constituted a definite part of this trend: styles were usually based, [Veblen] charged, on pretense and display, as well as on shelter and personal expression. The values of waste, expense, and elevation from 'familiarity with vulgar life' represented the principal determinants of form" (Wright, 1980, 113).
29 "A consequence of the so-called 'separation of home and work' . . . was the development of new gendered definitions of domesticity, in which the prime function of the home was to provided shelter; physical shelter in the traditional sense of a roof over one's head, but beyond that a private, almost spiritual shelter from the outside masculinized world of work" (Moira, 1999, 103).
30 "In maintaining a clean, artistic, personalized setting for the family's activities, the good wife was guiding her husband and children, forming their characters through the "influence" of the home environment. Dark suggestions that the saloon, the club, the office, or the bright lights of the city might intrude made this domestic mission all the more critical" (Wright, 1980, 10).
31 S. J. Kleinberg provides a critique of this generalized view of women's passive domesticity during the Victorian era, revisiting Charlotte Perkins Gilman's 1891 novel, *The Yellow Wallpaper*. The latter provides the quintessential image of women's imprisonment within the domicile: "The wallpaper, with its blotches and stains, accentuates her post-partum depression, as do the threats to send her to Dr. S. Weir Mitchell, an anti-feminist physician who prescribed inactivity as the cure for neurasthenic women" (Kleinberg, 1999, 150).
32 Sarah Winchester's interest in these kinds of mechanical and operational features may have reflected a larger cultural response to "environmental" diseases like tuberculosis, which had taken her husband. Gwendolyn Wright chronicles this Victorian concern for health and hygiene as it entered the domestic realm and became a particular preoccupation of women. In 1885, for example, a "Mrs. H. M. Plunkett, editor of the Sanitary Department of the New York Independent, published a morality tale about a woman whose inadequate care of her basement led to her husband's untimely death. She then went on to explain in detail what women should look for in terms of pipes, cisterns, and water tables when they bought or built a house" (Wright, 1980, 31).
33 No public records exist to illustrate the furnishings of Sarah Winchester's home during her tenure there.
34 See, for example, Walter Benjamin's (1999, 212–227) convolute on "The Interior, The Trace" concerning this period of residential architecture.

35 Also, see Freud, S. (1953). Draft K, The Neuroses of Defence from Extracts from the Fliess Papers. *SE I*, London: Hogarth Press, 228–229. (Originally published 1892); Freud, S. (1953). Some General Remarks on Hysterical Attacks. *SE IX*, London: Hogarth Press, 234. (Originally published 1909); Freud, S. (1953). Five Lectures on Psycho-analysis. *SE XI*, London: Hogarth Press, 20. (Originally published 1910).

36 Abraham and Torok (1984) observe, "Should the child have parents 'with secrets,' parents whose speech is not exactly complementary to their unstated repressions, he will receive from them a gap in the unconscious, an unknown, unrecognized knowledge, a *nescience*, subjected to a form of 'repression' before the fact.

"The buried speech of the parent becomes (a) dead (gap) without a burial place, in the child. This unknown phantom comes back to haunt from the unconscious and leads to phobias, madness, and obsessions. Its effect can persist through several generations and determine the fate of an entire family line" (footnote, 222).

37 In *Attention and Interpretation*, Bion (1970) similarly distinguishes what is missing from the emotional residua—the present-absence—left in place of that actual thing/object that was lost: "[I]f the geometer's concept of space derives from *an experience of* 'the place where something was', . . . it is in my experience meaningful to say that 'a feeling of depression' is 'the place where a breast or other lost object was' and that 'space' is 'where depression, or some other emotion, used to be'" (10, our italics).

38 See Bleger, J. (2013). *Symbiosis and Ambiguity*. London: Routledge. (First published in 1967 as *Simbiosis y ambigüedad: Estudio psicoanalítico* by Paidós, Buenos Aires.)

39 As above, this aligns with Abraham and Torok's (1984) concept of "encrypted identifications."

40 "Grievability" is a concept that Butler has developed across several essays (see for example "Melancholy gender, refused identification" in *The psychic life of power* (1997). Stanford, CA: Stanford University Press; *Precarious life: The powers of mourning and violence* (2004). London and New York: Verso Press). In *Frames of War* (2010) she associates grievability with another of her core concepts, "precariousness." "To say that life is injurable, for instance, or that it can be lost, destroyed, or systematically neglected to the point of death, is to underscore not only the finitude of a life (that death is certain) but also its precariousness (that life requires various social and economic conditions to be met in order to sustain life). Precariousness implies living socially, that is, the fact that one's life is always in some sense in the hands of the other. . . . Precisely because a living being may die, it is necessary to care for that being so that it may live. Only under conditions in which loss would matter does the value of the life appear. Thus, grievability is a presupposition for the life that matters. . . . The future anterior, 'a life has been lived', is presupposed at the beginning of a life that has only begun to be lived. In other words 'this will be a life that will have been lived' is the presupposition of a grievable life . . . Without grievability there is no life, or, rather, there is something living that is other than life. Instead, 'there is a life that will never have been lived,' sustained by no regard, no testimony, and ungrieved when lost."

41 See footnote 40, above. See footnote 40, above. For clarification, the conceptualization and form of Butler's "frame" differs from what is commonly understood as the "psychoanalytic frame." However, it may be interesting to contemplate potential resonances, as well as dissonances, in the ways these two notions of "frame" function.

42 The Second Amendment to the US Constitution, which has all but assumed mythic status in our culture, articulates another vertex of the aporia we characterize here—minus the entertainment value: "A well regulated Militia, being necessary to the security of a free State, the right of the people to keep and bear Arms, shall not be infringed." By obfuscating the link between self and state, the law reifies a paranoid conflation between an individual's sense of his right to defend himself, and the *responsibility* of all citizens—militia and civilians alike—to "the security of a free state."

(Source: http://www.law.cornell.edu/wex/second_amendment *accessed 6 July 2014, 12:13 PST)*

43 "Yet the press superimposed guilt on Sarah Winchester after the turn of the century. Since she benefited from the repeater, she would also be considered responsible for it. It was as if she personified a conscience, one that was so guilt-racked over countless deaths that she suffered her way into madness in a burgeoning and ghost-infested mansion" (Ignoffo, 2008, 141).

44 On her death certificate, Sarah Winchester's personal companion listed Sarah's occupation as "housewife" (Ignoffo, 2008, 197).

45 Faust (2008) calculates that "the Civil War's rate of death, its incidence in comparison with the size of the American population, was six times that of World War II. A similar rate, about 2 percent, in the United States today would mean six million fatalities" (*xi*).

46 While it is possible to find consistent estimates of the number of soldiers killed in the Civil War, it is not possible to find such consistent data on the numbers of deaths of American slaves or of Native Americans killed around that time period. As *uncountable*, these lives fall under the rubric of Butler's "ungrievable;" they are relegated outside the margins of lives considered "precarious" in conventional historical accounts (see footnote 40, above for an explanation of Butler's use of these terms).

To appreciate the wide variations in statistics, see for example Thornton, Russell (1987). *American Indian holocaust and survival*. Norman, Oklahoma: University of Oklahoma Press, 104–108; Michno, Gregory (2003). *Encyclopedia of Indian wars: Western battles and skirmishes, 1850–1890*. Missoula, MT: Mountain Publishing Press, 353–369; Stannard, David (1993). *American holocaust: Columbus and the conquest of the new world*. New York: Oxford University Press; Lewy, Guenter (2004). *Were American Indians the victims of genocide?* History News Network: George Mason University, http://historynewsnetwork.org/article/7302 *accessed 13 December 2104, 17:15 PST*; Mintz, S. *Facts about the slave trade and slavery*. The Gilder Lehrman Institute on American History, http://www.gilderlehrman.org/history-by-era/slavery-and-anti-slavery/resources/facts-about-slave-trade-and-slavery *accessed 14 December 2014, 14:35 PST;* 'Shahadah, Alik (2005). *African holocaust: Not just history, but legacy*. http://www.africanholocaust.net/html_ah/holocaustspecial.htm *accessed 14 December 2014, 15:00 PST.*

Bibliography

Abraham, N., & Torok, M. (1984). "The lost object—me": Notes on identification within the crypt. *Psychoanalytic Inquiry*, 4: 221–242.

Abraham N., & Torok, M. (1994). *The shell and the kernel*. Chicago: University of Chicago Press.

Benjamin, W. (1999). *The arcades project*. Trans. H. Eiland & K. McLaughlin. Cambridge, MA and London: The Belknap Press of Harvard University.

Bion, W. (1970). *Attention and interpretation*. London: Tavistock Publications.

Butler, J. (2010). *Frames of war*. London and New York: Verso.

Civitarese, G. (2010). *The intimate room*. London and New York: Routledge.

Davoine, F., & Gaudilliere, J. M. (2004). *History beyond trauma: Whereof one cannot speak, thereof one cannot remain silent*. New York: Other Press.

Evans, D. (2005). *An introductory dictionary of Lacanian psychoanalysis*. London and New York: Routledge.

Faust, D. G. (2008). *This republic of suffering: death and the American civil war*. New York: Random House.

Freud, S. (1953a). Mourning and melancholia. *SE XIV*, London: Hogarth Press, 244–245. (Originally published 1917.)

Freud, S. (1953b). Remembering, repeating and working through. *SE XII*, London: Hogarth Press, 145–156. (Originally published 1914.)

Freud, S. (1953c). The “Uncanny”. *SE XVII*, London: Hogarth Press, 217–256. (Originally published 1919.)
Gerson, S. (2009). When the third is dead: Memory, mourning, and witnessing in the aftermath of the holocaust. *International Journal of Psychoanalysis*, 90: 1341–57.
Grosz, E. (1994). *Volatile bodies*. Bloomington and Indianapolis: Indiana University Press.
Grosz, E. (2002). *Architecture from the outside: Essays of virtual and real spaces*. Cambridge, MA: The MIT Press.
Ignoffo, M. J. (2010). *Captive of the labyrinth: Sarah Winchester heiress to the rifle fortune*. Columbia, MO: University of Missouri Press.
Kant, I. (2005). *Prolegomena to any future metaphysics*. Trans. P. Lucas and G. Zoller. New York: Oxford University Press. (Originally published 1783.)
Kleinberg, S. J. (1999). ‘Gendered space: Housing, privacy and domesticity in the nineteenth-century United States’ In I. Bryden & J. Floyd (eds.), *Domestic space: Reading the nineteenth-century interior*. Manchester and New York: Manchester University Press, 142–161.
Lacan, J. (1992). *Seminar VII: The ethics of psychoanalysis, 1959–60*. Trans. D. Porter. New York: W.W. Norton and Company, Inc.
Massicotte, C. (2014). Psychical transmissions: Freud, spiritualism, and the occult. *Psychoanalytic Dialogues*, 24: 88–102.
Milner, M. (2002). *The suppressed madness of sane men*. Hove and New York: Brunner-Routledge.
Moira, D. (1999). Tranquil havens? Critiquing the idea of home as the middle-class sanctuary. In I. Bryden & J. Floyd (eds.), *Domestic space: Reading the nineteenth-century interior*. Manchester and New York: Manchester University Press.
Proust, M. (1913). *Remembrance of things past: Swann's Way*. Paris: Grasset and Gallimard.
Saussure, F. de. (2000). *Course in general linguistics*. Trans. Roy Harris. Chicago: Open Court Publishing, Inc. (Originally published 1912.)
Wigley, M. (1992). Untitled: The housing of gender. In B. Colomina (ed.), *Sexuality and space*. New York: Princeton Architectural Press, 327–389.
Wright, G. (1980). *Moralism and the model home: Domestic architecture and cultural conflict in Chicago*. New York and Chicago: The University of Chicago Press.

Chapter 9

First kiss, last word

Stairway to heaven

Adrienne Harris

June 23, 2011. My husband, the film historian Robert Sklar, and I are having dinner in Madrid, winding down after an afternoon of demonstrations in the streets. Students, citizens, older couples, babies in strollers pushed by parents, all have been demonstrating and we have marched with them. I had decided to try to teach the demonstrators a chant from the 1960s, a remnant of that heightened politicized time in America, still lodged in my memory.

I cannot seem to make the chant rhyme in Spanish. "2–4–6–8. Organize and smash the state." I remember the cadence, the feeling of shouting in the streets, the feeling of '68, our youth, mirrored in the intense young faces on that Madrid street, over 40 years later. The photos I took then from the demonstration stay circling on my computer. That day was the beginning of a celebratory trip to Spain. We were also on our way to a conference where I and a group of colleagues were giving papers on ghosts.

Later that day, we are at dinner, thinking of all the spirit and history, personal and collective that we were infused with. We are going the next day to Barcelona, a city we love being in. The conference will begin back in Madrid after the weekend and we will meet up with my fellow panelists, members of a group I had initiated. I find myself talking to Bob about this group's project—ghosts—the uncanny. Ghosts, I say to him, are connected, in some way, to the disruption of mourning.

So, a little backstory. The book in which this essay now sits, was developed within an on-going supervision group which found itself steeped in the uncanny. Undoubtedly, we were under the collective influence of Sam Gerson's paper "When the Third is Dead" (2009), but also, as we were to discover, under the pressure of individual histories. However this project began, our ongoing clinical discussions focused on a set of questions. What happens when objects are neither fully internal nor external? What happens when spatial cues, or cues of temporalities move off their conventional axes and we find ourselves living in familiar but strange situations? What makes time stop, or rather what allows or requires a person to step outside of the flow of time and history, transmitting the past into the present through oddness of gait, or speech, or thought? How is the experience of haunting so inexorably passed on from parent to child?

Increasingly in clinical worlds, we become more and more familiar with these migrant forms of life and memory and anguish. Four years ago, when our group undertook to look at ghosts in the consulting room, thanks to Gerson and contemporary writing on intergenerational transmission of trauma, we felt in new territory. That night in Madrid, I gave Bob a road map into this clinical world we were crafting. Our group had found itself following the train of history: the séances and mediums after the Civil War and the First World War, and from there I found my way back into the world of cinema, a keen and lively place for ghosts.

What I remember then is that we start talking about the postwar era, stimulated by a mélange of topics on our minds. We had been at a show of contemporary art at Reine Sofia, provocatively titled "Who won the war?" an exhibit looking at the political struggle between abstract expressionism and the more political outlier art produced in the postwar era in Spain and in Latin America. We were also talking about the book Bob was in the midst of writing on postwar cinema, and we talked about my ghost project. His book was tentatively titled *Nightmare Factory: American Cinema from 1945–1960*. My posse was working on ghosts, zombies, and dybbuks. The show at the Reine Sofia was a critical look at postwar abstract art and its political, often Situationist accompaniments in Spain and Europe and Latin America after the war. We had both been struck by the struggle, in the art and in the curated show, to come to terms with the '30s and '40s in Spain, and thus to the presence of unsettled ghosts.

We had been reading an article in the paper while we were in Madrid, recounting the recovery of the poet/hero Lorca's body and perhaps also the discovery of his killer. Pain and dissociation flowed in many directions and across many histories. It was impossible in that time in Spain not to feel the residue of so much unprocessed trauma.

When I tell Bob that our group, which is coming to Madrid, wants to do a book on ghosts in the consulting room, he suddenly remembers a film from 1946. *Stairway to Heaven* is its American title, though it is from the British director Michael Powell and the Hungarian screenwriter Emil

Pressberger. The film sits in the tradition of odd, quirky, British war films, inflected through Central Europe. Other flights. Other fights. Other losses. In England, the film is called *A Matter of Life and Death.*

What I held onto from that June night's conversation and Bob's reverie, is that *Stairway to Heaven* was a film in which David Niven appears at first as a doomed, dying British airman, magically saved from death through an error made in heaven, but really, finally, saved by love in the form of the intense longing of a woman, an American wireless operator—Kim Hunter—with whom Niven talks, as he sits in his doomed, smoking airplane.

Over a year later, when I finally see the film myself, I am plunged into the opening scene of the film as Niven and the wireless operator (Kim Hunter) talk on the wireless, as his damaged plane circulates the English coastline, ominously lurching and belching fire. We learn that the plane has already been deserted by one of the crew, presumably fallen to his death, while a remaining man lies in the cockpit, already dead, and staring blank-eyed at the camera. The plane circles down towards the sea, heading for the English coastline.

There is desperation and lyrical sensuality in these voices as the pilot and the American woman talk on the wireless. Love blossoms between the Yankee girl and the romantic hero. Niven is gloriously, glamorously, saying goodbye. This man knows death approaches as he falls out of the plane into the sea. The camera is high above a long flat beach that seems to be caressed with furling slow waves. We hear the woman's voice. We hear that she is desperate to save him. She begs him to stay alert and stay with her. She will guide him to life.

In the deathly danger of that moment and their talk, the airman and the wireless operator fall in love. He falls. And then a magical fantasy of reunion, and survival ensues. Heaven and earth battle for the fallen pilot. Love is in struggle with death. Can the clock be turned back, can a death notice be rescinded? It is 1946 when this film appears.

The 1950s, when Bob and I actually might have seen this film (he in California, I in Canada), is the world of his and my adolescence. It is the complex era that comes before our generation's politicized life in the '60s and '70s. Much of Bob's and my adult life included a dawning understanding of how deeply we (and our different professions: cinema studies and psychoanalysis) had been shaped by that era, even as we had also imagined ourselves in rebellion from the period.

On that evening in Madrid, I am thinking, with pleasure, that Bob can write a chapter on this film for the book he is writing on American postwar cinema (1945–1960), and that this essay could also be in my ghost book project as well. But as you can see, it is I who am writing the chapter.

As we walk home to the hotel I have a very familiar thought, almost a mantra, it was so often repeated. It is a thought that I had continuously and consciously, over 30 years. It was an idea, a judgment about Bob that never varied: the pleasure of talking, the persistence of interest. Over thousands of dinners, everywhere, sitting across from each other, there was never a moment when I was not interested in what we might be talking about. I wanted always to know what he was thinking and always it was interesting. This essay on *Stairway to Heaven* is one of the legacies of that abiding intense shared conversations, life, love, and interest.

Four days later, in Barcelona, Bob has a fall. I don't see it happen, but he is coming back to consciousness as I circle back to him on my bicycle. He is lying on his back, breathing heavily, and then those beautiful blue eyes open. Later, we sit in the ambulance and then even later in the ER. It is quiet. Close. We talk. I remember using my phone as a stopwatch to register his heart rate. Neither of us appears to be frightened and as he tells me, quite matter of factly, he is not in pain. He gets sleepy and as the young doctors wheel him away in a gurney, I see he is falling asleep.

I have many ways to tell this story. A man falls from his bicycle on a sunny morning in Barcelona, later he falls asleep, and is never awake again. Surgery. Intensive care. Calls and efforts on both sides of the Atlantic. Family arriving. Bedside vigils. It is finally clear that nothing more can be done and the mechanical engines keeping heart and brain in tempo are stopped. Or perhaps his death actually occurs that first afternoon. Brain bleeds, impossible to stop. Perhaps the next days are just the rest of us catching up to him.

Nov 4, 2012. I find that finally I can bear to watch *Stairway to Heaven* on Netflix and I start to take notes. It is four days after the gruesome and terrifying Hurricane Sandy has ripped coastal towns around us on the east coast and the storm has left New Yorkers with power outages and darkness. It is three days after I have had a dream that Bob is alive but now dying a terrible death from cancer. The dream rewrites history and gives him the death I feared he would have, long before Barcelona. *Nachtraglichkeit* in many directions. I am dreaming and living in the strange multiple and distorting time lines that have seemed endemic to my state since Bob's death. The run-up to the hurricane had plunged me into a strange dissociative state much like Barcelona in that week, taking me from the fall from his bicycle to the moment of silence when the machines and apparatus in the ICU are stopped.

May 2, 1945. We hear the date right at the outset of the film. A voice speaks to us over a soundtrack of romantic nostalgia-riddled music and a visual screen made up of a vast universe of stars, clouds, and specks of light. The opening narration sets the film's enigmatic premises and projects in motion. Is this a story of the supernatural, of a battle that heaven somehow came to be able to allow between love and death? Or are we in the mind and dreamy, near-death imagination of a soldier, "an airman in a world of war," as Niven describes himself?

As the film begins, the camera pans in, tracking through space and stars to the moon, towards our planet, and then towards the familiar terrain of earth, and finally with no sounds of guns and yet a cockpit full of smoke and flame, we join the "airman" later found to be a poet (homage to Wilfred Owen) named Peter Carter. He is talking to a woman at HQ who is trying to guide him to safety. The pilot "knows" he is headed for death. So, perhaps inevitably, love flowers in the breathless conversation between Peter and the woman whose name, he learns, is June.

We are in the timeless, beautiful world of war films, the staple of my childhood (b. 1941) and Bob's (b. 1936) when, in different but overlapping contexts, we became the enthralled witnesses of endless British and American accounts of the war, accounts of loves won and lost, and often of love in suspended time.

Peter Carter is lying in the shallow, beautiful surf on the English coast, waves quietly sliding into the shore. The camera pans in to the quiet, still body lying in the shallow water, and then those beautiful blue eyes open. He wakes, gets up, and walks into an English coastal scene. He and we don't know whether the little boy playing a flute with animals around him is heavenly, magical, or real. Peter Carter is imagining that this is heaven, and that he has died. He walks along the beach and sees the wireless operator riding her bicycle along a coastal road. They meet. They have, we know, already met. *Petit objet a*. Peter and June arrive in a Technicolor world of the living. Peter is surprised but also pleased to see dogs in heaven, and then surprised to be alive. And then, surprised and delighted to be in love.

This is one of the key primal scenes of our generation, the moment of heroic return, of the fantastical repair of fractured love, the luscious surprise of reunion. But every moment of reunion and transcendant love is also a moment of warding off trauma: the disaster of separation, the splits between fantasy and reality that doomed so many reunions of soldier and beloved and longed-for mate.

Everything in this film is familiar to me. The sound track is brimming with violins and nostalgic romantic music and longing. There is the voice of a narrator, God-like, comforting, and instructing. There is a particular characteristic cadence of romantic speech in films of that period, the way the actors' voices ache and tremble with promise and uncertainty. The acting hits notes of melodrama, romance, all against the hopelessness of war, and its inexorable, though often invisible costs.

In the opening scene in the burning plane, and on the wireless, the two not-yet-lovers imagine the lost future. Everything is intensified. The airman tries, in a brief speech, to tell the girl on the wireless something about himself. He loves his mother very much. He has sisters. If only, if only. As love starts up, death beckons as surely it must have those previous six years in England and Europe and America. (The film appears in 1946).

As Peter and June talk, she keeps crying out. "I can't understand. Signals coming in; don't leave me." Love across difference and incomprehension and imagination: the pattern of a million scenes of love and love lost or spoiled, as the war winds down. At one point, Peter says, intending to be comforting. "I'll be a ghost. Don't be frightened. I'll come and see you." I saw this film several times before I actually listened to those sentences. The benevolent specter. The accompanying figure from the spirit world. The fantasy of the exquisite corpse. Not dead, but sleeping. Reunion, going on being, the raw stuff of melancholy. I see that I can barely write about this in proper sentences.

I begin to track the role of melancholy in the experience of my childhood: fathers and husbands away and in persistent danger of dying. The fantasy, a core part of the traumatized soldiers' experience—frozen just before the bad thing happened—appears in all melancholic formations. Omnipotence trumps helplessness. Time stops. Willy Baranger (2009) has a great paper on this topic: *The dead-alive: object structure in mourning and depressive states*.

Peter and June, in this film, and I and so many others in the real-life task of mourning, hold onto the object as that which "the ego must keep alive at any price" (Freud, 1917). Peter, as the surviving shell-shocked airman, lives both with the hope of reunion/love but also the guilt and persecutory anxiety of being somehow responsible for his crew's deaths.

Guilt and depression, as Baranger points out, hold the melancholic subject in a tight grip. These thoughts arise, along with images and affects generated by the film, which live in my mental space beyond and before language. My father had gone away to the war in early 1941, four months before my birth, and he returned four and a half years later. In the interim, the picture of the handsome, uniformed serious man carried many of my hopes for my own repair and my mother's. Later, and from the late 40s onward, I was a determined enthralled consumer of war films (British and American, films that triggered the erotic, somewhat hopeless fervor of '50s era girlhoods).

As I had discovered in developing the ghost project with my group, the experience of mass death created many crises in the societies and individuals that were surviving. In the aftermath of wars and massive losses, there were outbreaks of religious visions, sightings of the Virgin Mary, intermingled with massive and inexorable civilian deaths and with the specter of dead comrades. Séances occurred in great number after the Civil War in America and after the First World War in Europe. Mediums flourished, offering ways to meet the dead, reunion necessary for letting go.

So I read this film in the context of the particular tensions of postwar experience and try to imagine what would have been stirred in an audience of people taking the measure of losses and an unknown future.

In *Stairway to Heaven*, the "*medium*" is film itself, as the narrative bifurcates, with a fantastical and stylized sequence set in heaven, running in parallel to a "realistic" world in England as the woman, June, tries to help Peter recover from the war trauma that has convinced him he should be dead. In perhaps a comic touch, Heaven is in Black and White, England and the living world in Technicolor.

The film-makers are English and European, but the sensibility is the great musical productions of Hollywood of the prewar era. Heaven also evokes modernist industrial beauty, the aesthetics of mass corporations and centers of commerce or government. We are in the imaginary timeless past/present. One soldier arriving through the great doors of heaven asks: "I wonder where do I report." Peter, wandering around an army hospital in England has the same question.

Heaven is like Harrods, or Saks, or the Four Seasons, or some modernist palace set in a Busby Berkeley musical. Huge doors admit a flood of the newly dead: refugees, soldiers, and civilians. Men of many eras and cultures mingle together. Heaven is also, we see, circa 1946, segregated, with black soldiers seated together. The dead man we saw first in Peter's plane has now arrived in Heaven and is flirting with one of the angels. He looks around for his leader, Peter, who has mysteriously not arrived. Glamorous angels direct traffic and manage life in heaven, and then, to much consternation, the elegant attendants and seraphs struggle to sort out a problem that only Hollywood could have devised.

We learn that the rule, in heaven, is that someone escorts you from death to the afterworld and on this occasion, an elegant French aristocrat (presumably a casualty of the French revolution), sent as Peter Carter's escort, gets lost in an English fog, like "pea soup," as he says disdainfully. An error has been made and in that space—the space of the unconscious, the limenal, the uncanny—something unbidden and unexpected has happened. The not-yet-transmitted-to-heaven airman has fallen in love.

After much argument and handwringing, God and some senior angels decide on a trial in order to determine if love should trump death.

In the narrative back on earth in England, Jill and Peter, try to settle into love and life. Peter is afraid he is mad, he has headaches, and often thinks he may be or should be dead (he needs to be with his comrades). June takes him to a friend, an army psychiatrist, and he is gradually absorbed into a military hospital.

Now we are in the standard narrative of the war-wounded, traumatized soldier, caught in the moment before the bad thing happened, and poised as much for death as life. When the emissary from Heaven arrives to talk to Peter, time and action in the world of the living present, are stopped. All the characters, except Peter and the Frenchman from Heaven, are frozen like figures from a ward of war-damaged soldiers, so much pictured from the First World War. We learn that Peter's father died in the First World war in 1917 and I think, at once, of Bion who famously wrote: "I died on August 7th, 1917, on the Amiens-Roye Road" (Bion 1982, p. 265).

Or to think in another language, is the freeze of time and space a sign of dissociation? There is a split away from reality and vitality as the traumatized man tries to discover if he is more attached to life or death. In the scene in England, as Peter comes to be in an army hospital and under the care of a worried and kindly psychiatrist, we watch what would have been repeated in many such settings in America and Europe in the postwar era. A mind-fractured man is coaxed back to life. If treatment works, the living come to be as important as the dead. Of this possibility, this psychoanalyst holds some doubt.

Entering the world of army hospitals and psychiatry, there are clues that we are in the world of fantasy. The psychiatrist has a "hobby" of building *camera obscuras*, and the spectator comes to look through tiny apertures to see a world of moving figures. Is this scene a strip of film or reality? Later patients and staff stage a production of *A Midsummer Night's Dream*. The casting of spells, the illusion of reality, the power of imagination and dream, offer a clue to reading the film. It is a product of the soldier's broken mind. Or perhaps this film narrative is the loving woman's dream/hope. He will come back. Love will come back. Love will bring him back.

The whole center section of the film plays out a doubled, intermingled encounter of worlds. On earth, the task at the military hospital Peter has entered is to cure his war neurosis. A neurologist/psychiatrist interested in his case helps support his "hallucinations" that he has escaped assignment to heaven, but begins to plan for his surgery. In heaven, a trial is convened and various political and cultural wars (Old world vs the new one) are fought. The trial is over the question heaven and Hollywood are willing to entertain: would love overcome death? In the 24 hours of cheating death, Peter has fallen in love. Is this enough to save him?

The two worlds, heaven and earth, are linked by a fabulous moving staircase, modern, mechanical, aesthetically spare, and elegant. As the trials and the surgery unfolds, the two worlds begin to intermingle. In one of a series of strange twists, the treating psychiatrist dies in a motorcycle accident on his way to try and save Peter and get him help. In a magical cinematic Hollywood touch, the doctor arrives in heaven just in time and now that dead man's job transfers to heaven he is enlisted to help with the trial. At the end of the film, we see that the actor who plays God in the trial sequence in heaven is also the surgeon operating on Peter's brain on earth.

We can always read this film as Peter's hallucination, his dream to suspend life. We can equally situate ourselves in the melancholic solution that love defeats death. The staircase is the route to mourning and the escape from mourning.

Heaven, in Powell/Pressberger's film is a modernist dream. A stark exquisite vision, looking like Hollywood's filmic fantastical vision of new space and structure. A moving staircase: delivering thousands of dead—soldiers, refugees, black airmen, British, American. Arrivals to heaven report in, get assignments, and are seamlessly and easily serviced by women, in lovely 40s hairdos.

We are left to wonder. Is Peter's rescue from death and the trial in heaven his hallucination, his guilty horror at survival? Is the surgery and the trial, both ending in victory and survival, June's hallucination to beat back the horror of the fall and the death of the beloved she could not protect? Another way to consider these alternatives is to think through the forms of the melancholic solution and the forms of mourning.

In the imaginary world of cinema, happily and with heaven now practicing a new ethos of democracy, melancholy and love win. On earth, Peter Carter, head bandaged after surgery, opens those beautiful blue eyes, again, as he does on that flat open English beach, and he is reunited with June. Love stops death, trumps it. We are left to sort out what has happened. The fantasy of death's defeat? A case of shellshock and PTSO cured by medicine and by love? The war and its horrors really just a dream? What is dream and what real and who falters under the burden of grief?

The film seems to me to settle on the romance of mourning; mourning as romance, really not mourning but melancholy. I think of the rise of spiritism and séances after wars of great loss and death. The siren call of the imaginary.

June 26, 2011. Bob lies on the pavement, I see that his breathing is shallow, his eyes flutter. I feel unsettled, confused, and then those lovely blue eyes open. We sit together until the ambulance arrives. I will say this over and over again. I tell this story over and over, I write it in many versions, in part to make it real but also I write it so that one time, it will come out differently.

> Journal entry: With him on the pavement. In the ambulance. In the ER. Familiar by now. His health wavering.
> Quiet,close. Using my iPhone as a stopwatch. Monitering his heart. Quiet.
> What happened?
> Sitting side by side in the ER but later I register that they are telling me it is the presurgery ER.
> I remember my odd surprise.
> Only later I realize that they had been working on this since Bob gave the list of meds in the ambulance.
> Kissing the top of his head. His shoulder. Close. Don't sleep. Concussion?
> You can doze, says the nurse.
> I am getting sleepy. He says. Yawning. Again, I am getting sleepy. When they come to put him onto the gurney, I am not consciously worried and only later do I realize that I have noticed his legs are omninously limp.

> Many lessons in Nachtraglichkeit.
> Then he is asleep. They – docs and nurses - are moving fast.
> They tell me (with translators hovering) that they will take him to the ICU and then they say they will come back and talk to me. I watch him wheel past. I kiss his head. Touch him.

This scene replays over hours, days, months, and now over years. It remains, at an important level, still not believable. But I often think, even if with suspended belief, that he dies then. He goes and we spend the next days catching up to him. This matter of repetition. Revisiting, re-writing, reading medical documents, looking at photos, inhabiting the iterative spaces of memory, memorializing, recording. This process seems always poised between life and death, between retreat and movement. I feel between destruction and creation, perhaps: between melancholy and mourning, certainly. This focus on what happened, whether relived in a film, a journal, an internal monolog, a narrative you tell and retell is both to start up time and hold it hostage. *Stairway to Heaven* lives and does its magic in these kinds of liminal spaces.

At the time and in the years of re-releases and happy re-encounters with the film, most critical reading centers on the role of ideology. In the formation of the film, most critics were interested in the explicit engagement of Powell and Pressberger in an anti-communist and Cold War project. This analysis centers on the trial in heaven as a site of Anglo-American relations in the light of the Cold War. From the trivial (enmity for the American G.I.s' ways with English girls) to the profound (alliances of the west against Russia, founding of new possibilities for social democracy, pace Tony Judt).

None of this occurred to me at first sighting of this film but I have been thinking about how the ghostly tasks of mourning and mourning suspended interweave with the crafting of ideological projects of alliance and remaking of a political world. Seeing the trial with its rather blatant ideological commitment to new ideas and freedom and its more undercover installation of the Cold War came to me after attending a conference honoring Bob Sklar at NYU where we screened and discussed the John Huston documentary *Let There be Light*, a film about the treatment of US soldier's war trauma in the Second World, made at the Long Island Hospital Mercy General in 1948.

At that conference, Hannah Zeavin and Noah Tikis read papers on the efforts in and out of the military to prepare the postwar culture for new/old forms of gender and in particular masculinity. Their work seemed relevant to this film. The girl on the wireless becomes the loving attendant care-giving woman, the man goes from collapsed to robust. Love, technologies of care, and benevolent forces on high, save the day.

I think of the themes in Bob's book, *Nightmare Factory*, his view that the 50s be read not as an era of security or hegemonic orderliness but as an era of anxiety and above all, resentment. *Stairway to Heaven*, seen in this light, airbrushes postwar alienation between and among the genders, classes, races. A celebration of new forms of freedom (hard won in war) covers death: the 50s as a melancholic solution.

From the perspective of psychoanalysis and trauma theory, this film catches viewers in the romance of melancholy, the suspension of mourning, the stopping of time. A number of critics note the lovely touch of reality in the English countryside in luscious technicolor while heaven, the site of political debate and also the space in which time is stopped, death reversed, is in the austere formalist world of black and white, a prewar scene where hairstyle, costume, and vocal cadence melds time and space and historical movement into an exquisite architectural modernist palace. Heaven, in part, represents the unconscious, in short, the world of psychic equivalence.

The scenes in heaven—the trial in particular—magically conjure a new world where all is restored and death suspended. This repression, this suppression of death is required for the launch of the postwar socio/political world, And I don't forget that this film is doing the work of the occult, the management of the ghosts from unmetabolizable death.

July 3, 2011. Bob's story and mine end differently from the Hollywood/ Powell/Pressberger/fantasy. It seems to me that the film's reception must have been complex, at a deep level, both to those whose mates had been lost and to those faced with the ambiguities of postwar reunions. Becky Okrent, who had been with me in the hospital in Barcelona, writes a poem:

Caprice in Barcelona

A holiday bike ride in Barcelona is no time to die.
We should be taken from our desks,
swiftly lifted from our tasks to rest.

Here we are so full of life—Gaudi, olives and tomatoes—
we're sure it's the surgeon's uneasiness with English
(not failure) that keeps him from offering hope.

So we hold Bob's hands, rub his feet, admiring his god-like profile.
We regale him with remembrances, whisper our affection, and watch
the monitors clock their own labors at mechanical existence.

Back in the hotel my hip is the hill you climb in sleep.
Your knee rests there; your arm finds purchase on my shoulder
lifting you from deep drowse. Holding fast you murmur to my back:

"Where do you keep this stuff?" as if this well-traversed terrain
were still uncharted even after thirty-five years' proximity.

Though naked, I am aproned in unshakable secrecy, wakeful,
grateful for love's constancy. Afraid.

Rebecca Okrent (2011)

My journals:
In preparation of silencing these machines we take our goodbyes. I locate the line reverberating in my mind: Romeo And Juliet. Of course I have had to use google to find it.

'Eyes, look your last,'

His eyes have not opened. No last look, no reunion, no trial in heaven where the right of love over death might be claimed.

Coda: I begin to write this essay in the fall of 2012. Whenever I sit to work on it, I play a CD that Jim and Shelley Hoberman made at the end of 2011. They make one every year, dedicating it to friends or figures in the film/culture world who have died that year. 2011's CD is dedicated to Suzie Rottola, the lovely girl on the cover of the Freewheeling Bob Dylan, to a film colleague of Jim's, and to Bob Sklar. Dylan, the Pogues, lots of music from 1950s westerns. Memory. Time suspended. That CD is the score for this essay.

As I work on the last pieces of care for Bob, I turn to his book. A wonderful and justly celebrated mentor and supporter to students, family, and definitely to wives, Bob was astonishingly generous. At the same time, alive, Bob liked to think of his work as *his work*. We talked about work and writing often, as on those nights in Spain just before his death. And we talked very explicitly about his book *Nightmare Factory*, which I felt carried his definitive and to me very original ideas about the 1950s. And as in so much, his ideas were very influential on my work, and on what I was trying to say about the 1950s in psychoanalysis.

All well and good, but he did also like differentiation, this man with whom I lived such a bonded entangled, immersed life. So, in all likelihood, against his wishes in life, I write this essay, and I push on to finish the book he was working on.

But it is not the end. Never the end. In **June 2013**, our grandson, Jake, and I go to Governor's Island to be part of an art project.

> Journal
>
> A young poet talks about the island, the history, how ephemeral the words and worlds and dwellings there really are. This island is the opening for migration and arrival. From the old world, from away. And onward towards . . . Something.
>
> We are invited to use paint and crayons and markers and to write on the walls. Yes. Write on the walls. Write anything. Anything.
>
> Jake is looking bored and I wonder what he has taken in. We choose a quiet wall with a window looking out into a garden. The lovely old houses of Governor's Island set in a graceful world so far from Manhattan. White walls on which we can write . . . anything
>
> We write a message to Bob. We describe him using the words of the project, the words the poet used and some of our own words.
>
> "Adrienne and Jake send love to Bob."
>
> And on a separate section of the wall.
>
> "Bob: from New Jersey via Hungary and the Ukraine
Adrienne: from Canada
Jake: native of Manhattan"
>
> Now, our next task is to think of words for Bob.
We write;
Bob: safe,
ephemeral,
continuous,
achieving, (Jake chooses this word)
giving us a love of baseball and movies. (I choose this sentence)

Later we walk to the ferry and are plunged into an intense talk. I suddenly think: "but these words should go on the wall inside the house." But its too late to go back, so I write down the words here.

Adrienne: You know, thanks for coming with me and writing about Bob. I like to send him messages.

Quiet

Jake: I wish he could send one back. Could be a text. On the iPhone. Maybe the text would say "heaven, heaven, heaven, heaven."

Silence.

Jake: Is there language in heaven?

Now I realize he has been paying attention to the poet.

Quiet.

Jake: Or is there even heaven . . .

Adrienne: I hope so.

Jake: Or hell or demons. You need demons.

Adrienne: Really.

We write on walls, we dream, we revive fantasy baseball. We go to the movies and wish we could be asking Bob: so what did you think? And in that fantasy, we live in the relieving world of melancholy. But I see and feel that increasingly, for Jake, Bob is a benevolent specter. At the beginning Jake was worried about reading material in heaven and so he put a copy of the Sports and the Culture section of the *New York Times* into his grandfather's grave. Now, Jake is deep into an identificatory immersion in baseball stats and list making of favorite teams and players. On the other hand, we hope that a message might arrive on the iphone. Heaven, heaven, heaven, heaven. Mourning and melancholia.

But, in a deep link with this film, I mostly live in a melancholy space. The film banishes "never" for both the lovers, really until a very far away old age. In 1946, this fascinating film commits to a scenario of death cheated, love victorious. Reality and mourning are airbrushed away.

In Bob's last unfinished book, *Nightmare Factory* he writes about *Let There Be Light*, a documentary of shell-shocked World War Two soldiers.

That film, rather notoriously, was suppressed by the Army that commissioned John Huston to make the film. It remained almost entirely unseen for 40 years. Davoine and Gaudilliere (2004), working on the terrible psychic consequences of these negations of history, say it takes half a century to process a war. We have the documentary film back in circulation now, but in so many places of postwar life we are so often only at the beginning.

Our ghost project takes up the question of intergenerational transmission of trauma, the leaking of experience and anguish from one generation to the next. The impossibility of fully internalizing and bearing loss, blocked by culture, by mental limits, by the deep defenses of omnipotence, means that our psyches and our films and cultural projects are brimming with these haunting ghostly figures, both friendly and ominous. My colleague Bob Bartlett, reading this paper, talked about the way the film and the paper search for a container. There is, in all these structures—film, paper, journal, psychic life—an experience of excess. Ghosts signify the inevitable presence of excess, of the uncontained. The longing and deep call of the imaginary in *Stairway to Heaven* speaks to that excess as it must have welled up and overwhelmed so many mourners in postwar culture.

Finally, I would say about this film that it both normalizes and idealizes the melancholic solution. Melancholy, in the standard canonical argument in psychoanalysis is the hopefully not too long way station on the path to mourning. Joel Whitebook (2014), in a paper attesting to the importance of reading Freud's secularism, notes that at bedrock Freud meant by mourning the acceptance of the reality of death and along with that a commitment to death's finality, no afterlife, no heaven. The world of "never." This question of "never" had come up in a long period of impasse and difficulty in a treatment where a patient angrily challenged me to take up this question of "never" in my own circumstances. I had proposed that she and I think of what it might mean if the she could mobilize the word "never" in regard to sobriety and giving up drugs. Even if one failed, fell down, fell off the wagon, could you at least commit to the idea that you would try for "never?" Really, came the retort. You try it. Try saying "never" about Bob. Indeed.

From this film and from now four years of work with my personal and professional communities, many experiences with patients who, alongside their analyst, have losses to metabolize, I have come to appreciate the massiveness, the pervasiveness, and the durability of melancholy. Perhaps theoretically and clinically, we might make more space for melancholy, see its opportunities as well as its defensive manoevers. I think that melancholy lurks in our intense preoccupations with omnipotence, a professional hazard of healers, as I have written elsewhere (Harris, 2009).

Omnipotence banishes need and loss, a hopeless task as it turns out. Omnipotence also carries the imaginary power to change outcomes, heal and repair and shape outcomes. As such, omnipotence trails, in its wake, deep caverns of guilt. If I am omnipotent, I can restart time, turn it back, undo death. But if I am omnipotent then I must be responsible for whatever happens. So omnipotence freezes us in a stance of guilt, a stance that is painful but necessary. Yet how curious that guilt seems preferable to the acceptance entailed in mourning. In the film, the melancholic solution suspends trauma and loss. The couple's future is in Technicolor.

Loss must be assimilated over and over. One fights very fiercely the "never" that accompanies the experience of death, and the helplessness in that experience. I think of the Fitzgerald quote from the end of *The Great Gatsby*. I read these lines from Fitzgerald at Bob's memorial and I put them on his tombstone.

> "So we beat on, boats against the current, borne back ceaselessly into the past." (Fitzgerald, 1925, p. 180)

But I give him the last word. From his manuscript *American Nightmare*, it is his judgment and conclusion about *Let There be Light*, the documentary where the real airmen and soldiers struggled to regain their footing.

> "*Let There Be Light* "became in the postwar years a symbol of a silence. It cast a shadow over the bright scenes of war reminiscence and peacetime expurgation, a shadow that darkened Hollywood, as much as, and even more than other centers of cultural industry. Under and through that shadow, the Dream Factory transformed itself into a Nightmare Factor, rendering what lay unspoken beneath the complacent surfaces of American postwar life." (Sklar, in prep, ms)

References

Abraham, N. (1987). Notes on the Phantom: A Complement to Freud's Metapsychology Critical Inquiry Vol. 13, No. 2, *The Trials of Psychoanalysis*, University of Chicago Press (Winter 1987), 287–292.

Baranger, W. (2009). The dead-alive objects. In *The Work of Confluence*. Willy and Madalin Baranger. London: Karnac Books, 202–219.

Bion, W. (1982). *The Long Weekend: 1897–1919 (Part of a Life)*, Bion F, editor. Abingdon: Fleetwood Press.

Davoine, F. and Gauadilliere, J.M. (2004). *History beyond Trauma*. New York: Other Press.

Fitzgerald, F. Scott (1925). *The Great Gatsby*. New York: Scribner.

Freud, S. (1917), Mourning and Melancholia, *S.E.* vol 14: 233–258.

Gerson, S. (2009). When the Third is Dead: Memory, Mourning, and Witnessing in the Aftermath of the Holocaust. *Int. J. Psycho-Anal.*, 90: 1341–1357.

Harris, A. (2009). You Must Remember This. *Psychoanal. Dialog*. vol 19: 2–21.

Sklar, R. (in prep). *Nightmare Factory, American Cinema from 1945–1960*. Ms.

Whitebook, Joel (2014). "'Imagine': Zur Verteidigung des Säkularismus der Psychoanalyse,"*Psyche: Zeitschrif für Pscyhoanalyse und Ihre Anwendungen*, Heff 12, December 2014, 1167–1195.

Afterword

Sam Gerson

> *"Something occurred inside of him then, something mysterious and definitive that uprooted him from his own time and carried him adrift through an unexplored region of his memory".*
>
> Gabriel Garcia Marquez, *One Hundred Years of Solitude*

Ours is a fragile existence; and forever, we live in the wake of this knowledge.

We are all surrounded and saturated with personal, familial, cultural, and historical pasts that propel us into the future—time simultaneously receding and shaping the form of our experience. Hurtling along in the anything but linear trajectories of time, we move within the constraints of our finite bodies and journey within the limitlessness of our imagination. Throughout, we engage with essences that evade material presence, and yet remain continuously formative of our being.

The essays in this volume represent a project replete with paradox, as each author attempts to capture this enduring presence of the absent in our lives. Their work creates a lexicon that illuminates those nuances of lived experience that cannot be easily relegated to the domains of reality, fantasy, or dream. Throughout, we are reminded that our hearts, and minds, and souls often inhabit locales, times, and sensibilities that are felt as profoundly real, while simultaneously eluding current representation and habitation. These are the ephemeral essences that haunt us even as we may welcome their company—these are our ghosts, forever and everywhere, filling time and space, and that are both the shadows and the light of our existence. These are the ineffable presences of absences that, however elusive, are known viscerally and that leave us feeling touched by something untouchable. In their often unbidden emergence, the revenants of the past signal the inchoate and the unsettled in our existence, the ruptures that dislocate us from our familiar domains and sensibilities.

Indeed, it may be this potential state of disruption that most troubles our comfort and creates the haunting inventions that populate the emptiness, articulate our fear, and provide meaning and continuity in the void.

The multiple forms and functions of ghostly presences, and their ubiquitous existence across ages and cultures, may each signify a unique amalgam of danger and of safety. As felt or as fantasized, as myth or as metaphor, ghosts may be invoked to create meaning when belief is threatened with dissolution. They emerge from an abyss, from the gaps between life and death, from the fissures of bodies, between sensibilities of liveliness and deadness, escaping the dimensions of past and future time, lurking in shadows between darkness and light as they float between heaven and hell and promise a potential transit between despair and hope.

When faith begins to evaporate into the ether, ghosts may fill the absences with purpose. The ghosts that haunt also carry promise as they evoke both destruction and survival—they signal the impoverishments of traumatic loss as well as the sustenance of re-creation. And, as such, they may herald a morphing of memory into novel movement as the spirits of the past are wakened and, by their insistent claims to remember, arouse us from the illusory stillness of our sleep. In their spectral existence, ghosts may be imagined as inhabiting the realms between Eros and Thanatos.

Entering this vast territory, and anchored in the breadth and depths of psychoanalytic history, theory, and practice, the authors of this volume have all responded to the demands of the "undead" to be heard and they have joined in a quest to give voice to these forbidden, yet not forgotten, claims of the past. The clinical and historical material of this set of essays moves through the project of recognition and reclamation of ghostly presences by traversing four major yet intertwined realms. First are issues related to mourning, and, in particular, the challenges of mourning the ruptures in experience that are deeply etched in our patients, in ourselves, in our psychoanalytic traditions, and in the world as a consequence of traumatic loss and the dehumanization. Second, are the intriguing yet mysterious phenomena whereby unresolved loss, and the remnants of all the losses that cannot find resolution, are manifest in the psychological dynamics of future generations. Third, is how this transmission of trauma across generations can be mitigated, and even transformed, through acts of therapeutic witnessing. And fourth is the cumulative impact of histories of injustice on all who would pause and reflect on the terrors and triumphs that mark the struggle for life.

In all of these domains, the authors arrived at their creative expression only after having entered into the lives and histories of their subjects in ways that could only be accomplished through their own steadfast availability to be startled, disturbed, and moved by the emergence of their own (and that of the psychoanalytic profession's), sequestered pasts. The editors captured this compelling project when they wrote that "Ghosts haunt analyst and analysand, participating in impasses and uncanny experiences in the countertransference and in the transference. While more traditional spiritual practices involving hauntings seek to expel ghosts and demons, psychoanalysis and psychotherapies – drawing on trauma work – rather seek to have ghosts readmitted and repatriated (p. 9; Harris, Kalb, & Klebanoff)".

This transformation of the gravitational pull of ghostly presences into a livable history and a creative future is a truly radical endeavor; one that requires the courage of another person who chooses to remain available in the midst of the unspeakable horrors and the numbing ennui of uninhabitable zones of experience. The process of becoming a living presence, which may draw the other from their netherworlds, inevitably involves inviting their unspeakable realms to stimulate one's own ghostly presences, and, in that resonance, to find a way to remain engaged, a way to hold on through the storms and the doldrums. And then, together, to come to know the old in a new way.

The perils and promise of active and therapeutic witnessing that I am sketching out here is most poignantly conveyed in the clinical work described by the authors in this book. Each vignette is an eloquent and inspiring testament to the awesome responsibility and reward of remaining present in the haunted fields of absence. And each of the quotations below is an exemplar of dedicated, live witnessing:

> I was pulled into Sophie's netherworld early on in treatment, where time and space were occluded, and we floated along together in a morass of melancholia (Klebanoff, p.45)

> My own unformulated loss, and its attendant shame, collided with Frank's desperate pleas to be held and deeply understood in his despairing depths. (Ferguson, p.76)

> To create a live analytic third . . . I would have to lead the way, remembering and acknowledging my own ghosts before Aaron could begin thinking about his. (Feldman, p.)

> The shadow of loss that fell across my life because it fell across my mother's had not been fully nameable for me, leaving me both inside and outside of it. It sensitized me to the trauma and shame the women I work with experience, but it also intensified my concerns about intrusion and trespass. (Kraemer & Steinberg, p.70)

> When she calls me she is calling out to some remembered universe of the human, in which there is the possibility of a living human bond. She calls in the possibility that she can be alive. (Grand, p.134)

In these therapeutic engagements, ghostly hauntings are navigated, their origins and sequella are known, and the terror or numbness they evoked is altered into recognizable and habitable affect and memory through the enlivening presence of an other who exists as a witnessing third to the traumatized person and to the unbearable event.

Haunted histories affect institutions and cultures no less than they do individuals. And the excavation of the buried but undead phantoms in the development of psychoanalysis requires a similar willingness to become deeply engaged, both emotionally and intellectually, with that which was both impossible to fully permit and impossible to completely forget. Indeed, it is a voyage infused with the "uncanny." Freud (1919) described the uncanny as being "in reality nothing new or alien, but something which is familiar and old-established in the mind and which has become alienated from it only through the process of repression" (p. 241).

Freud's portrait of the uncanny should be extended from the individual to include those that are embedded in the political choices, as well as the psychological dynamics, of the founders of psychoanalysis and of the traditions and practices that evolved from these origins. Reclaiming the neglected, banished, and devalued contributors to our field requires that current adherents acknowledge the harms of exclusion practiced by their forebears, so that its legacy is not a shadow darkening our contemporary practices but acts as a light illuminating paths away from hierarchical and prejudicial organizational ethics. Yet, it must also be acknowledged that contending with the force of the group to silence and obscure that which is threatening requires a similar courage to that of the clinician who deigns to enter the realms of a patient's repressions. As Butler, in his contribution in this volume put it: "The group elicits a fear of becoming a phantom to oneself. It elicits a fear of becoming a no-body engulfed by the vastness of the intangible group skin . . . Bearing witness to the trauma of the group requires facing such fear" (p. 43).

And in this process of bearing witness, be it with patient or institution, it is well for us to hold in mind that such acts constitute the well-being of the witness as well as of the witnessed. Each participates in the creative act of altering the hauntings of the past into a base from which development may proceed—and so each, witness and witnessed, partakes in the project Leowald (1960) so aptly described as the movement of ghosts into ancestors.

References

Freud, S. (1919). The Uncanny. *Standard Edition*, 17:217–248. London: Hogarth Press, 1955.

Loewald, H. (1960). The Therapeutic Action of Psychoanalysis. In: *Papers on Psychoanalysis*. New Haven, CT: Yale University Press, 221–226.

Index

9/11 memorial 7

Aaron (case study) 52–75
abjection 97, 98, 111–12, 146, 171
Abraham, N. 11, 39, 52, 55, 58, 59, 62, 84, 171
absent presences: definition of ghosts 156–7; ghosts vs. demons distinction 9; at heart of clinical trauma 3, 10, 11; loss of the analytic third 1, 43, 55–7, 70, 126, 181
adoption 101, 103
affective intersection 37, 44, 72
affective links, restoration of 98
affective residua 169
affiliation 136–8
alcoholism 100
alienation 42, 127, 136, 192
Allen, Woody 121
alpha-functioning 81
altruism, window of 154 n.5
Alvarez, A. 93, 141
ambivalence 40, 121–2, 123
American Civil War 6, 28, 160, 174, 187
American Nightmare (Sklar) 197
American Psychoanalytic Association (AsPA) 125, 127, 129
analytic third 1, 3, 19, 43, 55–7, 66, 70, 126, 181, 201–3
ancestors, turning ghosts into 5, 76, 83–4, 119, 203; Aaron (case study) 65; Frank (case study) 48
angels 46, 154 n.7
anger, repressed 37, 39, 42, 143, 150–1
anti-Semitism 29–30, 63, 124
anxiety 86, 91, 105–6, 170, 192
Anzieu, D. 90
aporias 171
Apprey, M. 20
architecture 163–9, 170–1, 173
attachment: analyst-analysand 69, 72, 104–5, 107; and disembodiment 106; vs. flight 69; and historical trauma 54, 102; to mother 29, 41, 43, 48, 104; to place 28–9, 65; Rosa (case study) 102
attunement of significant other 70, 79
Aulagnier, P. 79
authoritarian figures 21
autism (Omri case) 76–8, 89–92

Baranger, M. 3, 54, 55
Baranger, W. 3, 54, 55, 186–7
Barrows, K. 85
Barthes, R. 4
Bartlett, Bob 196
bastions 54, 56, 57, 67, 69
beta-elements 81
Beyond the Pleasure Principle (Freud, 1920) 115
Bion, W.R. 4–5, 126, 128, 129, 178 n.37, 188
bi-personal unconscious 2
black holes 38–40, 84, 88
Blechner, M.J. 124
Bleger, J. 55, 170
blind spots 23, 44, 126, 144
body: and architecture 164, 167–8; Chimerism 82, 88–93; disembodiment 100–1, 105–7, 110; dismantling behaviors 91; early life narratives 79;

embodied witnessing 59; female bodies 118, 164; ghost worlds 55; imprint of traumatic past on 6, 36, 41; lost links and ethical markers 99–105; memory of history 78; preverbal development phase 82; self-hatred 100, 103, 105, 106; sense phenomena 79, 91, 118, 156, 161–2, 168–9, 171; and shame 37, 42, 148; and space 164
body language 54–5
Bohleber, W. 84
Bollas, C. 2, 151
Botella, C. 82, 91
Botella, S. 82, 91
Bourne, S. 144
Breger, L. 136
bridge worlds 4, 140
bright spots 23, 43, 44, 58–9
Bromberg, P. 38
Brooklyn, New York: Aaron (case study) 56, 58, 61, 65–6; Rosa (case study) 99–100, 104, 111
Brothers, D. 37, 42
Brown, L. 43
Burrow, Trigant 126–30
Butler, J. 42, 171

care, ethos of 97–8, 192
Caruth, C. 2
child analysis 117–18
child development 79, 80, 82, 117–18
Chimerism 76, 82, 88–93
cinema and film 181–98
Civil War, American 6, 28, 160, 174, 187
Civitarese, Guiseppe 170, 171
claustrum 78, 140
Coates, S. 153
Coburn, W. 37
co-creative processes 44, 129, 156
Cohen, M. 142
collective denial 156
collectivities, haunting of 11, 171, 202
collectivization of ghosts 171
commonalities, assumptions of 58–9
companion volume 1, 9
compassion 98, 112
containers 21, 32–3, 55, 68, 93
containing mind 55–6, 59
containment 7, 45, 81–2, 83, 84, 165
control, seeking 54–5, 56, 67, 70, 123
core-consciousness 82
countertransference: and capacity for rescue 57; identification of secret histories 2, 3, 54; maternal countertransference 23–4; victim status 57–8
crunches 42–5
crypts 84–5, 109, 149
culture: collectivization of ghosts 157–81; film and cinema 181–98; haunting of 202; melancholy 6; popular culture and ghosts 6, 7–8, 187

Damasio, A. 82
Davoine, F. 4, 7, 22, 53, 54, 59, 140, 170, 196
defensiveness 21, 27, 29
definitions of ghosts 1–2, 9, 156–7
delayed reactions 20
demons 3, 9–10
Demons in the Consulting Room: Echoes of Genocide, Slavery and Extreme Trauma in Psychoanalytic Practice 9–10
De M'Uzan, M. 82
denial 30
depression: fear of losing 41; and melancholia 23, 187; and nostalgia 29, 30; Oscar (case study) 85–8; parents' 37–8, 39; Rosa (case study) 100, 105
depth mind 169
Descartes, Réné 176 n.18
development, child 79, 80, 82, 117–18
developmental second chances 44–5
De Waal, E. 141, 146
Dewey, John 129
disavowal 3, 136; Aaron (case study) 54, 56, 58–9, 61; Frank (case study) 37, 39; Sophie (case study) 29
disembodiment 100–1, 105–7, 110
dismantling behaviors 91
displacement 41, 42, 105, 160
disruption 11, 84, 136, 181, 200; Aaron (case study) 56; Frank (case study) 46, 48
dissociation: and defensiveness 21; gaps in narrative 55; in NICU 152, 153; as response to trauma 11, 97, 136–8, 185, 188; vs. use of term 'ghosts' 3

Doka, K. 141
dopplegangers 9
Dora (Freud case) 133
double loss 40
double time, traumatic states lived in 45–8
drama 69–70
dread to repeat 42
dreams: Aaron (case study) 57, 67, 73; analysts' 36, 38, 43–4, 45, 151, 184–5; Frank (case study) 47–8; and living with a shadow 81; recurrent childhood 62; Rosa (case study) 111; Sophie (case study) 32
Drescher, J. 124
drugs 120, 123, 132
Duberman, Martin 124
Durban, J. 10
dybbuks 3

ego: closed-off place within 85; early development of 79; and ghost worlds 55; and mourning 186; overwhelmed by unintegrated trauma 84
Ehrenzweig, Anton 169
Eissler, Kurt 132–3
Eliot, T.S. 141, 146
embodiment: embodied witnessing 59; ghost worlds 55; imprint of traumatic past 6, 36, 41; lost links and ethical markers 99–105; of shame 148
empathy 44, 47, 84
empty circles 84, 98
encrypted identification 11
ending treatment 57
Eros 3, 105–12
errands 20, 21, 43
escape, need for 56–7, 67
ethical markers 98–105
Etkind, A. 116
Evans, D. 163
excess/the uncontained 4, 118, 196
exile 65–6
expulsion vs. readmission/repatriation of ghosts 10–11
exquisite corpse 47
external vs. internal hauntings 10
extinction, pull of 20

Faimberg, H. 54, 57, 58, 85
fantasies: contemporary popular culture 8; filling gaps 62; in film 187, 188–9, 190; Freud on 120, 137; mirroring 47, 104; and the personal bastion 54; and shame 42; transformative 118; and trauma 25–6, 29–33, 137, 186, 195; unconscious 41, 47, 62, 65, 79; unconscious phantasies of psycho-genetic heritage 80–2; to ward off helplessness 41, 47, 54
fathers: Aaron (case study) 52, 57–8, 59, 62–6, 72; analysts' 21, 37–8, 58, 62–6, 187; Frank (case study) 39, 40; in NICU 149–51, 152; Oscar (case study) 77, 86; Rosa (case study) 102, 104; Sabina Spielrein 116
Faulkner, William 29
Faust, D. 161, 174, 176 n.16
Ferenczi, S. 6, 118, 126, 128, 152, 175 n.14
Ferro, A. 4
figure-background confusion 90–1
figure/ground matrices 9
film and cinema 181–98
First World War 6, 56, 60, 187, 188
Fitzgerald, F. Scott 197
flight 52–3, 56–7, 62, 67, 69
food 41, 52, 54, 56, 103–5
Foucault, Michel 127
Foulkes, S.H. 127
Fraiberg, S. 81
Frank (case study) 36–51
freezing of traumatic states 11, 39, 46, 186, 188
Freud, Anna 132–4
Freud, Sigmund: anti-Americanism 129; *Beyond the Pleasure Principle* (1920) 115; gaps 169; ghosts 3, 83; haunting presence on psychoanalytical profession 11, 120–4; heritage 79; on homosexuality 124; hostility to film industry 132; and the kinetic dimension 129; and memory 122–3, 161, 169; on mourning 2, 10, 161–2, 169–70, 186, 196; *Mourning and Melancholia* (1953) 169–70; own traumatic history 136–8; *Psychopathology of Everyday Life, The*

121; and Sabina Spielrein 115, 119; and spiritualism 175 n.14; theories of general psychology 117; thought transference 6; and Trigant Burrows 127, 129; uncanny 170, 202; *Vorstellung* 176 n.20
Freud: The Secret Passion (Huston, 1962) 131–5
frustration 122
future already present 6

Gabbard, G. 132
Gabbard, K. 132
Gaines, R. 8, 46
Galt, A. S. 127
Gampel, Y. 80, 85
gaps 53–9, 84, 141, 168, 169–71
Gaudilliere, J.M. 7, 22, 53, 54, 59, 170, 196
gender 164–6, 173
Gerson, Sam 1–2, 10, 55, 126, 169, 181, 182
ghosting (online context) 9
ghosts, definitions of 1–2, 9, 156–7
ghosts in the nursery 81
ghost stories 171–3
ghost worlds 55
Gilman, C.P. 177 n.31
Goldberger, M. 43, 44, 58
Goldman, S. 124
Goldner, V. 47
goodbyes, importance of 24–5, 41
good ghosts 154 n.7, 186
Gordon, A. 140
Gourevitch, P. 151
Grand, S. 3, 97, 112
grandparents: as good ghosts 154 n.7; language 58, 60–1, 63; losses passed down via parents 28; presence in the consulting room 54; Rosa (case study) 101, 103, 111; telescoping of generations 54, 60, 62–6
Great Depression 61
Green, A. 32, 36, 46
Greenson, Ralph 131, 132–4
grief: approaching grieving parents 142–3; disenfranchised grief 141; framing of violence 172; and Freud 161; ghosts as embodiment of grief 157; 'grievable' lives 172; opening space for 45, 46; perinatal 139–55; silent holding of 32 *see also* mourning
Grossmark, R. 70
Grotstein, James 5, 79
group analysis 127–8, 130
guilt: and melancholy 187; in NICU 145, 147, 149, 151; and omnipotence 197; and satisfaction 123
Guirand, F. 88
gun violence 156, 160–1, 172–3
Gurevich, H. 130

Hagman, G. 40
hallucinatory experiences 161, 189
Harris, A. 2, 4, 5, 36, 42, 45–6, 116, 140, 152, 153, 154 n.5
hidden projects 46
history: after war 7; analysts' own 135–8; angels in the nursery 46; collapses of time, space and history 53–4; embodied memory of history 78; gradual discovery of 141; and the group 130; identification of secret histories 54; as the larger context for the personal 53, 58, 59; and memory 4–5, 161; rediscovery of 44–5; 'shadows of the past' 83–5; and temporality 4–5; of violence 97
Hoberman, Jim and Shelley 193
Hoffman, E. 146
hollows in the real 169, 170
Hollywood 131–5, 187
Holocaust 7, 30, 57, 58, 63–4, 86–7
homosexuality 124–5
Houzel, D. 89–90
Hug-Hellmuth, H. 117
hunger 52, 56, 73, 83, 108
Huston, John 131, 132–3, 191, 196

idealization 11, 29, 38–41, 85, 98, 106, 196
identification 3, 11, 80–5, 126, 151, 169; Aaron (case study) 54–66, 69; Frank (case study) 39, 42, 43–4, 46, 47–8; projective identification 80–5; Sophie (case study) 23, 26, 29, 31
identity: balance of identity and heritage 58–9, 83–4; construction of self-identity 79–80, 102; gender shame 148
ideology 191

Ignoffo, M.J. 158–9, 161, 166, 179 n.43
illusions 163
impasse, clinical 42–4, 53, 55, 61–2
incest 102–3, 108–9
infant-caregiver relationship 70, 139–55
insomnia 52, 54, 62, 64, 68, 103
intergenerational trauma 54, 60, 62–6, 85, 97
interiors 27, 99, 107, 157, 165–7
internalization 6, 25, 38, 70, 153, 164, 196
internet 9
intersubjective disjunctions 43, 47
intimacy: desire for 67–8, 70, 105; dread of 100
intrapsychic 1, 12, 136
introjection 55, 84, 85, 118
Isaacs, S. 79
Isay, Richard 124

Jewish identity 30, 52, 58, 59–66, 86, 101
jokes 56, 100, 108, 121–2
Jung, C. 11, 115, 119, 175 n.14

Kahn, S. 126
Kant, Immanuel 163
Kaufman, Charles 132–3
kinetic dimensions 129
Kleinberg, S.J. 177 n.31
Kraemer, S. 141
Kriegman, D. 44–5
Kris, Marianne 134

Lacan, Jacques 126, 127, 163
language: as barrier between analyst-analysand 54–5, 63, 66, 106; and child analysis 117–18; common language 53; as connection 66; development of individuals with a shadow 83; grandparents 58, 60–1, 63; physical language 70; preverbal development phase 55, 80, 82; role of 58, 60–1, 63, 65–6; unconscious archaic elements 117; "watery speech" 87
Laub, D. 98
Lawtoo, N. 128
Let There Be Light (Huston) 191, 195–6, 197
Lewes, K. 124
Lewin, Kurt 129
Lewis, E. 144
Lewis, H.B. 147
Lewis, M. 148
Lichtenberg, J.D. 40, 41
Lieberman, A. 46
liminal spaces: architecture 156–7, 168, 172; bridge worlds 4, 140; film and cinema 191; in NICU 140, 146, 148
Lin, Maya 7
Lincoln, President Abraham 161
linkages, restoration of 98
Little, Margaret 6
living through 38
Loewald, H. 3, 5, 37, 48, 83, 119, 203
loneliness 5; Frank (case study) 41–2; Rosa (case study) 97, 100, 103, 104, 112
Lost 8
lost homelands 65
love 98, 121–2, 161, 183, 190, 192; Aaron (case study) 67; Frank (case study) 36, 41, 47; Oscar (case study) 86
Luria, Alexander 115

madness 53–4, 101, 103, 107, 156, 171
malignancy 63, 77, 82, 89, 97
Mankiewicz, J.L. 53
Marquez, Gabriel Garcia 199
marriage breakdown 39, 40
Massicotte, C. 175 n.14
Matter of Life and Death, A (1946) 183
McLaughlin, J. 44
Mead, George Herbert 129
meaning: attunement of significant other 79; disrupted by trauma 84; and Freud 123; in NICU 152–3
media portrayals: popular culture and ghosts 7; of psychiatry 132; of trauma 8; of violence 171–2
medication/pharmaceuticals 120, 123, 132
mediums, spiritual 160–1, 187
melancholia/melancholy: in culture 4, 6; going on being 186; and guilt and depression 187; making clinical space for 196–7; and mourning 5–6, 10, 11, 23, 176 n.17, 196; pathology of 23; power of melancholic state 10; as refusal

of grief 42; romance of 190, 192; as suspended grieving 36–7
Meltzer, D. 78, 91, 140
memorials 7–8, 27
memory: embodied memory of history 78; and Freud 122–3, 161, 169; and gaps 55, 169; and grief 161–2; management of 151; recursivity of 141; sense-memory 162, 170–1; and the significant other 79
mentalization 76–8, 89, 93
metabolization 7–8, 12, 39, 42, 48, 66, 196
metaphor 81, 83–4, 93, 171, 200; Aaron (case study) 64; Frank (case study) 37, 41, 48
migration, perpetual 52–75
Milner, Marion 169
mirroring self-object experience 45
Mitchell, J. 52
Mitchell, S. 42
model scenes 40–1
Moira, D. 177 n.29
Monroe, Marilyn 131–5
Moor, Paul 124
morality 8, 28, 172, 177
mothers: abandonment by 22, 24, 44; attachment to 29, 41, 43, 48, 104; attunement of significant other 79; celebrating and mourning 46; competition with other siblings for 68; dead mothers 32, 36, 46; death of 20–35, 36–7, 39, 46; early separation from 88; identification with 43–4; and 'lost' babies 143–4; mother-daughter relationships 24, 27; mother-infant relationships 70, 126, 128–9; in NICU 142–3, 147–53; Oscar (case study) 86; primary maternal preoccupation 143; Rosa (case study) 101–2, 103–4; separation from 88, 92
mourning: blocking of 26; and clinical stalemates 42–3; in the consulting room 169; forestalled 37–8; vs. haunting 161–2; and melancholia/melancholy 5–6, 10, 11, 23, 176 n.17, 196; necessity of witnessing 48; in NICU 143–4; vs. public memorials 8; relational mourning 47; resolution of 9–10; as romance 190, 192; of transgenerational transmission 97; unending nature of 6; unresolved mourning (Frank case) 36–51; unresolved mourning (Sophie case) 19–35
Mourning and Melancholia (Freud, 1953) 169–70
multiple losses 19–20
mutuality 126

Nachtraglichkeit 184, 191
narrative: as antidote to haunting 11, 63; gaps 55–9, 141; ghost stories 171–2; holding up of time 191; in NICU 152–3; projective identification 80; recursivity of 141; unconscious narratives of being 79–82
Nazis 77, 86, 102, 124
neuroscience 123
neutral analyst 128
never 196, 197
new beginnings, hope for 42
Newton, Isaac 176 n.18
NICU (neonatal intensive care unit) 139–55
Nightmare Factory (Sklar) 192, 193, 195–6
Niven, David 183, 185
non-figurability 91
non-representation 91
nostalgia 29, 121
numbness, psychic 52

objects: Chimerism 82; malicious vs. good 84; and memory 161; new persecutory objects 97; object constancy 106; psycho-genetic heritage 78, 81; and self-identity 80; and telescoping of the generations 85
obsessive-compulsive behavior 86, 87
Odyssey 83
Oedipal complex 41
Ogden, T. 2, 43
Okrent, Becky 192–3
omnipotence 186, 196–7; Aaron (case study) 54, 56, 68, 71; Frank (case study) 45; Oscar (case study) 87; Sophie (case study) 26
Omri (case study) 76–8, 88–92, 93
one-person psychoanalysis 127–8

Orange, D. 44
Ornstein, A. 33, 40, 42, 98
Oscar (case study) 77–8, 85–8, 93
Owen, Wilfrid 185

Palimpsest 141
paranoia 86
parents: presence in the consulting room 54; transfer of losses 28, 37–8 *see also* fathers; grandparents; mothers
partial answers 62
Perlswig, Ellis 124
personal bastions 54, 56, 57, 67, 69
personification 80
Pertegato, E. 129
Pertegato, G.O. 129
phantom limb pain 31
physical appearance 85–6
Piaget, Jean 117
pipe personalities 81, 89
Podell, D 98
Powell, Michael 182–3, 189, 191
pre-birth experiences 82, 92, 128–9
preconsciousness 126, 128–9
premature babies 142–3, 148–9
present absences: in the consulting room 22, 169; definition of ghosts 156–7; ghosts vs. demons distinction 9; loss of the analytic third 1–2, 55; sense-memory 162; unresolved mourning as 46
Pressberger, Emil 182–3, 189, 191
preverbal development phase 55, 80, 82
primary maternal preoccupation 143
professional PTSD 8, 11
projection 55
projective identification 80, 81, 83–4
proto-mental phenomenon 126, 129
proto-self 82
proto-signification 80, 82
Proust, Marcel 161
psychic retreat 40
psychic skin/membrane 89
psychoactive drugs 120, 123, 132
psycho-genetic heritage 78, 80–94
Psychopathology of Everyday Life, The (Freud) 121
psychosis 79
PTSD 8, 21, 190

racism 160
Racker, Heinrich 4
radical empathy 47
radioactive identification 85
rape 109–10, 111
Raphael-Leff, J. 144
readmission/repatriation of ghosts 10, 152, 201
refuge 54, 57, 67
registration of experience 6
Reiff, D. 148
Reis, B. 3, 59, 71, 72, 149
relational mourning 47
relational psychoanalysis iii–iv, 126, 128
relational 't' trauma 47
religion 27, 58, 87, 102, 175 n.12, 200
repair 5–6, 11, 44, 46
reparative quests 42
repetition 61, 72, 98, 171, 191, 197
representation 6, 176 n.20
repression 122, 192
resilience 97–8
resurrection 27
retraumatization 7
reunion 185–6
Rey, J.H. 5, 46
romanticization 29
romantic relationships 30, 37, 42, 47
Rosa (case study) 99–105
Roughton, Ralph 124
Russell, P. 44
Rustin, J. 44

Salomonsson, B. 83
Saussure, F. de 176 n.21
scaffolding 62, 142
Schafner, Bertram 124
secrets: burial of 59, 61, 62, 63, 84–5, 101; disorientation of secrecy 53; exhumation of 169; identification of secret histories 54; and narrative gaps 55
seduction theory 136
Self, early development of 79
self-analysis, therapist's 43
self-hatred 40, 42, 45, 100
self-isolation 104
sense phenomena 79, 91, 118, 156, 161–2, 168–9, 171

sensitivity 21, 91
separation: black holes 88; construction of self-identity 80; fear of 25, 40, 44; painful process of 169; vs. reunion 186; trauma of 65
sexual abuse 102–3, 108–9, 137 n.2
sexual life: Aaron (case study) 57; Frank (case study) 40–1, 42, 45, 47; Freud 120; Rosa (case study) 100, 105, 110; and transformation 118
Shabad, P. 23, 38, 46
shadows: being the shadow 82; living under a shadow of a ghost 81, 83–5; types of 10
shame: Aaron (case study) 56, 59, 61, 69, 71; analysts' 24, 36, 37–8, 56, 62; and the body 37, 42, 148; and fantasies 42; and Freud 121; gender shame 148; and grief 28, 61; and guilt 38; and the NICU 141, 143, 145, 147–9, 151; and power 56; and sexuality 118; transformation into grief 61; undoing 42
Shane, E. 40
Shane, M. 40
Shaw, D. 44
Shields, Clarence 128
Shoa 93
sibling relationships 149; Aaron (case study) 52, 68; Frank (case study) 40; Oscar (case study) 86–7; Rosa (case study) 101, 104; Sophie (case study) 21
significant other 79
silence: in the consulting room 69; and family secrets 102; and gaps 141, 169; at heart of clinical trauma 10, 11; silent holding of grief 32; and witnessing 61–2, 70–1
sister relationship (analyst-analysand) 47
Siva 25, 143
Sklar, Bob 181–98
slavery 160
Slavin, M.O. 44–5, 47
social unconscious 126, 127
Sodre, I. 80
somaticity 6, 38, 55, 64, 79, 104, 110
Sophie (case study) 19–35
Sopranos 121–2
space: architecture 163–9, 170–1, 173; collapses of time, space and history 53–4; and haunting 162–9; liminal spaces 4, 140, 146, 148, 156–7, 168, 172, 191; of psychoanalytic work 169–71
spectral presentations 55
Spielrein, Sabina 115–20
spiritism 6, 190
Spiritualism 160–1, 173, 174, 187
splitting 55, 91
Staehle, A. 78
Stairway to Heaven (1946) 182–3, 184–98
stalemates, clinical 42–3
Stanford family 161
step-relations 26
Stern, D. 153, 154 n.5
stillbirths 144–5
Stolorow, R. 46
subject formation/deformation 128
suicidal thoughts 23, 39, 42
Sullivan, Harry Stack 127, 136–8
survival in extreme conditions 54, 55, 61, 97–8
suspended states 25, 31, 36, 39
Swensen, Cole 135
Szjer, M. 143

tears 32
telephone sessions 105
telescoping of generations 54, 60, 62–6, 85
temporality 2, 4, 11, 118, 162
Thanatos 3, 105–12, 200
theater 69–70
third, the analytic 1, 3, 19, 43, 55–7, 66, 70, 126, 181, 201–3
thought transference 6
Tikis, Noah 191–2
time: collapses of time, space and history 53–4; history and temporality 4–5; stopping of 186, 191, 192; time traveling 60, 64; traumatic states lived in double time 45–8
Torok, M. 11, 39, 47, 84, 171
trance-like states 52–3
transformation 118, 135
transgenerational trauma 54, 60, 62–6, 85, 97
transplantation 93
traumatic assault 152

travel fever 52–75
treatment crunch 44
Trethewey, N. 19
Troise, D. 136
Tustin, F. 79, 89, 92

uncanny 170, 181, 202
unconscious communication 7, 37
unconscious gaps 55
unconscious narratives of being 79–81
unconscious phantasies of psycho-genetic heritage 80–2
unconscious transmission 56
uncontained/excess 4, 118, 196
unformulated experiences 43
unmarked graves 8
unthought knowns 151

vampires 3, 6
victim status 57–8, 61, 62, 64
videoconferencing 57, 66–8
Vietnam War 7
Vorstellung 176 n.20
vulnerability 69, 163
Vygotsky, L. 115, 117

war 6, 171–2, 182–3, 185–7, 190, 196; Aaron (case study) 53–4, 58, 61–6 *see also specific wars*
watery speech 88
welding 91–2
"When the Third is Dead" (Gerson, 2009) 1–2, 55, 181
Whitebook, Joel 196
white holes 88–92
Wigley, Mark 164
Willoughby, R. 140
Winchester Mystery House™ 156, 157–61, 165–6, 170, 172–4
Winnicott, D. W. 22, 126
witnessing: as antidote to haunting 11, 201–3; becoming a phantom to oneself 126; and definitions of ghosts 1–2; embodied witnessing 59; as goal of analysis 169; joint witnessing 53; living out non-represented feelings 38; loss of the analytic third 55; of mourning 48; in NICU 153; rediscovery of the past 45; refusal of 61–2; silent witnessing 61–2, 70–1; of strengths 98; as therapy 23; of transgenerational transmission 97; value of 10; via Internet 70; via physical language 70–1; via theater 70
work, ceaseless 52, 54, 62, 193
World War I 6, 56, 60, 187, 188
World War II 7, 182–3, 184–98; Aaron (case study) 52, 57, 59; Oscar (case study) 86–7
Wright, Gwendolyn 165

Zeavin, Hannah 191–2